MW01627951

GREAT ENCYCLICALS *of* POPE LEO XIII

VOLUME ONE: THE SOCIAL LETTERS

THE GREAT ENCYCLICALS

VOLUME ONE: THE SOCIAL LETTERS

POPE LEO XIII

Compiled and with an Introduction by
LEO L. CLARKE

CLUNY
Providence, Rhode Island

CLUNY EDITION, 2024

This Cluny edition of the Encyclical Letters of Pope Leo XIII follows, in the main, the text of the 1903 Benzinger Brothers edition of *The Great Encyclical Letters of Pope Leo XIII*, in conjunction with the English translation available from the Libreria Editrice Vaticana.

For this edition, citation and reference styles in the original text have been modified, as needed, for clarity and accessibility.

For more information regarding this title
or any other Cluny Media publication,
please write to info@clunymedia.com, or to
Cluny Media, P.O. Box 1664, Providence, RI 02901

ONLINE AT WWW.CLUNYMEDIA.COM

ISBN: 978-1685953683

Cover design by Clarke & Clarke
Cover image: Vincent van Gogh, *The Old Tower at Nuenen* (detail), 1884, oil on canvas
Courtesy of Google Arts & Culture

CONTENTS

INTRODUCTION

THIS VOLUME contains fourteen of the eighty-six encyclicals Pope Leo XIII issued during his twenty-five years as Pontiff. The letters presented here address subjects of fundamental importance to the development of Western civilization. They range in scope from the threats to religion and the Church presented by the rise of liberalism, Freemasonry, and nationalism, to the proper relationships between labor and capital and the respective roles in society of the Church, government, the family, and individuals.

Our companion volume, *The Great Encyclicals of Pope Leo XIII, Volume Two: The Spiritual Letters,* presents an additional seventeen encyclicals, primarily addressing issues of theology, philosophy, ecclesiology, and Mariology. Of course, the subjects covered in any one encyclical often belie this artificial distinction. After all, there is no clear distinction between an individual's duties as a Catholic and as a member of society. Indeed, much of Leo's writing in these encyclicals bemoans the fallacies of liberalism, modernism, statism, and Freemasonry in attempting to draw a clear distinction between religion and public life. For this reason, some of the encyclicals included in the companion volume, such as *Aeterni patris* (*On Christian Philosophy*) are sometimes included among the "social encyclicals" because they address concerns that extend beyond the Church.

Before proceeding to introduce Pope Leo and his writings in more detail, it may be beneficial to clarify why this book includes only "encyclicals." "Encyclical," from the Greek word for circle, generally refers to a letter meant for wide circulation. A "Papal Encyclical" is commonly defined as a letter written by a Pope to the bishops and other prelates of the universal Church on matters of faith, morals, or ecclesial discipline. Broadly considered, a communication is termed an encyclical if it deals with a topic of concern to the Church at large and treats that topic with some depth and scholarship. Encyclicals, it is important to note, seldom offer new infallible, *ex cathedra* teaching. They are, however, part of the Church's "ordinary magisterium"; Catholics are obliged to accept an encyclical's teaching on faith and morals (but not necessarily matters of politics or economics) and such teaching should not be considered debatable among theologians.[1]

An "encyclical" is just one of many classifications of papal documents. A papal communication can also be an "apostolic constitution," an "apostolic letter," a "bull," a "brief," a "*motu proprio*," a mere "letter" or—even more modestly—a "message." The classification appears to depend in large part upon the Papal author's discretion.

The one document included here that is not listed as an encyclical may clarify the point. Leo's teaching on "Americanism" is an example of the subtleties in distinguishing the classification of papal communications. *Longinqua oceani* ("On Catholicism in the United States"), an 1895 letter addressed to "the Archbishops and Bishops of the United States," is classified as an encyclical although it is fewer than two thousand words. In contrast, Leo's 1899 *Testem benevolentiae nostrae* ("On New Opinions, Virtue, Nature and Grace, with Regard to Americanism") is over four thousand words long and treats the issue of the relationships of Catholics and the Church in America to the predominant Protestant culture in more depth. *Testem*, however, is listed as an "Apostolic Letter," presumably because it is addressed solely to James Cardinal Gibbons of Baltimore. Thus, a communication may address

1. See Pope Pius XII, Encyclical Letter *Humani generis* (August 12, 1950).

the same subject as an encyclical and present that Pope's authoritative views on that subject, but it will not be listed as an "encyclical" if addressed to a single prelate or, perhaps, to the bishops of a single country.

The sheer number of Pope Leo's encyclicals complicated our selection process. His prolific output of eighty-six encyclicals dwarfed that of his predecessors—Leo's immediate predecessor, Pius IX, for example, wrote only thirty-six encyclicals in his thirty-one years. Nor have Leo's successors approached his average output of over three encyclicals per year. Pope St. Pius X wrote only sixteen encyclicals in his eleven years as Pope, and the annual output of encyclicals has continued to drop over time.

Of course, the development of other means of communication has reduced the need and effect of long, formal treatments of important issues. Certainly, the written output of Pope St. John Paul II far exceeds the total documentary library of Pope Leo XIII over a papacy of a similar length. And when John Paul II's speeches and homilies are added to the mix, there is no doubt that he reached a far larger audience with far more content than Leo could have ever dreamed of. After all, Leo was writing in Latin, and translations were communicated only through the Catholic press in a period of much lower literacy and access to that press. In contrast, Pope John Paul II was a polyglot who had full access to radio, television and, at the end of his Papacy, to the Internet. Today, what Pope Francis might say during an interview on an airplane is instantly available to a global audience and subject to immediate analysis and criticism.

But that does not mean that Leo was not a global figure or that his encyclicals were not read and effective. The Church had lost the Papal States just eight years before Leo's coronation, but it still had nuncios in most countries, and the bishops around the world read and disseminated his letters not just to their clergy but throughout their dioceses. Moreover, Leo negotiated throughout his Papacy with the anti-Catholic governments of some of the most powerful countries in the world, including Germany, Russia, France, and Spain. He was also energetic in re-establishing the Church in England and Scotland and in expanding it in the Americas. Non-Catholic world leaders like Kaiser Wilhelm II and King Edward II visited him at the Vatican, and his twenty-fifth Jubilee as Pope was celebrated throughout the world. Of particular note is the fact that his encouragement to Catholics to learn and advance science gave the Church new credibility in universities and among scientists. Finally, the size and importance of the Catholic population in most countries of Europe and the Americas ensured that his letters were taken into account by governments and business leaders even if not accepted or followed.

Full appreciation for Leo's encyclicals requires some understanding of his origins and what led him to the Papacy. Born Gioacchino [Joachim] Vincenzo Raffaele Luigi Pecci in Carpineto Romano in 1810, he was the son of a minor noble—so minor that a twenty-two-year-old Pecci, after he attained his doctorate in theology from the Roman College, had to write a brief proving the family's nobility when applying for entrance to the Academy of Noble Ecclesiastics in Rome. After studying canon and civil law, he served briefly as a bureaucrat in the Ministry of the Interior of the Papal States under his "protector" Cardinal Sala. Encouraged by Sala that he would have a bright future, he was ordained a priest at the end of 1837. Barely a month later, shortly before his twenty-eighth birthday, he was appointed by Pope Gregory XVI to be the civil governor of Benevento. Benevento, a city in the Kingdom of Naples under papal jurisdiction, was a hotbed of brigands and smugglers. Within three years, Pecci had stamped out brigandage, reformed the tax system, and built new roads. Pope

Gregory then sent him to Perugia, a larger jurisdiction and one overrun by anti-Papal revolutionaries. Within two years, Pecci had restored order. Not quite thirty-three, he was then appointed as nuncio to Belgium and consecrated as an archbishop.

As a nuncio, Pecci was fairly popular and successful, but the politics of the time created tensions between the Church and the growing liberalism within the Belgian government. Pecci's support of the Belgian bishops and his attempt to mediate a dispute between the Jesuits and professors at the University of Louvain resulted in complaints from his opponents to the Vatican.[2] The see of Perugia was then vacant and the Perugians were lobbying for his return. Pecci was invited by the dying Pope Gregory to abandon diplomacy, an invitation Pecci accepted.

Gregory died in June 1846, and Pius IX was elected shortly before Pecci arrived in Perugia. For the next thirty-two years, Pecci served as the archbishop of Perugia, which at the time had about two hundred parishes for a population of around one hundred thousand people. This was hardly a dynamic post for one made a cardinal when he was forty-three, especially since Perugia was an archdiocese only on account of Pecci's prior status. Nevertheless, he earned universal respect for his work reforming the educational system, especially his seminary; his promotion of a revival of Thomism; his pastoral letters that argued for a closer relationship between Catholicism and contemporary culture; and his general outspokenness on a wide range of matters ecclesial and secular. These were also turbulent times politically. In 1860, Perugia was separated from the Papal States, and Cardinal Pecci had to deal directly with the new political powers. In doing so, he showed great courage and force of personality in

2. This biographical sketch relies heavily on Henri-Daniel Rops, *The Church of the Revolutionary Age: A Fight for God,* vol. 1 (Providence, RI: Cluny, 2024), pp. 40–51, as well as on standard reference works.

opposing even General Giuseppe Garibaldi and sheltering refugee seminarians in his own house.

In particular, Cardinal Pecci was greatly admired by Pope Pius IX, who repeatedly offered him more significant dioceses closer to Rome. But he had a very powerful adversary in Pius's Secretary of State, Cardinal Antonelli, who may have mistrusted Pecci's potentially conciliatory political views or who simply may have considered him a rival. In any event, it was only after Antonelli died that Pius brought Cardinal Pecci to Rome as Camerlengo, the administrator of the property and the revenues of the Holy See. This appointment was taken in some circles as a sign Pius favored Pecci as his successor.

Pius IX died in February 1878. This was the first papal succession since the loss of the Papal States in 1870, and the first conclave in which the proliferation of railroads and steamships allowed Cardinals from distant sees to participate. The conclave elected Cardinal Pecci on the third ballot, impressed with his execution of his role as *camerlengo*, his pastoral experience in Perugia, and his pastoral letters on issues political and economic.

The new Pope took the name Leo in memory of Leo XII, the Pope of his youth, whom he said he had always admired for his interest in education, for his conciliatory attitude toward temporal governments, and for his desire to create links with Christians who had separated from the Roman Catholic Church. But this choice of name did not vouchsafe a favorable environment. Leo XII was terribly unpopular when he died in 1828, and Pius IX had died recognizing his own unpopularity within Rome and Italy as a whole. In fact, Pius IX is reported to have said: "My successor will have to draw inspiration from my attachment to the Church and from my desire to do good. For the rest, everything has changed around me; my system and my policies have had their day; but I am too old to think and do otherwise—that must be the work of my successor."

Volume One • The Social Letters

As his encyclicals establish beyond doubt, Leo XIII was a vibrant and courageous intellectual with a dedication to strengthening the Church in its relationships with the outside world. As Pius IX had hoped, Leo's pontificate was characterized by a new spirit. The encyclicals in this volume demonstrate that spirit. Here are four examples:

(1) His first Encyclical, *Inscrutabili Dei consilio,* issued very soon after his coronation, set out a vision and a detailed program. The new Pope did not counsel changing the Church's doctrine, and he left no room for equivocation. The letter denounced the weakening of the Church's authority, the abandonment of Christian rules, and "the excesses of unbridled and perverted liberty." He described modern "civilization," with its immorality and atheism, as "[B]ut a phantom of civilization; the word stands for no reality." Indeed, his description of the ideal Christian society presages John Paul II's "civilization of love" by a century: "[T]he very notion of civilization is a fiction of the brain if it rest not on the abiding principles of truth and the unchanging laws of virtue and justice, and if unfeigned love knit not together the wills of men, and gently control the interchange and the character of their mutual service."

(2) Leo also devoted several letters to the nature of government and its role in society. *Quod apostolici muneris* condemned socialism, communism, and nihilism/anarchy in words reminiscent of Pius IX. *Diuturnum illud* recognized the legitimacy of democracy in certain conditions but set out the limits of a democratic government's role in religion. *Immortale Dei* defined the relative roles of civil government and the Church and demonstrated that all civil power comes from God alone. *Libertas* set out the limits of human liberty in the context of our responsibility to God and established that the Church is, and can be, the sole custodian of liberty. A thread running through all these letters is the Catholic's duty to

obey legitimate government as a power authorized by God. But that obedience has its limits as explicated in *Sapientiae Christianae*: "If, in administering public affairs, it [the government] is wont to put God aside and show no solicitude for the upholding of moral law, it deflects woefully from its right course and from the injunctions of nature; nor should such a gathering together of an association of men be accounted as a commonwealth, but only as a deceitful imitation and make-believe of civil organization." In short, the duty of the Catholic citizen to obey laws extends only to those laws which do not conflict with God's law.

(3) Leo XIII was the first pope to address the disparity of wealth and the plight of the working class resulting from the Industrial Revolution. His most famous encyclical, *Rerum novarum*, boldly set out the Church's teaching on the relationship between labor and capital and their respective rights and responsibilities, including the rights of capitalists *and* laborers to private property. The Pope stressed the necessity of a just wage that permits the laborer to afford not just housing and food for his family, but education for his children and a margin for savings so that he could eventually become a property owner in his own right. Leo denounced liberal economics including its equating human labor with raw materials, and he held such liberalism responsible for the unjust misery of workers and for class conflict. In short, *Rerum novarum* deprived socialism's sole claim to key arguments it was using for its own ends. For this encyclical alone, he deservedly became known as the "workers' Pope."

(4) Nor did Leo shy away from the threats to Catholics and the Church of private societies like the Freemasons and of the growth of secular democratic societies, especially in countries that were no longer, or had never been, essentially Catholic. *Humanum genus* stands as the most severe condemnation ever against Freemasonry, describing its members as "the real abettors of evil in our age." Softer in tone, but just as clear and firm, was his denunciation in *Longinqua*

oceani of a nascent heresy sometimes called "Americanism," which claims that the Church should soften its teachings and "go along to get along" in predominantly Protestant or other non-Catholic countries. *Longinqua* and its subsequent Letter *Testem benevolentiae nostrae* quashed any such notion and made it clear that both the clergy and the laity had the duty to protect the Deposit of Faith and that a slide to indifferentism was a real threat that must be overcome.

Pope Leo's teaching in these and other encyclicals did not present any new truths. His social teaching drew solely on Scripture, the Church Fathers, and Thomistic theology and philosophy. His contribution and his innovation were his recognition that Revelation and the doctrines and philosophy derived from them were timeless and always applicable to the Church, to Catholics, and to society at large. Thus, in *Testem benevolentiae nostrae,* Leo quoted the Letter to the Hebrews: "Christ is the same yesterday, today and tomorrow" (13:8). In short, Leo's genius was to apply his experiences and his studies to identify the fallacies presented by the enemies of the Truth. Each of the encyclicals in this volume shows Leo's desire to go beyond just criticizing error and instead to provide solutions for his Venerable Brothers and the laity to protect their religion from becoming subservient to politics and economics.

More than a century later, the need for such solutions is no less pressing, for the problems we face remain no less troubling and destructive in our own age than they did in Leo's time. In fact, in the decades since the papacy of Leo XIII, the problems that confront the individual, society, and the Church have neither disappeared nor diminished; instead, they have endured, increased, and assumed new and aggravated proportions: rampant materialism, unabashed consumerism, economic stagnation that overwhelmingly affects the working classes' ability to accumulate assets and achieve financial security; abuse of political power that ignores subsidiarity and scorns the interests of religion; widespread antipathy for the sanctity of human life, typified by abortion, contraception, and pornography; endemic drug abuse and addiction; racial animus and marginalization; and the protraction of "forever" wars and internecine conflicts.

Time has neither abated the existence of these evils nor the need for effective solutions to them. The world may be different, but evil remains evil; yet so too do goodness, truth, and justice, because God remains God and man, man—the image and likeness of his Creator.

With clarity and force, Pope Leo XIII gives profound expression to those truths. Both instructive and persuasive, his encyclicals are valuable reminders that the triumph of secularism, materialism, relativism, is by no means inevitable. Instead, in the words of that great American contemporary of Leo XIII, Abraham Lincoln, "It is for us the living, to be here dedicated to the great task remaining before us." That *living*, as Leo saw it, is not to be done in a state of religious indifference or unwitting reliance on secular humanism. Rather, that living is to be done with a clear-eyed recognition of God's omnipotence and His infinite love for His creatures, coupled with the courageous readiness to reveal God in the events and encounters of everyday life.

To the question, then, of whether the words of Pope Leo XIII offer anything in the way of practical usefulness, the answer ought to be resoundingly and unequivocally in the affirmative. In substance and style alike, Pope Leo XIII extends the means to combat economic, social, and political evil and indifference. All that is needed is faith in Christ, hope in the face of indifference and animosity, and charity for the sake of our neighbors.

Leo L. Clarke
Western Massachusetts
Saint Robert Bellarmine, 2024

GREAT ENCYCLICALS *of* POPE LEO XIII

VOLUME ONE: THE SOCIAL LETTERS

ENCYCLICAL LETTER

INSCRUTABILI DEI CONSILIO

OF THE SUPREME PONTIFF

LEO XIII

TO THE PATRIARCHS, PRIMATES, ARCHBISHOPS, AND BISHOPS OF THE CATHOLIC WORLD IN GRACE AND COMMUNION WITH THE APOSTOLIC SEE ON THE EVILS OF SOCIETY

1. When by God's unsearchable design, We, though all unworthy, were raised to the height of apostolic dignity, at once We felt Ourselves moved by an urgent desire and, as it were, necessity, to address you by letter, not merely to express to you Our very deep feeling of love, but further, in accordance with the task entrusted to Us from heaven, to strengthen you who are called to share Our solicitude, that you may help Us to carry on the battle now being waged on behalf of the Church of God and the salvation of souls.

2. From the very beginning of Our pontificate, the sad sight has presented itself to Us of the evils by which the human race is oppressed on every side: the widespread subversion of the primary truths on which, as on its foundations, human society is based; the obstinacy of mind that will not brook any authority however lawful; the endless sources of disagreement, whence arrive civil strife, and ruthless war and bloodshed; the contempt of law which molds characters and is the shield of righteousness; the insatiable craving

for things perishable, with complete forgetfulness of things eternal, leading up to the desperate madness whereby so many wretched beings, in all directions, scruple not to lay violent hands upon themselves; the reckless mismanagement, waste, and misappropriation of the public funds; the shamelessness of those who, full of treachery, make semblance of being champions of country, of freedom, and every kind of right; in sum, the deadly kind of plague which infects in its inmost recesses, allowing it no respite and foreboding ever fresh disturbances and final disaster.[1]

3. Now, the source of these evils lies chiefly, We are convinced, in this, that the holy and venerable authority of the Church, which in God's name rules mankind, upholding and defending all lawful authority, has been despised and set aside. The enemies of public order, being fully aware of this, have thought nothing better suited to destroy the foundations of society than to make an unflagging attack upon the Church of God, to bring her into discredit and odium by spreading infamous calumnies and accusing her of being opposed to genuine progress. They labor to weaken her influence and power by wounds daily inflicted, and to overthrow the authority of the Bishop of Rome, in whom the abiding and unchangeable principles of right and good find their earthly guardian and champion. From these causes have originated laws that shake the structure of the Catholic Church, the enacting whereof we have to deplore in so many lands; hence, too, have flowed forth contempt of episcopal authority; the obstacles thrown in the way of the discharge of ecclesiastical duties; the dissolution of religious bodies; and the confiscation of property that was once the support of the Church's ministers and of the poor. Thereby, public institutions, vowed to charity and benevolence, have

1. This description of what is usually called a "corrupt government" or the government of a "corrupt party" is, in fact, the description of what necessarily happens to any government, or ruling party, when it rejects the moral rules taught by the Church. A religious error is the main root of all social and political evils.

been withdrawn from the wholesome control of the Church; thence, also, has arisen that unchecked freedom to teach and spread abroad all mischievous principles, while the Church's claim to train and educate youth is in every way outraged and baffled. Such, too, is the purpose of the seizing of the temporal power, conferred many centuries ago by divine providence on the Bishop of Rome, that he might without let or hindrance use the authority conferred by Christ for the eternal welfare of the nations.[2]

4. We have recalled to your minds, Venerable Brothers, this deathly mass of ills, not to increase the sorrow naturally caused by this most sad state of things, but because We believe that from its consideration you will most plainly see how serious are the matters claiming our attention as well as devotedness, and with what energy We should work and, more than ever, under the present adverse conditions, protect, so far as in Us lies, the Church of Christ and the honor of the apostolic see—the objects of so many slanders—and assert their claims.

5. It is perfectly clear and evident, Venerable Brothers, that the very notion of civilization is a fiction of the brain if it rest not on the abiding principles of truth and the unchanging laws of virtue and justice, and if unfeigned love knit not together the wills of men, and gently control the interchange and the character of their mutual service. Now, who would make bold to deny that the Church, by spreading the Gospel throughout the nations, has brought the light of truth amongst people utterly savage and steeped in foul superstition, and has quickened them alike to recognize the divine Author of nature and duly to respect themselves? Further, who will deny that the Church has done away with the curse of slavery and restored men to the original dignity of their noble nature; and—by uplifting the

2. An allusion to the capture of the Papal States by the Piedmontese army (1860) and to the usurpation of the temporal power of the Popes by King Victor Emmanuel II, in 1870. (EDITOR)

standard of redemption in all quarters of the globe, by introducing, or shielding under her protection, the sciences and arts, by founding and taking into her keeping excellent charitable institutions which provide relief for ills of every kind—has throughout the world, in private or in public life, civilized the human race, freed it from degradation, and with all care trained it to a way of living such as befits the dignity and the hopes of man? And if anyone of sound mind compare the age in which We live, so hostile to religion and to the Church of Christ, with those happy times when the Church was revered as a mother by the nations, beyond all question he will see that our epoch is rushing wildly along the straight road to destruction; while in those times which most abounded in excellent institutions, peaceful life, wealth, and prosperity the people showed themselves most obedient to the Church's rule and laws. Therefore, if the many blessings We have mentioned, due to the agency and saving help of the Church, are the true and worthy outcome of civilization, the Church of Christ, far from being alien to or neglectful of progress, has a just claim to all men's praise as its nurse, its mistress, and its mother.

6. Furthermore, that kind of civilization which conflicts with the doctrines and laws of holy Church is nothing but a worthless imitation and meaningless name. Of this those peoples on whom the Gospel light has never shown afford ample proof, since in their mode of life a shadowy semblance only of civilization is discoverable, while its true and solid blessings have never been possessed. Undoubtedly, that cannot by any means be accounted the perfection of civilized life which sets all legitimate authority boldly at defiance; nor can that be regarded as liberty which, shamefully and by the vilest means, spreading false principles, and freely indulging the sensual gratification of lustful desires, claims impunity for all crime and misdemeanor, and thwarts the goodly influence of the worthiest citizens of whatsoever class. Delusive, perverse, and misleading as are these principles, they cannot possibly have any inherent power to

perfect the human race and fill it with blessing, for "sin maketh nations miserable" (Prov. 14:34). Such principles, as a matter of course, must hurry nations, corrupted in mind and heart, into every kind of infamy, weaken all right order, and thus, sooner or later, bring the standing and peace of the State to the very brink of ruin.

7. Again, if We consider the achievements of the see of Rome, what can be more wicked than to deny how much and how well the Roman bishops have served civilized society at large? For Our predecessors, to provide for the peoples' good, encountered struggles of every kind, endured to the utmost burdensome toils, and never hesitated to expose themselves to most dangerous trials. With eyes fixed on heaven, they neither bowed down their head before the threats of the wicked, nor allowed themselves to be led by flattery or bribes into unworthy compliance. This apostolic chair it was that gathered and held together the crumbling remains of the old order of things; this was the kindly light by whose help the culture of Christian times shone far and wide; this was an anchor or safety in the fierce storms by which the human race has been convulsed; this was the sacred bond of union that linked together nations distant in region and differing in character; in short, this was a common center from which was sought instruction in faith and religion, no less than guidance and advice for the maintenance of peace and the functions of practical life. In very truth it is the glory of the supreme Pontiffs that they steadfastly set themselves up as a wall and a bulwark to save human society from falling back into its former superstition and barbarism.

8. Would that this healing authority had never been slighted or set aside! Assuredly, neither would the civil power have lost that venerable and sacred glory, the lustrous gift of religion, which alone renders the state of subjection noble and worthy of man; nor would so many revolutions and wars have been fomented to ravage the world with desolation and bloodshed; nor would kingdoms, once so flourishing, but now fallen from the height of prosperity, lie crushed

beneath the weight of every kind of calamity. Of this the peoples of the East also furnish an example, who, by breaking the most sweet yoke that bound them to this apostolic see, forfeited the splendor of their former greatness, their renown in science and art, and the dignity of their sway.

9. Of these remarkable benefits, however, which illustrious monuments of all ages prove to have flowed upon every quarter of the world from the apostolic see, this land of Italy has had the most abounding experience. For it has derived advantages from the see of Rome proportionate to the greater nearness of its natural situation. Unquestionably, to the Roman Pontiffs it is that Italy must own herself indebted for the substantial glory and majesty by which she has been preeminent amongst nations. The influence and fatherly care of the Popes have upon many occasions shielded her from hostile attack and brought her relief and aid, the effect of which is that the Catholic faith has been ever maintained inviolate in the hearts of Italians.

10. These services of Our predecessors, to omit mention of many others, have been witnessed to in a special manner by the records of the times of St. Leo the Great, Alexander III, Innocent III, St. Pius V, Leo X, and other Pontiffs,[3] by whose exertions or protection Italy has escaped unscathed from the utter destruction threatened by barbarians; has kept unimpaired her old faith, and, amid the darkness and defilement of the ruder age, has cultivated and preserved in vigor the luster of science and the splendor of art. To this, furthermore, bears witness Our own fostering city, the home of the Popes, which,

3. Pope St. Leo I, Leo the Great (440–461), caused Attila, King of the Huns, to retreat without having attacked Rome. Pope Alexander III (1159–1181) fought against the German Emperor Fredrick Barbarossa, to whom he opposed the Lombard League. Pope Innocent III (1198–1216) strongly resisted the French King Philip Augustus. St. Pius V was Pope from 1566 to 1572 and during his reign occurred the naval victory over the Turks at Lepanto in 1571. Leo X (John of Medici), Pope from 1513 to 1521, presided over one of the most brilliant epochs in history: the "century of Leo X." (EDITOR)

under their rule, reaped this special benefit, that it not only was the strong citadel of the faith, but also became the refuge of the liberal arts and the very abode of wisdom, winning for itself the admiration and respect of the whole world. As these facts in all their amplitude have been handed down in historical records for the perpetual remembrance of posterity, it is easy to understand that it is only with hostile design and shameless calumny—meant to mislead men—that anyone can venture in speech and in writing to accuse the apostolic see of being an obstacle to the civil progress of nations and to the prosperity of Italy.

11. Seeing, therefore, that all the hopes of Italy and of the whole world lie in the power, so beneficent to the common good and profit, wherewith the authority of the apostolic see is endowed, and in the close union which binds all the faithful of Christ to the Roman Pontiff, We recognize that nothing should be nearer Our heart than how to preserve safe and sound the dignity of the Roman see, and to strengthen ever more and more the union of members with the head, of the children with their father.

12. Wherefore, that We may above all things, and in every possible way, maintain the rights and freedom of this holy see, We shall never cease to strive that Our authority may meet with due deference; that obstacles may be removed which hamper the free exercise of Our ministry and that We may be restored to that condition of things in which the design of God's wisdom had long ago placed the Roman Pontiffs. We are moved to demand this restoration, Venerable Brethren, not by any feeling of ambition or desire of supremacy, but by the nature of Our office and by Our sacred promise confirmed on oath; and further, not only because this sovereignty is essential to protect and preserve the full liberty of the spiritual power, but also because it is an ascertained fact that, when the temporal sovereignty of the apostolic see is in question, the cause of the public good and the well-being of all human society in general are also at stake.

Hence, We cannot omit, in the discharge of Our duty, which obliges Us to guard the rights of holy Church, to renew and confirm in every particular by this Our letter those declarations and protests which Pius IX,[4] of sacred memory, Our predecessor, on many and repeated occasions published against the seizing of the civil sovereignty and the infringement of rights belonging to the Catholic Church. At the same time We address ourselves to princes and chief rulers of the nations, and earnestly beseech them in the august name of the Most High God, not to refuse the Church's aid, proffered them in a season of such need, but with united and friendly aims, to join themselves to her as the source of authority and salvation, and to attach themselves to her more and more in the bonds of hearty love and devotedness. God grant that—seeing the truth of Our words and considering within themselves that the teaching of Christ is, as Augustine used to say, "a great blessing to the State, if obeyed,"[5] and that their own peace and safety, as well as that of their people, is bound up with the safety of the Church and the reverence due to her—they may give their whole thought and care to mitigating the evils by which the Church and its visible head are harassed, and so it may at last come to pass that the peoples whom they govern may enter on the way of justice and peace, and rejoice in a happy era of prosperity and glory.

13. In the next place, in order that the union of hearts between their chief Pastor and the whole Catholic flock may daily be strengthened, We here call upon you, Venerable Brothers, with particular earnestness, and strongly urge you to kindle, with priestly zeal and pastoral care, the fire of the love of religion among the faithful entrusted to you, that their attachment to this chair of truth and justice

4. Pope Pius IX (1846–1878) proclaimed the dogmas of the Immaculate Conception and of the infallibility of the Popes in all matters related to faith and morals; published the *Syllabus*, or conspectus of modern errors; witnessed the usurpation by Victor Emmanuel II of the temporal power of the Popes, but never acknowledged it. (EDITOR)

5. *Letter* 138, to Marcellinus, 15 (*Patrologia Latina* [*PL*] 33:532).

may become closer and firmer, that they may welcome all its teachings with thorough assent of mind and will, wholly rejecting such opinion, even when most widely received, as they know to be contrary to the Church's doctrine. In this matter, the Roman Pontiffs, Our predecessors, and the last of all, Pius IX, of sacred memory, especially in the General Council of the Vatican, have not neglected, so often as there was need, to condemn wide-spreading errors and to smite them with the apostolic condemnation. This they did, keeping before their eyes the words of St. Paul: "Beware lest any man cheat you by philosophy and vain deceit, according to the tradition of men, according to the elements of the world and not according to Christ" (Col. 2:8). All such censures, We, following in the steps of Our predecessors, do confirm and renew from this apostolic seat of truth, whilst We earnestly ask of the Father of lights (James 1:17) that all the faithful, brought to thorough agreement in the like feeling and the same belief, may think and speak even as Ourselves. It is your duty, Venerable Brothers, sedulously to strive that the seed of heavenly doctrine be sown broadcast in the field of God, and that the teachings of the Catholic faith may be implanted early in the souls of the faithful, may strike deep root in them, and be kept free from the ruinous blight of error. The more the enemies of religion exert themselves to offer the uninformed, especially the young, such instruction as darkens the mind and corrupts morals, the more actively should we endeavor that not only a suitable and solid method of education may flourish but above all that this education be wholly in harmony with the Catholic faith in its literature and system of training, and chiefly in philosophy, upon which the direction of other sciences in great measure depends.[6] Philosophy seeks not the overthrow of divine revelation, but delights rather to prepare its way, and defend it against assailants, both by example and in written works, as the great

6. This point is developed in the Encyclical *Aeterni patris.* (EDITOR)

Augustine and the Angelic Doctor, with all other teachers of Christian wisdom, have proved to Us.

14. Now, the training of youth most conducive to the defense of true faith and religion and to the preservation of morality must find its beginning from an early stage within the circle of home life; and this family Christian training sadly undermined in these our times, cannot possibly be restored to its due dignity, save by those laws under which it was established in the Church by her divine Founder Himself. our Lord Jesus Christ, by raising to the dignity of a sacrament the contract of matrimony, in which He would have His own union with the Church typified, not only made the marriage tie more holy, but, in addition, provided efficacious sources of aid for parents and children alike, so that, by the discharge of their duties one to another, they might with greater ease attain to happiness both in time and in eternity. But when impious laws, setting at naught the sanctity of this great sacrament, put it on the same footing of mere civil contracts, the lamentable result followed, that, outraging the dignity of Christian matrimony, citizens made use of legalized concubinage in place of marriage; husband and wife neglected their bounden duty to each other; children refused obedience and reverence to their parents; the bonds of domestic love were loosened; and alas, the worst scandal and of all the most ruinous to public morality, very frequently an unholy passion opened the door to disastrous and fatal separations. These most unhappy and painful consequences, Venerable Brothers, cannot fail to arouse your zeal and move you constantly and earnestly to warn the faithful committed to your charge to listen with docility to your teaching regarding the holiness of Christian marriage, and to obey laws by which the Church controls the duties of married people and of their offspring.[7]

7. This point is developed in the Encyclical *Arcanum*. See also the Encyclical of Pope Pius XI, *Divini illius magistri* (December 31, 1929) (EDITOR)

15. Then, indeed, will that most desirable result come about, that the character and conduct of individuals also will be reformed; for, just as from a rotten stock are produced healthless branches or worthless fruits, so do the ravages of a pestilence which ruins the household spread wide their cruel infection to the hurt and injury of individual citizens. On the other hand, when domestic society is fashioned in the mold of Christian life, each member will gradually grow accustomed to the love of religion and piety, to the abhorrence of false and harmful teaching, to the pursuit of virtue, to obedience to elders, and to the restraint of the insatiable seeking after self-interest alone, which so spoils and weakens the character of men. To this end it will certainly help not a little to encourage and promote those pious associations which have been established, in our own times especially, with so great profit to the cause of the Catholic religion.

16. Great indeed and beyond the strength of man are these objects of our hopes and prayers, Venerable Brothers; but, since God has "made the nations of the earth for health,"[8] when He founded the Church for the welfare of the peoples, and promised that He will abide with her by His assistance to the end of the world, We firmly trust that, through your endeavors, the human race, taking warning from so many evils and visitations, will submit themselves at length to the Church, and turn for health and prosperity to the infallible guidance of this apostolic see.

17. Meanwhile, Venerable Brothers, before bringing this letter to a close, We must express Our congratulations on the striking harmony and concord which unites your minds among yourselves and with this apostolic see. This perfect union We regard as not merely an impregnable bulwark against hostile attacks, but also as an auspicious and happy omen, presaging better times for the Church; and,

---

8. Wis. 1:14: "For he created all things that they might be: and he made the nations of the earth for health: and there is no poison of destruction in them, nor kingdom of hell upon the earth."

while it yields great relief to Our weakness, it seasonably encourages Us to endure with readiness all labors and all struggles on behalf of God's Church in the arduous task which We have undertaken.

18. Moreover, from the causes of hope and rejoicing which We have made known to you We cannot separate those tokens of love and obedience which you, Venerable Brethren, in these first days of Our pontificate, have shown Our lowliness, and with you so many of the clergy and the faithful, who by letters sent, by offerings given, by pilgrimages undertaken, and by other works of love, have made it clear that the devotion and charity which they manifested to Our most worthy predecessor still lasts, so strong and steadfast and unchanged as not to slacken toward the person of a successor so much inferior. For these splendid tokens of Catholic piety We humbly confess to the Lord that He is good and gracious, while to you, Venerable Brothers, and to all Our beloved children from whom We have received them, We publicly, from the bottom of Our heart, avow the grateful feelings of Our soul, cherishing the fullest confidence that, in the present critical state of things and in the difficulties of the times, this your devotion and love and the devotion and love of the faithful will never fail Us. Nor have We any doubt that these conspicuous examples of filial piety and Christian virtue will be of such avail as to make Our most merciful God, moved by these dutiful deeds, look with favor on His flock and grant the Church peace and victory. But as We are sure that this peace and victory will more quickly and more readily be given Us, if the faithful are unremitting in their prayers and supplications to obtain it, We earnestly exhort you, Venerable Brothers, to stir up for this end the zeal and ardor of the faithful, taking the Immaculate Queen of Heaven as their intercessor with God, and having recourse as their advocates to St. Joseph, the heavenly patron of the Church, and to Sts. Peter and Paul, the Princes of the Apostles. To the powerful patronage of all these We humbly commit Our lowliness, all ranks of the ecclesiastical hierarchy, and all the flock of Christ our Lord.

19. For the rest, We trust that these days, on which We renew the memory of Jesus Christ, risen from the dead, may be to you, Venerable Brothers, and to all the fold of God, a source of blessing and salvation and fulness of holy joy, praying our most gracious God that by the blood of the Lamb without spot, which blotted out the handwriting that was against Us, the sins We have committed may be washed away, and the judgment We are suffering for them may mercifully be mitigated.

"The grace of our Lord Jesus Christ, and the charity of God, and the communion of the Holy Spirit be with you all" (2 Cor. 13:13), Venerable Brothers; to each and all of whom, as well as to Our beloved children, the clergy and faithful of your churches, as a pledge of Our special goodwill and as an earnest of the protection of heaven, We lovingly impart the Apostolic Benediction.

Given in Rome, at St. Peter's, on on the solemnity of Easter, the twenty-first day of April, 1878, in the first year of Our Pontificate.

LEO PP. XIII

ENCYCLICAL LETTER

QUOD APOSTOLICI MUNERIS

OF THE SUPREME PONTIFF

LEO XIII

TO THE PATRIARCHS, PRIMATES, ARCHBISHOPS, AND BISHOPS OF THE CATHOLIC WORLD IN GRACE AND COMMUNION WITH THE APOSTOLIC SEE ON SOCIALISM

1. At the very beginning of Our pontificate, as the nature of Our apostolic office demanded, we hastened to point out in an Encyclical Letter addressed to you, Venerable Brethren, the deadly plague that is creeping into the very fibers of human society and leading it on to the verge of destruction; at the same time We pointed out also the most effectual remedies by which society might be restored and might escape from the very serious dangers which threaten it. But the evils which We then deplored have so rapidly increased that We are again compelled to address you, as though we heard the voice of the prophet ringing in Our ears: "Cry, cease not, lift up thy voice like a trumpet" (Isa. 58:1). You understand, Venerable Brethren, that We speak of that sect of men who, under various and almost barbarous names, are called socialists, communists, or nihilists, and who, spread over all the world, and bound together by the closest ties in a wicked confederacy, no longer seek the shelter of secret meetings, but, openly and boldly marching forth in the light of day, strive to

bring to a head what they have long been planning—the overthrow of all civil society whatsoever.

Surely these are they who, as the sacred Scriptures testify, "Defile the flesh, despise dominion and blaspheme majesty" (Jude 1:8). They leave nothing untouched or whole which by both human and divine laws has been wisely decreed for the health and beauty of life. They refuse obedience to the higher powers, to whom, according to the admonition of the Apostle, every soul ought to be subject, and who derive the right of governing from God; and they proclaim the absolute equality of all men in rights and duties. They debase the natural union of man and woman, which is held sacred even among barbarous peoples; and its bond, by which the family is chiefly held together, they weaken, or even deliver up to lust. Lured, in sum, by the greed of present goods, which is "the root of all evils, which some coveting have erred from the faith" (1 Tim. 6:10), they assail the right of property sanctioned by natural law; and by a scheme of horrible wickedness, while they seem desirous of caring for the needs and satisfying the desires of all men, they strive to seize and hold in common whatever has been acquired either by title of lawful inheritance, or by labor of brain and hands, or by thrift in one's mode of life. These are the startling theories they utter in their meetings, set forth in their pamphlets, and scatter abroad in a cloud of journals and tracts. Wherefore, the revered majesty and power of kings has won such fierce hatred from their seditious people that disloyal traitors, impatient of all restraint, have more than once within a short period raised their arms in impious attempt against the lives of their own sovereigns.

2. But the boldness of these evil men, which day by day more and more threatens civil society with destruction, and strikes the souls of all with anxiety and fear, finds its cause and origin in those poisonous doctrines which, spread abroad in former times among the people, like evil seed bore in due time such fatal fruit. For you know,

Venerable Brethren, that that most deadly war which from the sixteenth century down has been waged by innovators against the Catholic faith, and which has grown in intensity up to today, had for its object to subvert all revelation, and overthrow the supernatural order, that thus the way might be opened for the discoveries, or rather the hallucinations, of reason alone. This kind of error, which falsely usurps to itself the name of reason, as it lures and whets the natural appetite that is in man of excelling, and gives loose rein to unlawful desires of every kind, has easily penetrated not only the minds of a great multitude of men but to a wide extent civil society, also. Hence, by a new species of impiety, unheard of even among the heathen nations, states have been constituted without any count at all of God or of the order established by him; it has been given out that public authority neither derives its principles, nor its majesty, nor its power of governing from God, but rather from the multitude, which, thinking itself absolved from all divine sanction, bows only to such laws as it shall have made at its own will. The supernatural truths of faith having been assailed and cast out as though hostile to reason, the very Author and Redeemer of the human race has been slowly and little by little banished from the universities, the lyceums and gymnasia—in a word, from every public institution. In sum, the rewards and punishments of a future and eternal life having been handed over to oblivion, the ardent desire of happiness has been limited to the bounds of the present. Such doctrines as these having been scattered far and wide, so great a license of thought and action having sprung up on all sides, it is no matter for surprise that men of the lowest class, weary of their wretched home or workshop, are eager to attack the homes and fortunes of the rich; it is no matter for surprise that already there exists no sense of security either in public or private life, and that the human race should have advanced to the very verge of final dissolution.

3. But the supreme pastors of the Church, on whom the duty

falls of guarding the Lord's flock from the snares of the enemy, have striven in time to ward off the danger and provide for the safety of the faithful. For as soon as the secret societies began to be formed, in whose bosom the seeds of the errors which we have already mentioned were even then being nourished, the Roman Pontiffs Clement XII and Benedict XIV did not fail to unmask the evil counsels of the sects, and to warn the faithful of the whole globe against the ruin which would be wrought. Later on again, when a licentious sort of liberty was attributed to man by a set of men who gloried in the name of philosophers, and a new right, as they call it, against the natural and divine law began to be framed and sanctioned, Pope Pius VI, of happy memory, at once exposed in public documents the guile and falsehood of their doctrines, and at the same time foretold with apostolic foresight the ruin into which the people so miserably deceived would be dragged. But, as no adequate precaution was taken to prevent their evil teachings from leading the people more and more astray, and lest they should be allowed to escape in the public statutes of States, Popes Pius VII and Leo XII condemned by anathema the secret sects,[1] and again warned society of the danger which threatened them. Finally, all have witnessed with what solemn words and great firmness and constancy of soul our glorious predecessor, Pius IX, of happy memory, both in his allocutions and in his Encyclical Letters addressed to the bishops of all the world, fought now against the wicked attempts of the sects, now openly by name against the pest of socialism, which was already making headway.

4. But it is to be lamented that those to whom has been committed the guardianship of the public weal, deceived by the wiles of wicked men and terrified by their threats, have looked upon the Church with a suspicious and even hostile eye, not perceiving that the attempts of the sects would be vain if the doctrine of the Catholic

1. See *Humanum genus*, §6.

Church and the authority of the Roman Pontiffs had always survived, with the honor that belongs to them, among princes and peoples. For "the church of the living God, which is the pillar and ground of truth" (1 Tim. 3:15), hands down those doctrines and precepts whose special object is the safety and peace of society and the uprooting of the evil growth of socialism.

5. For, indeed, although the socialists, stealing the very Gospel itself with a view to deceive more easily the unwary, have been accustomed to distort it so as to suit their own purposes, nevertheless so great is the difference between their depraved teachings and the most pure doctrine of Christ that none greater could exist: "For what participation hath justice with injustice or what fellowship hath light with darkness?" (2 Cor. 6:14). Their habit, as we have intimated, is always to maintain that nature has made all men equal, and that, therefore, neither honor nor respect is due to majesty, nor obedience to laws, unless, perhaps, to those sanctioned by their own good pleasure. But, on the contrary, in accordance with the teachings of the Gospel, the equality of men consists in this: that all, having inherited the same nature, are called to the same most high dignity of the sons of God, and that, as one and the same end is set before all, each one is to be judged by the same law and will receive punishment or reward according to his deserts. The inequality of rights and of power proceeds from the very Author of nature, "from whom all paternity in heaven and earth is named" (Eph. 3:15). But the minds of princes and their subjects are, according to Catholic doctrine and precepts, bound up one with the other in such a manner, by mutual duties and rights, that the thirst for power is restrained and the rational ground of obedience made easy, firm, and noble.

6. Assuredly, the Church wisely inculcates the apostolic precept on the mass of men: "There is no power but from God; and those that are, are ordained of God. Therefore he that resisteth the power resisteth the ordinance of God. And they that resist purchase to

themselves damnation." And again she admonishes those "subject by necessity" to be so "not only for wrath but also for conscience's sake," and to render "to all men their dues; tribute to whom tribute is due, custom to whom custom, fear to whom fear, honor to whom honor" (Rom. 13:1–7). For He who created and governs all things has, in His wise providence, appointed that the things which are lowest should attain their ends by those which are intermediate, and these again by the highest. Thus, as even in the kingdom of heaven He hath willed that the choirs of angels be distinct and some subject to others, and also in the Church has instituted various orders and a diversity of offices, so that all are not Apostles or doctors or pastors (1 Cor. 12:28), so also has He appointed that there should be various orders in civil society, differing in dignity, rights, and power, whereby the State, like the Church, should be one body, consisting of many members, some nobler than others, but all necessary to each other and solicitous for the common good.

7. But that rulers may use the power conceded to them to save and not to destroy, the Church of Christ seasonably warns even princes that the sentence of the Supreme Judge overhangs them, and, adopting the words of divine wisdom, calls upon all in the name of God: "Give ear, you that rule the people, and that please yourselves in multitudes of nations; for power is given you by the Lord, and strength by the Most High, who will examine your works, and search out your thoughts.... For a most severe judgment shall be for them that bear rule.... For God will not except any man's person, neither will he stand in awe of any man's greatness, for he hath made the little and the great; and he hath equally care of all. But a greater punishment is ready for the more mighty" (Wis. 6:3–4, 8–9). And if at any time it happen that the power of the State is rashly and tyrannically wielded by princes, the teaching of the Catholic church does not allow an insurrection on private authority against them, lest public order be only the more disturbed, and lest society take greater hurt

therefrom. And when affairs come to such a pass that there is no other hope of safety, she teaches that relief may be hastened by the merits of Christian patience and by earnest prayers to God. But, if the will of legislators and princes shall have sanctioned or commanded anything repugnant to the divine or natural law, the dignity and duty of the Christian name, as well as the judgment of the Apostle, urge that "God is to be obeyed rather than man" (Acts 5:29).

8. Even family life itself, which is the cornerstone of all society and government, necessarily feels and experiences the salutary power of the Church, which redounds to the right ordering and preservation of every State and kingdom. For you know, Venerable Brethren, that the foundation of this society rests first of all in the indissoluble union of man and wife according to the necessity of natural law, and is completed in the mutual rights and duties of parents and children, masters and servants. You know also that the doctrines of socialism strive almost completely to dissolve this union; since, that stability which is imparted to it by religious wedlock being lost, it follows that the power of the father over his own children, and the duties of the children toward their parents, must be greatly weakened. But the Church, on the contrary, teaches that "marriage, honorable in all" (Heb. 13:4), which God himself instituted in the very beginning of the world, and made indissoluble for the propagation and preservation of the human species, has become still more binding and more holy through Christ, who raised it to the dignity of a sacrament, and chose to use it as the figure of His own union with the Church.

Wherefore, as the Apostle has it (Eph. 5:23), as Christ is the head of the Church, so is the man the head of the woman; and as the Church is subject to Christ, who embraces her with a most chaste and undying love, so also should wives be subject to their husbands, and be loved by them in turn with a faithful and constant affection. In like manner does the Church temper the use of parental and domestic authority, that it may tend to hold children and servants to their duty, without going beyond bounds. For, according to Catholic teaching, the authority of our heavenly Father and Lord is imparted to parents and masters, whose authority, therefore, not only takes its origin and force from Him, but also borrows its nature and character. Hence, the Apostle exhorts children to "obey their parents in the Lord, and honor their father and mother, which is the first commandment with promise" (Eph. 6:1–2); and he admonishes parents: "And you, fathers, provoke not your children to anger, but bring them up in the discipline and correction of the Lord" (Eph. 6:4). Again, the apostle enjoins the divine precept on servants and masters, exhorting the former to be "obedient to their lords according to the flesh of Christ...with a good will serving, as to the Lord"; and the latter, to "forbear threatenings, knowing that the Lord of all is in heaven, and there is no respect of persons with God" (Eph. 6:5–9). If only all these matters were faithfully observed according to the divine will by all on whom they are enjoined, most assuredly every family would be a figure of the heavenly home, and the wonderful blessings there begotten would not confine themselves to the households alone, but would scatter their riches abroad through the nations.

9. But Catholic wisdom, sustained by the precepts of natural and divine law, provides with especial care for public and private tranquility in its doctrines and teachings regarding the duty of government and the distribution of the goods which are necessary for life and use. For while the socialists would destroy the "right" of property, alleging it to be a human invention altogether opposed to the inborn equality of man, and, claiming a community of goods, argue that poverty should not be peaceably endured, and that the property and privileges of the rich may be rightly invaded, the Church, with much greater wisdom and good sense, recognizes the inequality among men, who are born with different powers of body and mind, inequality in actual possession, also, and holds that the right of property and of ownership, which springs from nature itself, must not be

touched and stands inviolate. For she knows that stealing and robbery were forbidden in so special a manner by God, the Author and Defender of right, that He would not allow man even to desire what belonged to another, and that thieves and despoilers, no less than adulterers and idolaters, are shut out from the Kingdom of Heaven. But not the less on this account does our holy Mother not neglect the care of the poor or omit to provide for their necessities; but, rather, drawing them to her with a mother's embrace, and knowing that they bear the person of Christ Himself, who regards the smallest gift to the poor as a benefit conferred on Himself, holds them in great honor. She does all she can to help them; she provides homes and hospitals where they may be received, nourished, and cared for all the world over and watches over these. She is constantly pressing on the rich that most grave precept to give what remains to the poor; and she holds over their heads the divine sentence that unless they succor the needy they will be repaid by eternal torments. In sum, she does all she can to relieve and comfort the poor, either by holding up to the example of Christ, "who being rich became poor for our sake" (2 Cor. 8:9), or by reminding them of His own words, wherein He pronounced the poor blessed and bade them hope for the reward of eternal bliss. But who does not see that this is the best method of arranging the old struggle between the rich and poor? For as the very evidence of facts and events shows, if this method is rejected or disregarded, one of two things must occur: either the greater portion of the human race will fall back into the vile condition of slavery which so long prevailed among the pagan nations, or human society must continue to be disturbed by constant eruptions, to be disgraced by rapine and strife, as we have had sad witness even in recent times.

10. These things being so, then, Venerable Brethren, as at the beginning of Our pontificate We, on whom the guidance of the whole Church now lies, pointed out a place of refuge to the peoples and the princes tossed about by the fury of the tempest, so now, moved by

the extreme peril that is on them, We again lift up Our voice, and beseech them again and again for their own safety's sake as well as that of their people to welcome and give ear to the Church which has had such wonderful influence on the public prosperity of kingdoms, and to recognize that political and religious affairs are so closely united that what is taken from the spiritual weakens the loyalty of subjects and the majesty of the government. And since they know that the Church of Christ has such power to ward off the plague of socialism as cannot be found in human laws, in the mandates of magistrates, or in the force of armies, let them restore that Church to the condition and liberty in which she may exert her healing force for the benefit of all society.

11. But you, Venerable Brethren, who know the origin and the drift of these gathering evils, strive with all your force of soul to implant the Catholic teaching deep in the minds of all. Strive that all may have the habit of clinging to God with filial love and revering His divinity from their tenderest years; that they may respect the majesty of princes and of laws; that they may restrain their passions and stand fast by the order which God has established in civil and domestic society. Moreover, labor hard that the children of the Catholic Church neither join nor favor in any way whatsoever this abominable sect; let them show, on the contrary, by noble deeds and right dealing in all things, how well and happily human society would hold together were each member to shine as an example of right doing and of virtue. In sum, as the recruits of socialism are especially sought among artisans and workmen, who, tired, perhaps, of labor, are more easily allured by the hope of riches and the promise of wealth, it is well to encourage societies of artisans and workmen which, constituted under the guardianship of religion, may tend to make all associates contented with their lot and move them to a quiet and peaceful life.

12. Venerable Brethren, may He who is the beginning and end of every good work inspire your and Our endeavors. And, indeed, the

very thought of these days, in which the anniversary of our Lord's birth is solemnly observed, moves us to hope for speedy help. For the new life which Christ at His birth brought to a world already aging and steeped in the very depths of wickedness He bids us also to hope for, and the peace which He then announced by the angels to men He has promised to us also. For the Lord's "hand is not shortened that he cannot save, neither is his ear heavy that he cannot hear" (Isa. 59:1). In these most auspicious days, then, Venerable Brethren, wishing all joy and happiness to you and to the faithful of your churches, We earnestly pray the Giver of all good that again "there may appear unto men the goodness and kindness of God our Savior" (Titus 3:4), who brought us out of the power of our most deadly enemy into the most noble dignity of the sons of God. And that We may the sooner and more fully gain our wish, do you, Venerable Brethren, join with Us in lifting up your fervent prayers to God and beg the intercession of the Blessed and Immaculate Virgin Mary, and of Joseph her spouse, and of the blessed Apostles Peter and Paul, in whose prayers We have the greatest confidence. And in the meanwhile We impart to you, with the inmost affection of the heart, and to your clergy and faithful people, the Apostolic Benediction as an augury of the divine gifts.

Given at St. Peter's, in Rome, on the twenty-eighth day of December, 1878, in the first year of Our Pontificate.

LEO PP. XIII

ENCYCLICAL LETTER
DIUTURNUM
OF THE SUPREME PONTIFF
LEO XIII

TO THE PATRIARCHS, PRIMATES, ARCHBISHOPS, AND BISHOPS OF THE CATHOLIC WORLD IN GRACE AND COMMUNION WITH THE APOSTOLIC SEE ON THE ORIGIN OF CIVIL POWER

1. The long-continued and most bitter war waged against the divine authority of the Church has reached the culmination to which it was tending, the common danger, namely, of human society, and especially of the civil power on which the public safety chiefly reposes. In our own times most particularly this result is apparent. For popular passions now reject, with more boldness than formerly, every restraint of authority. So great is the license on all sides, so frequent are seditious and tumults, that not only is obedience often refused to those who rule states, but a sufficiently safe guarantee of security does not seem to have been left to them.

2. For a long time, indeed, pains have been taken to render rulers the object of contempt and hatred to the multitude. The flames of envy thus excited have at last burst forth, and attempts have been several times made, at very short intervals, on the life of sovereign princes, either by secret plots or by open attacks. The whole of Europe was lately filled with horror at the horrible murder of a most

powerful emperor.[1] Whilst the minds of men are still filled with astonishment at the magnitude of the crime, abandoned men do not fear publicly to utter threats and intimidations against other European princes.

3. These perils to commonwealth, which are before Our eyes, fill Us with grave anxiety, when We behold the security of rulers and the tranquility of empires, together with the safety of nations, put in peril almost from hour to hour. Nevertheless, the divine power of the Christian religion has given birth to excellent principles of stability and order for the State, while at the same time it has penetrated into the customs and institutions of States. And of this power not the least nor last fruit is a just and wise proportion of mutual rights and duties in both princes and peoples. For in the precepts and example of Christ our Lord there is a wonderful force for restraining in their duty as much those who obey as those who rule; and for keeping between them that agreement which is most according to nature, and that concord of wills, so to speak, from which arises a course of administration tranquil and free from all disturbance. Wherefore, being, by the favor of God, entrusted with the government of the Catholic Church, and made guardian and interpreter of the doctrines of Christ, We judge that it belongs to Our jurisdiction, Venerable Brethren, publicly to set forth what Catholic truth demands of everyone in this sphere of duty; thus making clear also by what way and by what means measures may be taken for the public safety in so critical a state of affairs.

4. Although man, when excited by a certain arrogance and contumacy, has often striven to cast aside the reins of authority, he has never yet been able to arrive at the state of obeying no one. In every

1. An allusion to Alexander II (1818–1881) Emperor of Russia, a liberally minded sovereign and a great social reformer, who was murdered March 13, 1881, by a group of nihilists, in St. Petersburg. (EDITOR)

association and community of men, necessity itself compels that some should hold pre-eminence, lest society, deprived of a prince or head by which it is ruled should come to dissolution and be prevented from attaining the end for which it was created and instituted. But, if it was not possible that political power should be removed from the midst of states, it is certain that men have used every art to take away its influence and to lessen its majesty, as was especially the case in the sixteenth century, when a fatal novelty of opinions infatuated many. Since that epoch, not only has the multitude striven after a liberty greater than is just, but it has seen fit to fashion the origin and construction of the civil society of men in accordance with its own will.

5. Indeed, very many men of more recent times, walking in the footsteps of those who in a former age assumed to themselves the name of philosophers,[2] say that all power comes from the people; so that those who exercise it in the State do so not as their own, but as delegated to them by the people, and that, by this rule, it can be revoked by the will of the very people by whom it was delegated. But from these, Catholics dissent, who affirm that the right to rule is from God, as from a natural and necessary principle.

6. It is of importance, however, to remark in this place that those who may be placed over the State may in certain cases be chosen by the will and decision of the multitude, without opposition to or impugning of the Catholic doctrine. And by this choice, in truth, the ruler is designated, but the rights of ruling are not thereby conferred. Nor is the authority delegated to him, but the person by whom it is to be exercised is determined upon.

7. There is no question here respecting forms of government, for there is no reason why the Church should not approve of the chief

---

2. The name of Philosophers is usually given to a group of eighteenth-century French writers, especially Voltaire, d'Alembert and Diderot. Their main views are contained in the *Encyclopédie* (1751–1772). (EDITOR)

power being held by one man or by more, provided only it be just, and that it tend to the common advantage. Wherefore, so long as justice be respected, the people are not hindered from choosing for themselves that form of government which suits best either their own disposition, or the institutions and customs of their ancestors.

8. But, as regards political power, the Church rightly teaches that it comes from God, for it finds this clearly testified in the sacred Scriptures and in the monuments of antiquity; besides, no other doctrine can be conceived which is more agreeable to reason, or more in accord with the safety of both princes and peoples.

9. In truth, that the source of human power is in God the books of the Old Testament in very many places clearly establish. "By me kings reign...by me princes rule, and the mighty decree justice" (Prov. 8:15–16). And in another place: "Give ear, you that rule the people...for power is given you of the Lord and strength by the Most High" (Wis. 6:3–4). The same thing is contained in the Book of Ecclesiasticus: "Over every nation he hath set a ruler" (Eccles. 7:14). These things, however, which they had learned of God, men were little by little untaught through heathen superstition, which even as it has corrupted the true aspect and often the very concept of things, so also it has corrupted the natural form and beauty of the chief power. Afterwards, when the Christian Gospel shed its light, vanity yielded to truth, and that noble and divine principle whence all authority flows began to shine forth. To the Roman governor, ostentatiously pretending that he had the power of releasing and of condemning, our Lord Jesus Christ answered: "Thou shouldst not have any power against me unless it were given thee from above" (John 19:11). And St. Augustine, in explaining this passage, says: "Let us learn what He said, which also He taught by His Apostle, that there is no power but from God."[3] The faithful voice of the Apostles, as an echo, repeats the

---

3. *Tract. in Joan* 116, n. 5 (*PL* 35:1942).

doctrine and precepts of Jesus Christ. The teaching of Paul to the Romans, when subject to the authority of heathen princes, is lofty and full of gravity: "There is not power but from God," from which, as from its cause, he draws this conclusion: "The prince is the minister of God" (Rom. 13:1–4).

10. The Fathers of the Church have taken great care to proclaim and propagate this very doctrine in which they had been instructed. "We do not attribute," says St. Augustine, "the power of giving government and empires to any but the true God."[4] On the same passage St. John Chrysostom says: "That there are kingdoms, and that some rule, while others are subject, and that none of these things is brought about by accident or rashly...is, I say, a work of divine wisdom."[5] The same truth is testified by St. Gregory the Great, saying: "We confess that power is given from above to emperors and kings."[6] Verily the holy doctors have undertaken to illustrate also the same precepts by the natural light of reason in such a way that they must appear to be altogether right and true, even to those who follow reason for their sole guide.

11. And, indeed, nature, or rather God who is the Author of nature, wills that man should live in a civil society; and this is clearly shown both by the faculty of language, the greatest medium of intercourse, and by numerous innate desires of the mind, and the many necessary things, and things of great importance, which men isolated cannot procure, but which they can procure when joined and associated with others. But now, a society can neither exist nor be conceived in which there is no one to govern the wills of individuals, in such a way as to make, as it were, one will out of many, and to impel them rightly and orderly to the common good; therefore, God has

---

4. *De civ. Dei*, 5, 21 (*PL* 41:167).
5. *In Epist. ad Rom.*, Homily 23, n. 1 (*Patrologiae Graeca* [*PG*] 60:615).
6. *In Epist.*, lib. 11, epist. 61.

willed that in a civil society there should be some to rule the multitude. And this also is a powerful argument, that those by whose authority the State is administered must be able so to compel the citizens to obedience that it is clearly a sin in the latter not to obey. But no man has in himself or of himself the power of constraining the free will of others by fetters of authority of this kind. This power resides solely in God, the Creator and Legislator of all things; and it is necessary that those who exercise it should do it as having received it from God. "There is one lawgiver and judge, who is able to destroy and deliver" (James 4:12). And this is clearly seen in every kind of power. That that which resides in priests comes from God is so acknowledged that among all nations they are recognized as, and called, the ministers of God. In like manner, the authority of fathers of families preserves a certain impressed image and form of the authority which is in God, "of whom all paternity in heaven and earth is named" (Eph. 3:15). But in this way different kinds of authority have between them wonderful resemblances, since, whatever there is of government and authority, its origin is derived from one and the same Creator and Lord of the world, who is God.

12. Those who believe civil society to have risen from the free consent of men, looking for the origin of its authority from the same source, say that each individual has given up something of his right,[7] and that voluntarily every person has put himself into the power of the one man in whose person the whole of those rights has been centered. But it is a great error not to see, what is manifest, that men, as they are not a nomad race, have been created, without their own free will, for a natural community of life. It is plain, moreover, that the pact which they allege is openly a falsehood and a fiction, and that it has no authority to confer on political power such great force,

7. An allusion to the doctrine of "Social contract," developed by Jean-Jacques Rousseau (1712–1778). According to this doctrine, all political power comes to rulers from the people. (EDITOR)

dignity, and firmness as the safety of the State and the common good of the citizens require. Then only will the government have all those ornaments and guarantees, when it is understood to emanate from God as its august and most sacred source.

13. And it is impossible that any should be found not only more true but even more advantageous than this opinion. For the authority of the rulers of a State, if it be a certain communication of divine power, will by that very reason immediately acquire a dignity greater than human—not, indeed, that impious and most absurd dignity sometimes desired by heathen emperors when affecting divine honors, but a true and solid one received by a certain divine gift and benefaction. Whence it will behoove citizens to submit themselves and to be obedient to rulers, as to God, not so much through fear of punishment as through respect for their majesty; nor for the sake of pleasing, but through conscience, as doing their duty. And by this means authority will remain far more firmly seated in its place. For the citizens, perceiving the force of this duty, would necessarily avoid dishonesty and contumacy, because they must be persuaded that they who resist State authority resist the divine will; that they who refuse honor to rulers refuse it to God Himself.

14. This doctrine the Apostle Paul particularly inculcated on the Romans; to whom he wrote with so great authority and weight on the reverence to be entertained toward the higher powers, that it seems nothing could be prescribed more weightily: "Let every soul be subject to higher powers, for there is no power but from God, and those that are, are ordained of God. Therefore he that resisteth the power resisteth the ordinance of God, and they that resist purchase to themselves damnation...wherefore be subject of necessity, not only for wrath, but also for conscience's sake" (Rom. 13:1–2, 5). And in agreement with this is the celebrated declaration of Peter, the Prince of the Apostles, on the same subject: "Be ye subject, therefore, to every human creature for God's sake; whether it be to the king as

excelling, or to governors, as sent by him for the punishment of evil-doers, and for the praise of the good, for so is the will of God" (1 Pet. 2:13, 15).

15. The one only reason which men have for not obeying is when anything is demanded of them which is openly repugnant to the natural or the divine law, for it is equally unlawful to command to do anything in which the law of nature or the will of God is violated. If, therefore, it should happen to anyone to be compelled to prefer one or the other, namely, to disregard either the commands of God or those of rulers, he must obey Jesus Christ, who commands us to "give to Caesar the things that are Caesar's, and to God the things that are God's" (Matt. 22:21), and must reply courageously after the example of the Apostles: "We ought to obey God rather than men" (Acts 5:29). And yet there is no reason why those who so behave themselves should be accused of refusing obedience; for, if the will of rulers is opposed to the will and the laws of God, they themselves exceed the bounds of their own power and pervert justice; nor can their authority then be valid, which, when there is no justice, is null.

16. But in order that justice may be retained in government it is of the highest importance that those who rule States should understand that political power was not created for the advantage of any private individual; and that the administration of the State must be carried on to the profit of those who have been committed to their care, not to the profit of those to whom it has been committed. Let princes take example from the Most High God, by whom authority is given to them; and, placing before themselves His model in governing the State, let them rule over the people with equity and faithfulness, and let them add to that severity, which is necessary, a paternal charity. On this account they are warned in the oracles of the sacred Scriptures, that they will have themselves some day to render an account to the King of kings and Lord of lords; if they shall fail in their duty, that it will not be possible for them in any way to escape the

severity of God: "The Most High will examine your work and search out your thoughts: because being ministers of his kingdom you have not judged rightly.... Horribly and speedily will he appear to you, for a most severe judgment shall be for them that bear rule.... For God will not accept any man's person, neither will he stand in awe of any man's greatness; for he made the little and the great, and he hath equally care of all. But a greater punishment is ready for the more mighty" (Wis. 6:4–6, 8–9).

17. And if these precepts protect the State, all cause or desire for seditions is removed; the honor and security of rulers, the quiet and well-being of societies will be secure. The dignity also of the citizen is best provided for; for to them it has been permitted to retain even in obedience that greatness which conduces to the excellence of man. For they understand that, in the judgment of God, there is neither slave nor free man; that there is one Lord of all, rich "to all that call upon Him" (Rom. 10:12), but that they on this account submit to and obey their rulers, because these in a certain sort bring before them the image of God, "whom to serve is to reign."

18. But the Church has always so acted that the Christian form of civil government may not dwell in the minds of men, but that it may be exhibited also in the life and habits of nations. As long as there were at the helm of the States pagan emperors, who were prevented by superstition from rising to that form of imperial government which We have sketched, she studied how to instill into the minds of subjects, immediately on their embracing the Christian institutions, the teaching that they must be desirous of bringing their lives into conformity with them. Therefore, the pastors of souls, after the example of the Apostle Paul, were accustomed to teach the people with the utmost care and diligence "to be subject to princes and powers, to obey at a word" (Titus 3:1), and to pray God for all men and particularly "for kings and all that are in a high station: for this is good and acceptable in the sight of God our Savior" (1 Tim. 2:1–3).

And the Christians of old left the most striking proofs of this; for, when they were harassed in a very unjust and cruel way by pagan emperors, they nevertheless at no time omitted to conduct themselves obediently and submissively, so that, in fact, they seemed to vie with each other: those in cruelty, and these in obedience.

19. This great modesty, this fixed determination to obey, was so well known that it could not be obscured by the calumny and malice of enemies. On this account, those who were going to plead in public before the emperors for any persons bearing the Christian name proved by this argument especially that it was unjust to enact laws against the Christians because they were in the sight of all men exemplary in their bearing according to the laws. Athenagoras thus confidently addresses Marcus Aurelius Antoninus and Lucius Aurelius Commodus, his son: "You allow us, who commit no evil, yea, who demean ourselves the most piously and justly of all toward God and likewise toward your government, to be driven about, plundered and exiled."[8] In like manner, Tertullian openly praises the Christians because they were the best and surest friends of all to the Empire: "The Christian is the enemy of no one, much less of the emperor, whom he knows to be appointed by God, and whom he must, therefore, of necessity love, reverence and honor, and wish to be preserved together with the whole Roman Empire."[9] Nor did he hesitate to affirm that, within the limits of the Empire, the number of enemies was wont to diminish just in proportion as the number of Christians increased.[10] There is also a remarkable testimony to the same point in the Epistle to Diognetus, which confirms the statement that the Christians at that period were not only in the habit of obeying the laws, but in every office they of their own accord did

8. *Legatio pro christianis*, 1 (*PG* 6:891b–894a).
9. *Apologia*, 35.
10. *Apologia*, 37 (*PL* 1:526a).

more, and more perfectly, than they were required to do by the laws. "Christians observe these things which have obtained the sanction of the law, and in the character of their lives they even go beyond the law."[11]

20. The case, indeed, was different when they were ordered by the edicts of emperors and the threats of praetors to abandon the Christian faith or in any way fail in their duty. At these times, undoubtedly, they preferred to displease men rather than God. Yet, even under these circumstances, they were so far from doing anything seditious or despising the imperial majesty that they took it on themselves only to profess themselves Christians and declare that they would not in any way alter their faith. But they had no thought of resistance, calmly and joyfully they went to the torture of the rack, in so much that the magnitude of the torments gave place to their magnitude of mind. During the same period the force of Christian principles was observed in like manner in the army. For it was a mark of a Christian soldier to combine the greatest fortitude with the greatest attention to military discipline, and to add to nobility of mind immovable fidelity towards his prince. But, if anything dishonorable was required of him, as, for instance, to break the laws of God, or to turn his sword against innocent disciples of Christ, then, indeed, he refused to execute the orders, yet in such wise that he would rather retire from the army and die for his religion than oppose the public authority by means of sedition and tumult.

21. But afterward, when Christian rulers were at the head of States, the Church insisted much more on testifying and preaching how much sanctity was inherent in the authority of rulers. Hence, when people thought of princedom, the image of a certain sacred majesty would present itself to their minds, by which they would be impelled to greater reverence and love of rulers. And on this account

11. *Ad Diognetum*, 10.

she wisely provides that kings should commence their reign with the celebration of solemn rites; which, in the Old Testament, was appointed by divine authority. (1 Kgs. 9:16; 10:1; 16:13).

22. But from the time when the civil society of men, raised from the ruins of the Roman Empire, gave hope of its future Christian greatness, the Roman Pontiffs, by the institution of the Holy Empire, consecrated the political power in a wonderful manner. Greatly, indeed, was the authority of rulers ennobled; and it is not to be doubted that what was then instituted would always have been a very great gain, both to ecclesiastical and civil society, if princes and peoples had ever looked to the same object as the Church. And, indeed, tranquility and a sufficient prosperity lasted so long as there was a friendly agreement between these two powers. If the people were turbulent, the Church was at once the mediator for peace. Recalling all to their duty, she subdued the more lawless passions partly by kindness and partly by authority. So, if, in ruling, princes erred in their government, she went to them and, putting before them the rights, needs, and lawful wants of their people, urged them to equity, mercy, and kindness. Whence it was often brought about that the dangers of civil wars and popular tumults were stayed.

23. On the other hand, the doctrines on political power invented by late writers have already produced great ills amongst men, and it is to be feared that they will cause the very greatest disasters to posterity. For an unwillingness to attribute the right of ruling to God, as its Author, is not less than a willingness to blot out the greatest splendor of political power and to destroy its force. And they who say that this power depends on the will of the people err in opinion first of all; then they place authority on too weak and unstable a foundation. For the popular passions, incited and goaded on by these opinions, will break out more insolently; and, with great harm to the common weal, descend headlong by an easy and smooth road to revolts and to open sedition. In truth, sudden uprisings and the boldest rebellions

immediately followed in Germany the so-called Reformation,[12] the authors and leaders of which, by their new doctrines, attacked at the very foundation religious and civil authority; and this with so fearful an outburst of civil war and with such slaughter that there was scarcely any place free from tumult and bloodshed. From this heresy there arose in the last century a false philosophy—a new right as it is called, and a popular authority, together with an unbridled license which many regard as the only true liberty. Hence we have reached the limit of horrors, to wit, communism, socialism, nihilism, hideous deformities of the civil society of men and almost its ruin. And yet too many attempt to enlarge the scope of these evils, and under the pretext of helping the multitude, already have fanned no small flames of misery. The things we thus mention are neither unknown nor very remote from us.

24. This, indeed, is all the graver because rulers, in the midst of such threatening dangers, have no remedies sufficient to restore discipline and tranquility. They supply themselves with the power of laws, and think to coerce, by the severity of their punishment, those who disturb their governments. They are right to a certain extent, but yet should seriously consider that no power of punishment can be so great that it alone can preserve the State. For fear, as St. Thomas admirably teaches, "is a weak foundation; for those who are subdued by fear would, should an occasion arise in which they might hope for immunity, rise more eagerly against their rulers, in proportion to the previous extent of their restraint through fear." And besides, "from too great fear many fall into despair; and despair drives men to attempt boldly to gain what they desire."[13] That these things are so we see from experience. It is therefore necessary to seek a higher and

12. Especially the Peasant Revolt and its repression by the German princes. Luther himself then had to stress the duty of the citizens to obey the civil power (*On the Civil Power,* 1523). (EDITOR)

13. *On the Governance of Rulers,* 1, 10.

more reliable reason for obedience, and to say explicitly that legal severity cannot be efficacious unless men are led on by duty and moved by the salutary fear of God. But this is what religion can best ask of them, religion which by its power enters into the souls and bends the very wills of men causing them not only to render obedience to their rulers, but also to show their affection and good will, which is in every society of men the best guardian of safety.

25. For this reason the Roman Pontiffs are to be regarded as having greatly served the public good, for they have ever endeavored to break the turbulent and restless spirit of innovators and have often warned men of the danger they are to civil society. In this respect we may worthily recall to mind the declaration of Clement VII to Ferdinand, King of Bohemia and Hungary: "In the cause of faith your own dignity and advantage and that of other rulers is included, since the faith cannot be shaken without your authority being brought down; which has been most clearly shown in several instances." In the same way the supreme forethought and courage of Our predecessors have been shown, especially of Clement XI, Benedict XIV, and Leo XII, who, when in their day the evil of vicious doctrine was more widely spreading and the boldness of the sects was becoming greater, endeavored by their authority to close the door against them. And We Ourselves have several times declared what great dangers are impending and have pointed out the best ways of warding them off. To princes and other rulers of the State we have offered the protection of religion, and we have exhorted the people to make abundant use of the great benefits which the Church supplies. Our present object is to make rulers understand that this protection, which is stronger than any, is again offered to them; and We earnestly exhort them in our Lord to defend religion, and to consult the interest of their Lord to defend religion, and to consult the interest of their States by giving that liberty to the Church which cannot be taken away without injury and ruin to the commonwealth.

26. The Church of Christ, indeed, cannot be an object of suspicion to rulers, nor of hatred to the people; for it urges rulers to follow justice, and in nothing to decline from their duty; while at the same time it strengthens and in many ways supports their authority. All things that are of a civil nature the Church acknowledges and declares to be under the power and authority of the ruler; and in things whereof for different reasons the decision belongs both to the sacred and to the civil power, the Church wishes that there should be harmony between the two so that injurious contests may be avoided. As to what regards the people, the Church has been established for the salvation of all men and has ever loved them as a mother. For it is the Church which by the exercise of her charity has given gentleness to the minds of men, kindness to their manners, and justice to their laws. Never opposed to honest liberty, the Church has always detested a tyrant's rule. This custom which the Church has ever had of deserving well of mankind is notably expressed by St. Augustine when he says that "the Church teaches kings to study the welfare of their people, and people to submit to their kings, showing what is due to all: and that to all is due charity and to no one injustice."[14]

27. For these reasons, Venerable Brethren, your work will be most useful and salutary if you employ with us every industry and effort which God has given you in order to avert the dangers and evils of human society. Strive with all possible care to make men understand and show forth in their lives what the Catholic Church teaches on government and the duty of obedience. Let the people be frequently urged by your authority and teaching to fly from the forbidden sects, to abhor all conspiracy, to have nothing to do with sedition, and let them understand that they who for God's sake obey their rulers render a reasonable service and a generous obedience. And as it is God "who gives safety to kings" (Ps. 152:11), and grants to the people "to

14. *De moribus ecclesiae*, 1, 30, 53 (*PL* 32:1236).

rest in the beauty of peace and in the tabernacles of confidence and in wealthy repose" (Isa. 37:18), it is to Him that we must pray, beseeching Him to incline all minds to uprightness and truth, to calm angry passions, to restore the long-wished-for tranquility to the world.

28. That we may pray with greater hope, let us take as our intercessors and protectors of our welfare the Virgin Mary, the great Mother of God, the help of Christians, and protector of the human race; St. Joseph, her chaste spouse, in whose patronage the whole Church greatly trusts; and the Princes of the Apostles, Peter and Paul, the guardians and protectors of the Christian name.

Given at St. Peter's, in Rome, the twenty-ninth day of June, 1881, the third year of Our Pontificate.

LEO PP. XIII

ENCYCLICAL LETTER

HUMANUM GENUS

OF THE SUPREME PONTIFF

LEO XIII

TO THE PATRIARCHS, PRIMATES, ARCHBISHOPS, AND BISHOPS OF THE CATHOLIC WORLD IN GRACE AND COMMUNION WITH THE APOSTOLIC SEE ON FREEMASONRY

1. The race of man, after its miserable fall from God, the Creator and the Giver of heavenly gifts, "through the envy of the devil," separated into two diverse and opposite parts, of which the one steadfastly contends for truth and virtue, the other of those things which are contrary to virtue and to truth. The one is the kingdom of God on earth, namely, the true Church of Jesus Christ; and those who desire from their heart to be united with it, so as to gain salvation, must of necessity serve God and His only-begotten Son with their whole mind and with an entire will. The other is the kingdom of Satan, in whose possession and control are all whosoever follow the fatal example of their leader and of our first parents, those who refuse to obey the divine and eternal law, and who have many aims of their own in contempt of God, and many aims also against God.

2. This twofold kingdom St. Augustine keenly discerned and described after the manner of two cities, contrary in their laws because striving for contrary objects; and with a subtle brevity he expressed

the efficient cause of each in these words: "Two loves formed two cities: the love of self, reaching even to contempt of God, an earthly city; and the love of God, reaching to contempt of self, a heavenly one."[1] At every period of time each has been in conflict with the other, with a variety and multiplicity of weapons and of warfare, although not always with equal ardor and assault. At this period, however, the partisans of evil seem to be combining together, and to be struggling with united vehemence, led on or assisted by that strongly organized and widespread association called the Freemasons. No longer making any secret of their purposes, they are now boldly rising up against God Himself. They are planning the destruction of holy Church publicly and openly, and this with the set purpose of utterly despoiling the nations of Christendom, if it were possible, of the blessings obtained for us through Jesus Christ our Savior. Lamenting these evils, We are constrained by the charity which urges Our heart to cry out often to God: "For lo, Thy enemies have made a noise; and they that hate Thee have lifted up the head. They have taken a malicious counsel against Thy people, and they have consulted against Thy saints. They have said, 'Come, and let us destroy them, so that they be not a nation'" (Ps. 82:24).

3. At so urgent a crisis, when so fierce and so pressing an onslaught is made upon the Christian name, it is Our office to point out the danger, to mark who are the adversaries, and to the best of Our power to make head against their plans and devices, that those may not perish whose salvation is committed to Us, and that the kingdom of Jesus Christ entrusted to Our charge may not stand and remain whole but may be enlarged by an ever-increasing growth throughout the world.

4. The Roman Pontiffs Our predecessors, in their incessant watchfulness over the safety of the Christian people, were prompt in

1. *De civ. Dei*, 14, 28 (*PL* 41:436).

detecting the presence and the purpose of this capital enemy immediately it sprang into the light instead of hiding as a dark conspiracy; and, moreover, they took occasion with true foresight to give, on their guard as it were, and not allow themselves to be caught by the devices and snares laid out to deceive them.

5. The first warning of the danger was given by Clement XII in the year 1738,[2] and his constitution was confirmed and renewed by Benedict XIV.[3] Pius VII followed the same path[4]; and Leo XII, by his apostolic constitution *Quo graviora*,[5] put together the acts and decrees of former Pontiffs on this subject, and ratified and confirmed them forever. In the same sense spoke Pius VIII,[6] Gregory XVI,[7] and, many times over, Pius IX.[8]

6. For as soon as the constitution and the spirit of the masonic sect were clearly discovered by manifest signs of its actions, by the investigation of its causes, by publication of its laws, and of its rites and commentaries, with the addition often of the personal testimony of those who were in the secret, this Apostolic See denounced the sect of the Freemasons, and publicly declared its constitution, as contrary to law and right, to be pernicious no less to Christendom than to the State; and it forbade anyone to enter the society, under the penalties which the Church is wont to inflict upon exceptionally guilty persons. The sectaries, indignant at this, thinking to elude or to weaken the force of these decrees, partly by contempt of them, and partly by calumny, accused the sovereign Pontiffs who had passed them either of exceeding the bounds of moderation in their decrees or of decreeing

---

2. Apostolic Constitution *In eminenti apostolatus specula* (April 24, 1738).
3. Apostolic Constitution *Providas Romanorum* (May 18, 1751).
4. Apostolic Constitution *Ecclesiam a Jesu Christo* (September 13, 1821).
5. Given March 13, 1825.
6. Encyclical Letter *Traditi humilitati* (May 21, 1829).
7. Encyclical Letter *Mirari vos* (August 15, 1832).
8. Encyclical Letter *Qui pluribus* (November 9, 1846); Allocution *Multiplices inter* (September 25, 1865); etc.

what was not just. This was the manner in which they endeavored to elude the authority and the weight of the apostolic constitutions of Clement XII and Benedict XIV, as well as of Pius VII and Pius IX. Yet, in the very society itself, there were to be found men who unwillingly acknowledged that the Roman Pontiffs had acted within their right, according to the Catholic doctrine and discipline. The Pontiffs received the same assent, and in strong terms, from many princes and heads of governments, who made it their business either to delate the masonic society to the Apostolic See, or of their own accord by special enactments to brand it as pernicious, as, for example, in Holland, Austria, Switzerland, Spain, Bavaria, Savoy, and other parts of Italy.

7. But, what is of highest importance, the course of events has demonstrated the prudence of Our predecessors. For their provident and paternal solicitude had not always and everywhere the result desired; and this, either because of the simulation and cunning of some who were active agents in the mischief, or else of the thoughtless levity of the rest who ought, in their own interest, to have given to the matter their diligent attention. In consequence, the sect of Freemasons grew with a rapidity beyond conception in the course of a century and a half, until it came to be able, by means of fraud or of audacity, to gain such entrance into every rank of the State as to seem to be almost its ruling power. This swift and formidable advance has brought upon the Church, upon the power of princes, upon the public well-being, precisely that grievous harm which Our predecessors had long before foreseen. Such a condition has been reached that henceforth there will be grave reason to fear, not indeed for the Church—for her foundation is much too firm to be overturned by the effort of men—but for those States in which prevails the power, either of the sect of which we are speaking or of other sects not dissimilar which lend themselves to it as disciples and subordinates.

8. For these reasons, We no sooner came to the helm of the Church than We clearly saw and felt it to be Our duty to use Our

authority to the very utmost against so vast an evil. We have several times already, as occasion served, attacked certain chief points of teaching which showed in a special manner the perverse influence of masonic opinions. Thus, in Our Encyclical Letter, *Quod Apostolici muneris,* We endeavored to refute the monstrous doctrines of the socialists and communists; afterwards, in another beginning "*Arcanum*," We took pains to defend and explain the true and genuine idea of domestic life, of which marriage is the spring and origin; and again, in that which begins "*Diuturnum*," We described the ideal of political government conformed to the principles of Christian wisdom, which is marvelously in harmony, on the one hand, with the natural order of things, and, in the other, with the well-being of both sovereign princes and of nations. It is now Our intention, following the example of Our predecessors, directly to treat of the masonic society itself, of its whole teaching, of its aims, and of its manner of thinking and acting, in order to bring more and more into the light its power for evil, and to do what We can to arrest the contagion of this fatal plague.

9. There are several organized bodies which, though differing in name, in ceremonial, in form and origin, are nevertheless so bound together by community of purpose and by the similarity of their main opinions, as to make in fact one thing with the sect of the Freemasons, which is a kind of center whence they all go forth, and whither they all return. Now, these no longer show a desire to remain concealed; for they hold their meetings in the daylight and before the public eye, and publish their own newspaper organs; and yet, when thoroughly understood, they are found still to retain the nature and the habits of secret societies. There are many things like mysteries which it is the fixed rule to hide with extreme care, not only from strangers, but from very many members, also; such as their secret and final designs, the names of the chief leaders, and certain secret and inner meetings, as well as their decisions, and the ways and means of carrying them

out. This is, no doubt, the object of the manifold difference among the members as to right, office, and privilege, of the received distinction of orders and grades, and of that severe discipline which is maintained.

Candidates are generally commanded to promise—nay, with a special oath, to swear—that they will never, to any person, at any time or in any way, make known the members, the passes, or the subjects discussed. Thus, with a fraudulent external appearance, and with a style of simulation which is always the same, the Freemasons, like the Manichees of old, strive, as far as possible, to conceal themselves, and to admit no witnesses but their own members. As a convenient manner of concealment, they assume the character of literary men and scholars associated for purposes of learning. They speak of their zeal for a more cultured refinement, and of their love for the poor; and they declare their one wish to be the amelioration of the condition of the masses, and to share with the largest possible number all the benefits of civil life. Were these purposes aimed at in real truth, they are by no means the whole of their object. Moreover, to be enrolled, it is necessary that the candidates promise and undertake to be thenceforward strictly obedient to their leaders and masters with the utmost submission and fidelity, and to be in readiness to do their bidding upon the slightest expression of their will; or, if disobedient, to submit to the direst penalties and death itself. As a fact, if any are judged to have betrayed the doings of the sect or to have resisted commands given, punishment is inflicted on them not infrequently, and with so much audacity and dexterity that the assassin very often escapes the detection and penalty of his crime.

10. But to simulate and wish to lie hid; to bind men like slaves in the very tightest bonds, and without giving any sufficient reason; to make use of men enslaved to the will of another for any arbitrary act; to arm men's right hands for bloodshed after securing impunity for the crime—all this is an enormity from which nature

recoils. Wherefore, reason and truth itself make it plain that the society of which we are speaking is in antagonism with justice and natural uprightness. And this becomes still plainer, inasmuch as other arguments, also, and those very manifest, prove that it is essentially opposed to natural virtue. For no matter how great may be men's cleverness in concealing and their experience in lying, it is impossible to prevent the effects of any cause from showing, in some way, the intrinsic nature of the cause whence they come. "A good tree cannot produce bad fruit, nor a bad tree produce good fruit" (Matt. 7:18). Now, the masonic sect produces fruits that are pernicious and of the bitterest savor. For, from what We have above most clearly shown, that which is their ultimate purpose forces itself into view—namely, the utter overthrow of that whole religious and political order of the world which the Christian teaching has produced, and the substitution of a new state of things in accordance with their ideas, of which the foundations and laws shall be drawn from mere naturalism.

11. What We have said, and are about to say, must be understood of the sect of the Freemasons taken generically, and in so far as it comprises the associations kindred to it and confederated with it, but not of the individual members of them. There may be persons amongst these, and not a few who, although not free from the guilt of having entangled themselves in such associations, yet are neither themselves partners in their criminal acts nor aware of the ultimate object which they are endeavoring to attain. In the same way, some of the affiliated societies, perhaps, by no means approve of the extreme conclusions which they would, if consistent, embrace as necessarily following from their common principles, did not their very foulness strike them with horror. Some of these, again, are led by circumstances of times and places either to aim at smaller things than the others usually attempt or than they themselves would wish to attempt. They are not, however, for this reason, to be reckoned as alien to the masonic federation; for the masonic federation is to be judged

not so much by the things which it has done, or brought to completion, as by the sum of its pronounced opinions.

12. Now, the fundamental doctrine of the naturalists, which they sufficiently make known by their very name, is that human nature and human reason ought in all things to be mistress and guide. Laying this down, they care little for duties to God, or pervert them by erroneous and vague opinions. For they deny that anything has been taught by God; they allow no dogma of religion or truth which cannot be understood by the human intelligence, nor any teacher who ought to be believed by reason of his authority. And since it is the special and exclusive duty of the Catholic Church fully to set forth in words truths divinely received, to teach, besides other divine helps to salvation, the authority of its office, and to defend the same with perfect purity, it is against the Church that the rage and attack of the enemies are principally directed.

13. In those matters which regard religion let it be seen how the sect of the Freemasons acts, especially where it is more free to act without restraint, and then let anyone judge whether in fact it does not wish to carry out the policy of the naturalists. By a long and persevering labor, they endeavor to bring about this result—namely, that the teaching office and authority of the Church may become of no account in the civil State; and for this same reason they declare to the people and contend that Church and State ought to be altogether disunited. By this means they reject from the laws and from the commonwealth the wholesome influence of the Catholic religion; and they consequently imagine that States ought to be constituted without any regard for the laws and precepts of the Church.

14. Nor do they think it enough to disregard the Church—the best of guides—unless they also injure it by their hostility. Indeed, with them it is lawful to attack with impunity the very foundations of the Catholic religion, in speech, in writing, and in teaching; and even the rights of the Church are not spared, and the offices with which

it is divinely invested are not safe. The least possible liberty to manage affairs is left to the Church; and this is done by laws not apparently very hostile, but in reality framed and fitted to hinder freedom of action. Moreover, We see exceptional and onerous laws imposed upon the clergy, to the end that they may be continually diminished in number and in necessary means. We see also the remnants of the possessions of the Church fettered by the strictest conditions and subjected to the power and arbitrary will of the administrators of the State, and the religious orders rooted up and scattered.

15. But against the Apostolic See and the Roman Pontiff the contention of these enemies has been for a long time directed. The Pontiff was first, for specious reasons, thrust out from the bulwark of his liberty and of his right, the civil princedom; soon, he was unjustly driven into a condition which was unbearable because of the difficulties raised on all sides; and now the time has come when the partisans of the sects openly declare, what in secret among themselves they have for a long time plotted, that the sacred power of the Pontiffs must be abolished, and that the papacy itself, founded by divine right, must be utterly destroyed. If other proofs were wanting, this fact would be sufficiently disclosed by the testimony of men well informed, of whom some at other times, and others again recently, have declared it to be true of the Freemasons that they especially desire to assail the Church with irreconcilable hostility, and that they will never rest until they have destroyed whatever the supreme Pontiffs have established for the sake of religion.

16. If those who are admitted as members are not commanded to abjure by any form of words the Catholic doctrines, this omission, so far from being adverse to the designs of the Freemasons, is more useful for their purposes. First, in this way they easily deceive the simple-minded and the heedless, and can induce a far greater number to become members. Again, as all who offer themselves are received whatever may be their form of religion, they thereby teach the great

error of this age—that a regard for religion should be held as an indifferent matter, and that all religions are alike. This manner of reasoning is calculated to bring about the ruin of all forms of religion, and especially of the Catholic religion, which, as it is the only one that is true, cannot, without great injustice, be regarded as merely equal to other religions.

17. But the naturalists go much further; for, having in the highest things entered upon a wholly erroneous course, they are carried headlong to extremes, either by reason of the weakness of human nature, or because God inflicts upon them the just punishment of their pride. Hence it happens that they no longer consider as certain and permanent those things which are fully understood by the natural light of reason, such as certainly are—the existence of God, the immaterial nature of the human soul, and its immortality. The sect of the Freemasons, by a similar course of error, is exposed to these same dangers; for, although in a general way they may profess the existence of God, they themselves are witnesses that they do not all maintain this truth with the full assent of the mind or with a firm conviction. Neither do they conceal that this question about God is the greatest source and cause of discords among them; in fact, it is certain that a considerable contention about this same subject has existed among them very lately. But, indeed, the sect allows great liberty to its votaries, so that to each side is given the right to defend its own opinion, either that there is a God, or that there is none; and those who obstinately contend that there is no God are as easily initiated as those who contend that God exists, though, like the pantheists, they have false notions concerning Him: all which is nothing else than taking away the reality, while retaining some absurd representation of the divine nature.

18. When this greatest fundamental truth has been overturned or weakened, it follows that those truths, also, which are known by the teaching of nature must begin to fall—namely, that all things were

made by the free will of God the Creator; that the world is governed by Providence; that souls do not die; that to this life of men upon the earth there will succeed another and an everlasting life.

19. When these truths are done away with, which are as the principles of nature and important for knowledge and for practical use, it is easy to see what will become of both public and private morality. We say nothing of those more heavenly virtues, which no one can exercise or even acquire without a special gift and grace of God; of which necessarily no trace can be found in those who reject as unknown the redemption of mankind, the grace of God, the sacraments, and the happiness to be obtained in heaven. We speak now of the duties which have their origin in natural probity. That God is the Creator of the world and its provident Ruler; that the eternal law commands the natural order to be maintained and forbids that it be disturbed; that the last end of men is a destiny far above human things and beyond this sojourning upon the earth: these are the sources and these the principles of all justice and morality. If these be taken away, as the naturalists and Freemasons desire, there will immediately be no knowledge as to what constitutes justice and injustice, or upon what principle morality is founded. And, in truth, the teaching of morality which alone finds favor with the sect of Freemasons, and in which they contend that youth should be instructed, is that which they call "civil," and "independent," and "free," namely, that which does not contain any religious belief. But, how insufficient such teaching is, how wanting in soundness, and how easily moved by every impulse of passion, is sufficiently proved by its sad fruits, which have already begun to appear. For wherever, by removing Christian education, this teaching has begun more completely to rule, there goodness and integrity of morals have begun quickly to perish, monstrous and shameful opinions have grown up, and the audacity of evil deeds has risen to a high degree. All this is commonly complained of and deplored; and not a few of those who by no means

wish to do so are compelled by abundant evidence to give not infrequently the same testimony.

20. Moreover, human nature was stained by original sin, and is therefore more disposed to vice than to virtue. For a virtuous life it is absolutely necessary to restrain the disorderly movements of the soul, and to make the passions obedient to reason. In this conflict human things must very often be despised, and the greatest labors and hardships must be undergone, in order that reason may always hold its sway. But the naturalists and Freemasons, having no faith in those things which we have learned by the revelation of God, deny that our first parents sinned, and consequently think that free will is not at all weakened and inclined to evil.[9] On the contrary, exaggerating rather the power and the excellence of nature, and placing therein alone the principle and rule of justice, they cannot even imagine that there is any need at all of a constant struggle and a perfect steadfastness to overcome the violence and rule of our passions.

Wherefore we see that men are publicly tempted by the many allurements of pleasure; that there are journals and pamphlets with neither moderation nor shame; that stage-plays are remarkable for license; that designs for works of art are shamelessly sought in the laws of a so-called verism; that the contrivances of a soft and delicate life are most carefully devised; and that all the blandishments of pleasure are diligently sought out by which virtue may be lulled to sleep. Wickedly, also, but at the same time quite consistently, do those act who do away with the expectation of the joys of heaven, and bring down all happiness to the level of mortality, and, as it were, sink it in the earth. Of what We have said the following fact, astonishing not so much in itself as in its open expression, may serve as a confirmation. For since generally no one is accustomed to obey crafty

9. Council of Trent, Session 6, *De justif.*, c. 1. Text of the Council of Trent: "*tametsi in eis* (sc. Judaeis) *liberum arbitrium minime extinctum esset, viribus licet attenuatum et inclinatum*."

and clever men so submissively as those whose soul is weakened and broken down by the domination of the passions, there have been in the sect of the Freemasons some who have plainly determined and proposed that, artfully and of set purpose, the multitude should be satiated with a boundless license of vice, as, when this had been done, it would easily come under their power and authority for any acts of daring.

21. What refers to domestic life in the teaching of the naturalists is almost all contained in the following declarations: that marriage belongs to the genus of commercial contracts, which can rightly be revoked by the will of those who made them, and that the civil rulers of the State have power over the matrimonial bond; that in the education of youth nothing is to be taught in the matter of religion as of certain and fixed opinion; and each one must be left at liberty to follow, when he comes of age, whatever he may prefer. To these things the Freemasons fully assent; and not only assent, but have long endeavored to make them into a law and institution. For in many countries, and those nominally Catholic, it is enacted that no marriages shall be considered lawful except those contracted by the civil rite; in other places the law permits divorce; and in others every effort is used to make it lawful as soon as may be. Thus, the time is quickly coming when marriages will be turned into another kind of contract—that is into changeable and uncertain unions which fancy may join together, and which the same when changed may disunite.

With the greatest unanimity the sect of the Freemasons also endeavors to take to itself the education of youth. They think that they can easily mold to their opinions that soft and pliant age and bend it whither they will; and that nothing can be more fitted than this to enable them to bring up the youth of the State after their own plan. Therefore, in the education and instruction of children they allow no share, either of teaching or of discipline, to the ministers of the Church; and in many places they have procured that the education of youth shall be exclusively in the hands of laymen, and that nothing which treats of the most important and most holy duties of men to God shall be introduced into the instructions on morals.

22. Then come their doctrines of politics, in which the naturalists lay down that all men have the same right and are in every respect of equal and like condition; that each one is naturally free; that no one has the right to command another; that it is an act of violence to require men to obey any authority other than that which is obtained from themselves. According to this, therefore, all things belong to the free people; power is held by the command or permission of the people, so that, when the popular will changes, rulers may lawfully be deposed and the source of all rights and civil duties is either in the multitude or in the governing authority when this is constituted according to the latest doctrines. It is held also that the State should be without God; that in the various forms of religion there is no reason why one should have precedence of another; and that they are all to occupy the same place.

23. That these doctrines are equally acceptable to the Freemasons, and that they would wish to constitute States according to this example and model, is too well known to require proof. For some time past they have openly endeavored to bring this about with all their strength and resources; and in this they prepare the way for not a few bolder men who are hurrying on even to worse things, in their endeavor to obtain equality and community of all goods by the destruction of every distinction of rank and property.

24. What, therefore, the sect of the Freemasons is, and what course it pursues, appears sufficiently from the summary We have briefly given. Their chief dogmas are so greatly and manifestly at variance with reason that nothing can be more perverse. To wish to destroy the religion and the Church which God Himself has established, and whose perpetuity He insures by His protection, and to bring back after a lapse of eighteen centuries the manners and customs

of the pagans, is signal folly and audacious impiety. Neither is it less horrible nor more tolerable that they should repudiate the benefits which Jesus Christ so mercifully obtained, not only for individuals, but also for the family and for civil society, benefits which, even according to the judgment and testimony of enemies of Christianity, are very great. In this insane and wicked endeavor, we may almost see the implacable hatred and spirit of revenge with which Satan himself is inflamed against Jesus Christ. So also the studious endeavor of the Freemasons to destroy the chief foundations of justice and honesty, and to cooperate with those who would wish, as if they were mere animals, to do what they please, tends only to the ignominious and disgraceful ruin of the human race.

The evil, too, is increased by the dangers which threaten both domestic and civil society. As We have elsewhere shown,[10] in marriage, according to the belief of almost every nation, there is something sacred and religious; and the law of God has determined that marriages shall not be dissolved. If they are deprived of their sacred character, and made dissoluble, trouble and confusion in the family will be the result, the wife being deprived of her dignity and the children left without protection as to their interests and well-being. To have in public matters no care for religion, and in the arrangement and administration of civil affairs to have no more regard for God than if He did not exist, is a rashness unknown to the very pagans; for in their heart and soul the notion of a divinity and the need of public religion were so firmly fixed that they would have thought it easier to have city without foundation than a city without God. Human society, indeed for which by nature we are formed, has been constituted by God the Author of nature; and from Him, as from their principle and source, flow in all their strength and permanence the countless benefits with which society abounds. As we

10. See Encyclical Letter *Arcanum*, §41.

are each of us admonished by the very voice of nature to worship God in piety and holiness, as the Giver unto us of life and of all that is good therein, so also and for the same reason, nations and States are bound to worship Him; and therefore it is clear that those who would absolve society from all religious duty act not only unjustly but also with ignorance and folly.

25. As men are by the will of God born for civil union and society, and as the power to rule is so necessary a bond of society that, if it be taken away, society must at once be broken up, it follows that from Him who is the Author of society has come also the authority to rule; so that whosoever rules, he is the minister of God. Wherefore, as the end and nature of human society so requires, it is right to obey the just commands of lawful authority, as it is right to obey God who ruleth all things; and it is most untrue that the people have it in their power to cast aside their obedience whenever they please.

26. In like manner, no one doubts that all men are equal one to another, so far as regards their common origin and nature, or the last end which each one has to attain, or the rights and duties which are thence derived. But, as the abilities of all are not equal, as one differs from another in the powers of mind or body, and as there are very many dissimilarities of manner, disposition, and character, it is most repugnant to reason to endeavor to confine all within the same measure, and to extend complete equality to the institutions of civic life. Just as a perfect condition of the body results from the conjunction and composition of its various members, which, though differing in form and purpose, make, by their union and the distribution of each one to its proper place, a combination beautiful to behold, firm in strength, and necessary for use; so, in the commonwealth, there is an almost infinite dissimilarity of men, as parts of the whole. If they are to be all equal, and each is to follow his own will, the State will appear most deformed; but if, with a distinction of degrees of dignity, of pursuits and employments, all aptly conspire for the common good,

they will present the image of a State both well constituted and conformable to nature.

27. Now, from the disturbing errors which We have described the greatest dangers to States are to be feared. For the fear of God and reverence for divine laws being taken away, the authority of rulers despised, sedition permitted and approved, and the popular passions urged on to lawlessness, with no restraint save that of punishment, a change and overthrow of all things will necessarily follow. Yea, this change and overthrow is deliberately planned and put forward by many associations of communists and socialists; and to their undertakings the sect of Freemasons is not hostile, but greatly favors their designs, and holds in common with them their chief opinions. And if these men do not at once and everywhere endeavor to carry out their extreme views, it is not to be attributed to their teaching and their will, but to the virtue of that divine religion which cannot be destroyed; and also because the sounder part of men, refusing to be enslaved to secret societies, vigorously resist their insane attempts.

28. Would that all men would judge of the tree by its fruit, and would acknowledge the seed and origin of the evils which press upon us, and of the dangers that are impending! We have to deal with a deceitful and crafty enemy, who, gratifying the ears of people and of princes, has ensnared them by smooth speeches and by adulation. Ingratiating themselves with rulers under a pretense of friendship, the Freemasons have endeavored to make them their allies and powerful helpers for the destruction of the Christian name; and that they might more strongly urge them on, they have, with determined calumny, accused the Church of invidiously contending with rulers in matters that affect their authority and sovereign power. Having, by these artifices, insured their own safety and audacity, they have begun to exercise great weight in the government of States; but nevertheless they are prepared to shake the foundations of empires, to harass the rulers of the State, to accuse, and to cast them out, as

often as they appear to govern otherwise than they themselves could have wished. In like manner, they have by flattery deluded the people. Proclaiming with a loud voice liberty and public prosperity, and saying that it was owing to the Church and to sovereigns that the multitude were not drawn out of their unjust servitude and poverty, they have imposed upon the people, and, exciting them by a thirst for novelty, they have urged them to assail both the Church and the civil power. Nevertheless, the expectation of the benefits which was hoped for is greater than the reality; indeed, the common people, more oppressed than they were before, are deprived in their misery of that solace which, if things had been arranged in a Christian manner, they would have had with ease and in abundance. But, whoever strive against the order which divine providence has constituted pay usually the penalty of their pride and meet with affliction and misery where they rashly hoped to find all things prosperous and in conformity with their desires.

29. The Church, if she directs men to render obedience chiefly and above all to God the sovereign Lord, is wrongly and falsely believed either to be envious of the civil power or to arrogate to herself something of the rights of sovereigns. On the contrary, she teaches that what is rightly due to the civil power must be rendered to it with a conviction and consciousness of duty. In teaching that from God Himself comes the right of ruling, she adds a great dignity to civil authority, and on small help towards obtaining the obedience and good will of the citizens. The friend of peace and sustainer of concord, she embraces all with maternal love; and, intent only upon giving help to mortal man, she teaches that to justice must be joined clemency, equity to authority, and moderation to lawgiving; that no one's right must be violated; that order and public tranquility are to be maintained; and that the poverty of those are in need is, as far as possible, to be relieved by public and private charity. "But for this reason," to use the words of St. Augustine, "men think, or would have it believed,

that Christian teaching is not suited to the good of the State; for they wish the State to be founded not on solid virtue, but on the impunity of vice."[11] Knowing these things, both princes and people would act with political wisdom, and according to the needs of general safety, if, instead of joining with Freemasons to destroy the Church, they joined with the Church in repelling their attacks.

30. Whatever the future may be, in this grave and widespread evil it is Our duty, Venerable Brethren, to endeavor to find a remedy. And because We know that Our best and firmest hope of a remedy is in the power of that divine religion which the Freemasons hate in proportion to their fear of it, We think it to be of chief importance to call that most saving power to Our aid against the common enemy. Therefore, whatsoever the Roman Pontiffs Our predecessors have decreed for the purpose of opposing the undertakings and endeavors of the masonic sect, and whatsoever they have enacted to enter or withdraw men from societies of this kind, We ratify and confirm it all by our apostolic authority; and trusting greatly to the good will of Christians, We pray and beseech each one, for the sake of his eternal salvation, to be most conscientiously careful not in the least to depart from what the Apostolic See has commanded in this matter.

31. We pray and beseech you, Venerable Brethren, to join your efforts with Ours, and earnestly to strive for the extirpation of this foul plague, which is creeping through the veins of the body politic. You have to defend the glory of God and the salvation of your neighbor; and with the object of your strife before you, neither courage nor strength will be wanting. It will be for your prudence to judge by what means you can best overcome the difficulties and obstacles you meet with. But, as it befits the authority of Our office that We Ourselves should point out some suitable way of proceeding, We wish it to be your rule first of all to tear away the mask from Freemasonry,

---

11. *Epist.* 137, *ad Volusianum*, 5, 20 (*PL* 33:525).

and to let it be seen as it really is; and by sermons and pastoral letters to instruct the people as to the artifices used by societies of this kind in seducing men and enticing them into their ranks, and as to the depravity of their opinions and the wickedness of their acts. As Our predecessors have many times repeated, let no man think that he may for any reason whatsoever join the masonic sect, if he values his Catholic name and his eternal salvation as he ought to value them. Let no one be deceived by a pretense of honesty. It may seem to some that Freemasons demand nothing that is openly contrary to religion and morality; but, as the whole principle and object of the sect lies in what is vicious and criminal, to join with these men or in any way to help them cannot be lawful.

32. Further, by assiduous teaching and exhortation, the multitude must be drawn to learn diligently the precepts of religion; for which purpose we earnestly advise that by opportune writings and sermons they be taught the elements of those sacred truths in which Christian philosophy is contained. The result of this will be that the minds of men will be made sound by instruction and will be protected against many forms of error and inducements to wickedness, especially in the present unbounded freedom of writing and insatiable eagerness for learning.

33. Great, indeed, is the work; but in it the clergy will share your labors, if, through your care, they are fitted for it by learning and a well-turned life. This good and great work requires to be helped also by the industry of those amongst the laity in whom a love of religion and of country is joined to learning and goodness of life. By uniting the efforts of both clergy and laity, strive, Venerable Brethren, to make men thoroughly know and love the Church; for the greater their knowledge and love of the Church, the more will they be turned away from clandestine societies.

34. Wherefore, not without cause do We use this occasion to state again what We have stated elsewhere, namely, that the Third

Order of St. Francis, whose discipline We a little while ago prudently mitigated,[12] should be studiously promoted and sustained; for the whole object of this Order, as constituted by its founder, is to invite men to an imitation of Jesus Christ, to a love of the Church, and to the observance of all Christian virtues; and therefore it ought to be of great influence in suppressing the contagion of wicked societies. Let, therefore, this holy sodality be strengthened by a daily increase. Amongst the many benefits to be expected from it will be the great benefit of drawing the minds of men to liberty, fraternity, and equality of right; not such as the Freemasons absurdly imagine, but such as Jesus Christ obtained for the human race and St. Francis aspired to: the liberty, We mean, of *sons of God*, through which we may be free from slavery to Satan or to our passions, both of them most wicked masters; the fraternity whose origin is in God, the common Creator and Father of all; the equality which, founded on justice and charity, does not take away all distinctions among men, but, out of the varieties of life, of duties, and of pursuits, forms that union and that harmony which naturally tend to the benefit and dignity of society.

35. In the third place, there is a matter wisely instituted by our forefathers, but in course of time laid aside, which may now be used as a pattern and form of something similar. We mean the associations of guilds of workmen, for the protection, under the guidance of religion, both of their temporal interests and of their morality. If our ancestors, by long use and experience, felt the benefit of these

12. The text here refers to the Encyclical Letter *Auspicato concessum* (September 17, 1882), in which Pope Leo XIII had recently glorified St. Francis of Assisi on the occasion of the seventh centenary of his birth. In this encyclical, the Pope had presented the Third Order of St. Francis as a Christian answer to the social problems of the times. The Constitution *Misericors dei filius* (June 23, 1883) expressly recalled that the neglect in which Christian virtues are held is the main cause of the evils that threaten societies. In confirming the rule of the Third Order and adapting it to the needs of modern times, Pope Leo XIII had intended to bring back the largest possible number of souls to the practice of these virtues.

guilds, our age perhaps will feel it the more by reason of the opportunity which they will give of crushing the power of the sects. Those who support themselves by the labor of their hands, besides being, by their very condition, most worthy above all others of charity and consolation, are also especially exposed to the allurements of men whose ways lie in fraud and deceit. Therefore, they ought to be helped with the greatest possible kindness, and to be invited to join associations that are good, lest they be drawn away to others that are evil. For this reason, We greatly wish, for the salvation of the people, that, under the auspices and patronage of the bishops, and at convenient times, these guilds may be generally restored. To Our great delight, sodalities of this kind and also associations of masters have in many places already been established, having, each class of them, for their object to help the honest workman, to protect and guard his children and family, and to promote in them piety, Christian knowledge, and a moral life. And in this matter We cannot omit mentioning that exemplary society, named after its founder, St. Vincent, which has deserved so well of the lower classes. Its acts and its aims are well known. Its whole object is to give relief to the poor and miserable. This it does with singular prudence and modesty; and the less it wishes to be seen, the better is it fitted for the exercise of Christian charity, and for the relief of suffering.

36. In the fourth place, in order more easily to attain what We wish, to your fidelity and watchfulness We commend in a special manner the young, as being the hope of human society. Devote the greatest part of your care to their instruction; and do not think that any precaution can be great enough in keeping them from masters and schools whence the pestilent breath of the sects is to be feared. Under your guidance, let parents, religious instructors, and priests having the cure of souls use every opportunity, in their Christian teaching, of warning their children and pupils of the infamous nature of these societies, so that they may learn in good time to beware

of the various and fraudulent artifices by which their promoters are accustomed to ensnare people. And those who instruct the young in religious knowledge will act wisely if they induce all of them to resolve and to undertake never to bind themselves to any society without the knowledge of their parents, or the advice of their parish priest or director.

37. We well know, however, that our united labors will by no means suffice to pluck up these pernicious seeds from the Lord's field, unless the Heavenly Master of the vineyard shall mercifully help us in our endeavors. We must, therefore, with great and anxious care, implore of Him the help which the greatness of the danger and of the need requires. The sect of the Freemasons shows itself insolent and proud of its success, and seems as if it would put no bounds to its pertinacity. Its followers, joined together by a wicked compact and by secret counsels, give help one to another, and excite one another to an audacity for evil things. So vehement an attack demands an equal defense—namely, that all good men should form the widest possible association of action and of prayer. We beseech them, therefore, with united hearts, to stand together and unmoved against the advancing force of the sects; and in mourning and supplication to stretch out their hands to God, praying that the Christian name may flourish and prosper, that the Church may enjoy its needed liberty, that those who have gone astray may return to a right mind, that error at length may give place to truth, and vice to virtue. Let us take as our helper and intercessor the Virgin Mary, Mother of God, so that she, who from the moment of her conception overcame Satan may show her power over these evil sects, in which is revived the contumacious spirit of the demon, together with his unsubdued perfidy and deceit. Let us beseech Michael, the prince of the heavenly angels, who drove out the infernal foe; and Joseph, the spouse of the most holy Virgin, and heavenly patron of the Catholic Church; and the great Apostles, Peter and Paul, the fathers and victorious champions of the Christian

faith. By their patronage, and by perseverance in united prayer, we hope that God will mercifully and opportunely succor the human race, which is encompassed by so many dangers.

38. As a pledge of heavenly gifts and of Our benevolence, We lovingly grant in the Lord, to you, Venerable Brethren, and to the clergy and all the people committed to your watchful care, Our Apostolic Benediction.

Given at St. Peter's, in Rome, the twentieth day of April, 1884, the sixth year of Our Pontificate.

LEO PP. XIII

ENCYCLICAL LETTER

IMMORTALE DEI

OF THE SUPREME PONTIFF

LEO XIII

TO OUR VENERABLE BRETHREN THE PATRIARCHS, PRIMATES, ARCHBISHOPS, BISHOPS, AND OTHER ORDINARIES IN PEACE AND COMMUNION WITH THE APOSTOLIC SEE

ON THE CHRISTIAN CONSTITUTION OF STATES

1. The Catholic Church, that imperishable handiwork of our all-merciful God, has for her immediate and natural purpose the saving of souls and securing our happiness in heaven. Yet, in regard to things temporal, she is the source of benefits as manifold and great as if the chief end of her existence were to ensure the prospering of our earthly life. And, indeed, wherever the Church has set her foot she has straightway changed the face of things and has tempered the moral tone of the people with a new civilization and with virtues before unknown. All nations which have yielded to her sway have become eminent by their gentleness, their sense of justice, and the glory of their high deeds.

2. And yet a hackneyed reproach of old date is leveled against her, that the Church is opposed to the rightful aims of the civil government and is wholly unable to afford help in spreading that welfare and progress which justly and naturally are sought after by every

well-regulated State. From the very beginning Christians were harassed by slanderous accusations of this nature, and on that account were held up to hatred and execration, for being (so they were called) enemies of the Empire. The Christian religion was moreover commonly charged with being the cause of the calamities that so frequently befell the State, whereas, in very truth, just punishment was being awarded to guilty nations by an avenging God. This odious calumny, with most valid reason, nerved the genius and sharpened the pen of St. Augustine, who, notably in his treatise, *The City of God*, set forth in so bright a light the worth of Christian wisdom in its relation to the public wealth that he seems not merely to have pleaded the cause of the Christians of his day, but to have refuted for all future times impeachments so grossly contrary to truth. The wicked proneness, however, to levy like charges and accusations has not been lulled to rest. Many, indeed, are they who have tried to work out a plan of civil society based on doctrines other than those approved by the Catholic Church. Nay, in these latter days a novel conception of law has begun here and there to gain increase and influence, the outcome, as it is maintained, of an age arrived at full stature, and the result of progressive liberty. But, though endeavors of various kinds have been ventured on, it is clear that no better mode has been devised for the building up and ruling the State than that which is the necessary growth of the teachings of the Gospel. We deem it, therefore, of the highest moment, and a strict duty of Our apostolic office, to contrast with the lessons taught by Christ the novel theories now advanced touching the State. By this means We cherish hope that the bright shining of the truth may scatter the mists of error and doubt, so that one and all may see clearly the imperious law of life which they are bound to follow and obey.

3. It is not difficult to determine what would be the form and character of the State were it governed according to the principles of Christian philosophy. Man's natural instinct moves him to live in

civil society, for he cannot, if dwelling apart, provide himself with the necessary requirements of life, nor procure the means of developing his mental and moral faculties. Hence, it is divinely ordained that he should lead his life—be it family or civil—with his fellow men, amongst whom alone his several wants can be adequately supplied. But, as no society can hold together unless someone be over all, directing all to strive earnestly for the common good, every body politic must have a ruling authority, and this authority, no less than society itself, has its source in nature, and has, consequently, God for its Author. Hence, it follows that all public power must proceed from God. For God alone is the true and supreme Lord of the world. Everything, without exception, must be subject to Him, and must serve him, so that whosoever holds the right to govern holds it from one sole and single source, namely, God, the sovereign Ruler of all. "There is no power but from God" (Rom. 13:1).

4. The right to rule is not necessarily, however, bound up with any special mode of government. It may take this or that form, provided only that it be of a nature of the government, rulers must ever bear in mind that God is the paramount ruler of the world, and must set Him before themselves as their exemplar and law in the administration of the State. For, in things visible, God has fashioned secondary causes in which His divine action can in some wise be discerned, leading up to the end to which the course of the world is ever tending. In like manner, in civil society, God has always willed that there should be a ruling authority, and that they who are invested with it should reflect the divine power and providence in some measure over the human race.

5. They, therefore, who rule should rule with evenhanded justice, not as masters, but rather as fathers, for the rule of God over man is most just and is tempered always with a father's kindness. Government should, moreover, be administered for the well-being of the citizens, because they who govern others possess authority solely for the

welfare of the State. Furthermore, the civil power must not be subservient to the advantage of any one individual or of some few persons, inasmuch as it was established for the common good of all. But, if those who are in authority rule unjustly, if they govern overbearingly or arrogantly, and if their measures prove hurtful to the people, they must remember that the Almighty will one day bring them to account, the more strictly in proportion to the sacredness of their office and preeminence of their dignity. "The mighty shall be mightily tormented" (Wis. 6:7). Then, truly, will the majesty of the law meet with the dutiful and willing homage of the people, when they are convinced that their rulers hold authority from God, and feel that it is a matter of justice and duty to obey them, and to show them reverence and fealty, united to a love not unlike that which children show their parents. "Let every soul be subject to higher powers" (Rom. 13:1). To despise legitimate authority, in whomsoever vested, is unlawful, as a rebellion against the divine will, and whoever resists that, rushes willfully to destruction. "He that resisteth the power resisteth the ordinance of God, and they that resist, purchase to themselves damnation" (Rom. 13:2). To cast aside obedience, and by popular violence to incite to revolt, is therefore treason, not against man only, but against God.

6. As a consequence, the State, constituted as it is, is clearly bound to act up to the manifold and weighty duties linking it to God, by the public profession of religion. Nature and reason, which command every individual devoutly to worship God in holiness, because we belong to Him and must return to Him, since from Him we came, bind also the civil community by a like law. For men living together in society are under the power of God no less than individuals are, and society, no less than individuals, owes gratitude to God who gave it being and maintains it and whose ever-bounteous goodness enriches it with countless blessings. Since, then, no one is allowed to be remiss in the service due to God, and since the chief duty of all men

is to cling to religion in both its reaching and practice—not such religion as they may have a preference for, but the religion which God enjoins, and which certain and most clear marks show to be the only one true religion—it is a public crime to act as though there were no God. So, too, is it a sin for the State not to have care for religion as a something beyond its scope, or as of no practical benefit; or out of many forms of religion to adopt that one which chimes in with the fancy; for we are bound absolutely to worship God in that way which He has shown to be His will. All who rule, therefore, would hold in honor the holy name of God, and one of their chief duties must be to favor religion, to protect it, to shield it under the credit and sanction of the laws, and neither to organize nor enact any measure that may compromise its safety. This is the bounden duty of rulers to the people over whom they rule. For one and all are we destined by our birth and adoption to enjoy, when this frail and fleeting life is ended, a supreme and final good in heaven, and to the attainment of this every endeavor should be directed. Since, then, upon this depends the full and perfect happiness of mankind, the securing of this end should be of all imaginable interests the most urgent. Hence, civil society, established for the common welfare, should not only safeguard the well-being of the community, but have also at heart the interests of its individual members, in such mode as not in any way to hinder, but in every manner to render as easy as may be, the possession of that highest and unchangeable good for which all should seek. Wherefore, for this purpose, care must especially be taken to preserve unharmed and unimpeded the religion whereof the practice is the link connecting man with God.

7. Now, it cannot be difficult to find out which is the true religion, if only it be sought with an earnest and unbiased mind; for proofs are abundant and striking. We have, for example, the fulfilment of prophecies, miracles in great numbers, the rapid spread of the faith in the midst of enemies and in face of overwhelming obstacles, the

witness of the martyrs, and the like. From all these it is evident that the only true religion is the one established by Jesus Christ Himself, and which He committed to His Church to protect and to propagate.

8. For the only-begotten Son of God established on earth a society which is called the Church, and to it He handed over the exalted and divine office which He had received from His Father, to be continued through the ages to come. "As the Father hath sent Me, I also send you" (John 20:21). "Behold I am with you all days, even to the consummation of the world" (Matt. 28:20). Consequently, as Jesus Christ came into the world that men "might have life and have it more abundantly" (John 10:10), so also has the Church for its aim and end the eternal salvation of souls, and hence it is so constituted as to open wide its arms to all mankind, unhampered by any limit of either time or place. "Preach ye the Gospel to every creature" (Mark 16:15).

9. Over this mighty multitude God has Himself set rulers with power to govern, and He has willed that one should be the head of all, and the chief and unerring teacher of truth, to whom He has given "the keys of the kingdom of heaven" (Matt. 16:19). "Feed my lambs, feed my sheep" (John 21:16–17). "I have prayed for thee that thy faith fail not" (Luke 22:32).

10. This society is made up of men, just as civil society is, and yet is supernatural and spiritual, on account of the end for which it was founded, and of the means by which it aims at attaining that end. Hence, it is distinguished and differs from civil society, and, what is of highest moment, it is a society chartered as of right divine, perfect in its nature and in its title, to possess in itself and by itself, through the will and loving kindness of its Founder, all needful provision for its maintenance and action. And just as the end at which the Church aims is by far the noblest of ends, so is its authority the most exalted of all authority, nor can it be looked upon as inferior to the civil power or in any manner dependent upon it.

11. In very truth, Jesus Christ gave to His Apostles unrestrained authority in regard to things sacred, together with the genuine and most true power of making laws, as also with the twofold right of judging and of punishing, which flow from that power. "All power is given to me in heaven and on earth: going therefore teach all nations...teaching them to observe all things whatsoever I have commanded you" (Matt. 28:18–20). And in another place: "If he will not hear them, tell the Church" (Matt. 18:12). And again: "In readiness to revenge all disobedience" (2 Cor. 10:6). And once more: "That...I may not deal more severely according to the power which the Lord hath given me, unto edification and not unto destruction" (2 Cor. 13:10). Hence, it is the Church, and not the State, that is to be man's guide to heaven. It is to the Church that God has assigned the charge of seeing to, and legislating for, all that concerns religion; of teaching all nations; of spreading the Christian faith as widely as possible; in short, of administering freely and without hindrance, in accordance with her own judgment, all matters that fall within its competence.

12. Now, this authority, perfect in itself, and plainly meant to be unfettered, so long assailed by a philosophy that submits obsequiously to the State, the Church, has never ceased to claim for herself and openly to exercise. The Apostles themselves were the first to uphold it, when, being forbidden by the rulers of the synagogue to preach the Gospel, they courageously answered: "We must obey God rather than men" (Acts 5:29). This same authority the holy Fathers of the Church were always careful to maintain by weighty arguments, according as occasion arose, and the Roman Pontiffs have never shrunk from defending it with unbending constancy. Nay, more, princes and all invested with power to rule have themselves approved it, in theory alike and in practice. It cannot be called in question that in the making of treaties, in the transaction of business matters, in the sending and receiving ambassadors, and in the interchange of other kinds of official dealings they have been wont to treat

with the Church as with a supreme and legitimate power. And, assuredly, all ought to hold that it was not without a singular disposition of God's providence that this power of the Church was provided with a civil sovereignty as the surest safeguard of her independence.

13. The Almighty, therefore, has given the charge of the human race to two powers, the ecclesiastical and the civil, the one being set over divine, and the other over human, things. Each in its kind is supreme, each has fixed limits within which it is contained, limits which are defined by the nature and special object of the province of each, so that there is, we may say, an orbit traced out within which the action of each is brought into play by its own native right. But, inasmuch as each of these two powers has authority over the same subjects, and as it might come to pass that one and the same thing—related differently, but still remaining one and the same thing—might belong to the jurisdiction and determination of both, therefore God, who foresees all things, and who is the author of these two powers, has marked out the course of each in right correlation to the other. "For the powers that are, are ordained of God" (Rom. 13:1). Were this not so, deplorable contentions and conflicts would often arise, and, not infrequently, men, like travelers at the meeting of two roads, would hesitate in anxiety and doubt, not knowing what course to follow. Two powers would be commanding contrary things, and it would be a dereliction of duty to disobey either of the two.

14. But it would be most repugnant to them to think thus of the wisdom and goodness of God. Even in physical things, albeit of a lower order, the Almighty has so combined the forces and springs of nature with tempered action and wondrous harmony that no one of them clashes with any other, and all of them most fitly and aptly work together for the great purpose of the universe. There must, accordingly, exist between these two powers a certain orderly connection, which may be compared to the union of the soul and body in man. The nature and scope of that connection can be determined only, as

We have laid down, by having regard to the nature of each power, and by taking account of the relative excellence and nobleness of their purpose. One of the two has for its proximate and chief object the well-being of this mortal life; the other, the everlasting joys of heaven. Whatever, therefore in things human is of a sacred character, whatever belongs either of its own nature or by reason of the end to which it is referred, to the salvation of souls, or to the worship of God, is subject to the power and judgment of the Church. Whatever is to be ranged under the civil and political order is rightly subject to the civil authority. Jesus Christ has Himself given command that what is Caesar's is to be rendered to Caesar, and that what belongs to God is to be rendered to God.

15. There are, nevertheless, occasions when another method of concord is available for the sake of peace and liberty. We mean when rulers of the State and the Roman Pontiff come to an understanding touching some special matter. At such times the Church gives signal proof of her motherly love by showing the greatest possible kindliness and indulgence.

16. Such, then, as We have briefly pointed out, is the Christian organization of civil society; not rashly or fancifully shaped out, but educed from the highest and truest principles, confirmed by natural reason itself.

17. In such organization of the State, there is nothing that can be thought to infringe upon the dignity of rulers, and nothing unbecoming them; nay, so far from degrading the sovereign power in its due rights, it adds to it permanence and luster. Indeed, when more fully pondered, this mutual coordination has a perfection in which all other forms of government are lacking, and from which excellent results would flow, were the several component parts to keep their place and duly discharge the office and work appointed respectively for each. And, doubtless, in the constitution of the State such as We have described, divine and human things are equitably shared; the

rights of citizens assured to them, and fenced round by divine, by natural, and by human law; the duties incumbent on each one being wisely marked out, and their fulfilment fittingly insured. In their uncertain and toilsome journey to the everlasting city, all see that they have safe guides and helpers on their way and are conscious that others have charge to protect their persons alike and their possessions and to obtain or preserve for them everything essential for their present life. Furthermore, domestic society acquires that firmness and solidity so needful to it from the holiness of marriage, one and indissoluble, wherein the rights and duties of husband and wife are controlled with wise justice and equity; due honor is assured to the woman; the authority of the husband is conformed to the pattern afforded by the authority of God; the power of the father is tempered by a due regard for the dignity of the mother and her offspring; and the best possible provision is made for the guardianship, welfare, and education of the children.

18. In political affairs, and all matters civil, the laws aim at securing the common good, and are not framed according to the delusive caprices and opinions of the mass of the people, but by truth and by justice; the ruling powers are invested with a sacredness more than human, and are withheld from deviating from the path of duty, and from overstepping the bounds of rightful authority; and the obedience is not the servitude of man to man, but submission to the will of God, exercising His sovereignty through the medium of men. Now, this being recognized as undeniable, it is felt that the high office of rulers should be held in respect; that public authority should be constantly and faithfully obeyed; that no act of sedition should be committed; and that the civic order of the commonwealth should be maintained as sacred.

19. So, also, as to the duties of each one toward his fellow men, mutual forbearance, kindliness, generosity are placed in the ascendant; the man who is at once a citizen and a Christian is not drawn

aside by conflicting obligations; and, lastly, the abundant benefits with which the Christian religion, of its very nature, endows even the mortal life of man are acquired for the community and civil society. And this to such an extent that it may be said in sober truth: "The condition of the commonwealth depends on the religion with which God is worshipped; and between one and the other there exists an intimate and abiding connection."[1]

20. Admirably, according to his wont, does St. Augustine, in many passages, enlarge upon the nature of these advantages; but nowhere more markedly and to the point than when he addresses the Catholic Church in the following words: "Thou dost teach and train children with much tenderness, young men with much vigor, old men with much gentleness; as the age not of the body alone, but of the mind of each requires. Women thou dost subject to their husbands in chaste and faithful obedience, not for the gratifying of their lust, but for bringing forth children, and for having a share in the family concerns. Thou dost set husbands over their wives, not that they may play false to the weaker sex, but according to the requirements of sincere affection. Thou dost subject children to their parents in a kind of free service, and dost establish parents over their children with a benign rule.... Thou joinest together, not in society only, but in a sort of brotherhood, citizen with citizen, nation with nation, and the whole race of men, by reminding them of their common parentage. Thou teachest kings to look to the interests of their people, and dost admonish the people to be submissive to their kings. With all care dost thou teach all to whom honor is due, and affection, and reverence, and fear, consolation, and admonition and exhortation, and discipline, and reproach, and punishment. Thou showest that all these are not equally incumbent on all, but that charity is owing

---

1. *Sacr. Imp. ad Cyrillum Alexand. et Episcopos metrop.* See Labbeus, *Collection of Councils*, vol. 3.

to all, and wrongdoing to none."[2] And in another place, blaming the false wisdom of certain time-serving philosophers, he observes: "Let those who say that the teaching of Christ is hurtful to the State produce such armies as the maxims of Jesus have enjoined soldiers to bring into being; such governors of provinces; such husbands and wives; such parents and children; such masters and servants; such kings; such judges, and such payers and collectors of tribute, as the Christian teaching instructs them to become, and then let them dare to say that such teaching is hurtful to the State. Nay, rather will they hesitate to own that this discipline, if duly acted up to, is the very mainstay of the commonwealth."[3]

21. There was once a time when States were governed by the philosophy of the Gospel. Then it was that the power and divine virtue of Christian wisdom had diffused itself throughout the laws, institutions, and morals of the people, permeating all ranks and relations of civil society. Then, too, the religion instituted by Jesus Christ, established firmly in befitting dignity, flourished everywhere, by the favor of princes and the legitimate protection of magistrates; and Church and State were happily united in concord and friendly interchange of good offices. The State, constituted in this wise, bore fruits important beyond all expectation, whose remembrance is still, and always will be, in renown, witnessed to as they are by countless proofs which can never be blotted out or ever obscured by any craft of any enemies. Christian Europe has subdued barbarous nations and changed them from a savage to a civilized condition, from superstition to true worship. It victoriously rolled back the tide of Mohammedan conquest; retained the headship of civilization; stood forth in the front rank as the leader and teacher of all, in every branch of national culture; bestowed on the world the gift of true and many-sided liberty;

2. *De moribus ecclesiae*, I, 30, 63 (*PL* 32:1336).
3. *Epist.* 138 *ad Marcellinum*, 2, 15 (*PL* 33:532).

and most wisely founded very numerous institutions for the solace of human suffering. And if we inquire how it was able to bring about so altered a condition of things, the answer is beyond all question, in large measure, through religion, under whose auspices so many great undertakings were set on foot, through whose aid they were brought to completion.

22. A similar state of things would certainly have continued had the agreement of the two powers been lasting. More important results even might have been justly looked for, had obedience waited upon the authority, teaching, and counsels of the Church, and had this submission been specially marked by greater and more unswerving loyalty. For that should be regarded in the light of an ever-changeless law which Ivo of Chartres wrote to Pope Paschal II: "When kingdom and priesthood are at one, in complete accord, the world is well ruled, and the Church flourishes, and brings forth abundant fruit. But when they are at variance, not only smaller interests prosper not, but even things of greatest moment fall into deplorable decay."[4]

23. But that harmful and deplorable passion for innovation which was aroused in the sixteenth century threw first of all into confusion the Christian religion, and next, by natural sequence, invaded the precincts of philosophy, whence it spread amongst all classes of society. From this source, as from a fountain-head, burst forth all those later tenets of unbridled license which, in the midst of the terrible upheavals of the last century, were wildly conceived and boldly proclaimed as the principles and foundation of that new conception of law which was not merely previously unknown, but was at variance on many points with not only the Christian, but even the natural law.

24. Amongst these principles the main one lays down that as all men are alike by race and nature, so in like manner all are equal in

---

4. *Epist.* 238, to Pope Paschal II (*PL* 162:246b).

the control of their life; that each one is so far his own master as to be in no sense under the rule of any other individual; that each is free to think on every subject just as he may choose, and to do whatever he may like to do; that no man has any right to rule over other men. In a society grounded upon such maxims all government is nothing more nor less than the will of the people, and the people, being under the power of itself alone, is alone its own ruler. It does choose, nevertheless, some to whose charge it may commit itself, but in such wise that it makes over to them not the right so much as the business of governing, to be exercised, however, in its name.

25. The authority of God is passed over in silence, just as if there were no God; or as if He cared nothing for human society; or as if men, whether in their individual capacity or bound together in social relations, owed nothing to God; or as if there could be a government of which the whole origin and power and authority did not reside in God Himself. Thus, as is evident, a State becomes nothing but a multitude which is its own master and ruler. And since the people is declared to contain within itself the spring-head of all rights and of all power, it follows that the State does not consider itself bound by any kind of duty toward God. Moreover, it believes that it is not obliged to make public profession of any religion; or to inquire which of the very many religions is the only one true; or to prefer one religion to all the rest; or to show to any form of religion special favor; but, on the contrary, is bound to grant equal rights to every creed, so that public order may not be disturbed by any particular form of religious belief.

26. And it is a part of this theory that all questions that concern religion are to be referred to private judgment; that everyone is to be free to follow whatever religion he prefers, or none at all if he disapprove of all. From this the following consequences logically flow: that the judgment of each one's conscience is independent of all law; that the most unrestrained opinions may be openly expressed as to the

practice or omission of divine worship; and that everyone has unbounded license to think whatever he chooses and to publish abroad whatever he thinks.

27. Now, when the State rests on foundations like those just named (and for the time being they are greatly in favor) it readily appears into what and how unrightful a position the Church is driven. For when the management of public business is in harmony with doctrines of such a kind, the Catholic religion is allowed a standing in civil society equal only, or inferior, to societies alien from it; no regard is paid to the laws of the Church, and she who, by the order and commission of Jesus Christ, has the duty of teaching all nations, finds herself forbidden to take any part in the instruction of the people. With reference to matters that are of twofold jurisdiction, they who administer the civil power lay down the law at their own will, and in matters that appertain to religion defiantly put aside the most sacred decrees of the Church. They claim jurisdiction over the marriages of Catholics, even over the bond as well as the unity and the indissolubility of matrimony. They lay hands on the goods of the clergy, contending that the Church cannot possess property. Lastly, they treat the Church with such arrogance that, rejecting entirely her title to the nature and rights of a perfect society, they hold that she differs in no respect from other societies in the State, and for this reason possesses no right nor any legal power of action, save that which she holds by the concession and favor of the government. If in any State the Church retains her own agreement publicly entered into by the two powers, men forthwith begin to cry out that matters affecting the Church must be separated from those of the State.

28. Their object in uttering this cry is to be able to violate unpunished their plighted faith, and in all things to have unchecked control. And as the Church, unable to abandon her chiefest and most sacred duties, cannot patiently put up with this, and asks that the pledge given to her be fully and scrupulously acted up to, contentions

frequently arise between the ecclesiastical and the civil power, of which the issue commonly is that the weaker power yields to the one which is stronger in human resources.

29. Accordingly, it has become the practice and determination under this condition of public polity (now so much admired by many) either to forbid the action of the Church altogether, or to keep her in check and bondage to the State. Public enactments are in great measure framed with this design. The drawing up of laws, the administration of State affairs, the godless education of youth, the spoliation and suppression of religious orders, the overthrow of the temporal power of the Roman Pontiff, all alike aim to this one end—to paralyze the action of Christian institutions, to cramp to the utmost the freedom of the Catholic Church, and to curtail her every single prerogative.

30. Now, natural reason itself proves convincingly that such concepts of the government of a State are wholly at variance with the truth. Nature itself bears witness that all power, of every kind, has its origin from God, who is its chief and most august source.

31. The sovereignty of the people, however, and this without any reference to God, is held to reside in the multitude; which is doubtless a doctrine exceedingly well calculated to flatter and to inflame many passions, but which lacks all reasonable proof, and all power of insuring public safety and preserving order. Indeed, from the prevalence of this teaching, things have come to such a pass that one may hold as an axiom of civil jurisprudence that seditions may be rightfully fostered. For the opinion prevails that princes are nothing more than delegates chosen to carry out the will of the people; whence it necessarily follows that all things are as changeable as the will of the people, so that risk of public disturbance is ever hanging over our heads. To hold, therefore, that there is no difference in matters of religion between forms that are unlike each other, and even contrary to each other, most clearly leads in the end to the rejection of

all religion in both theory and practice. And this is the same thing as atheism, however it may differ from it in name. Men who really believe in the existence of God must, in order to be consistent with themselves and to avoid absurd conclusions, understand that differing modes of divine worship involving dissimilarity and conflict even on most important points cannot all be equally probable, equally good, and equally acceptable to God.

32. So, too, the liberty of thinking, and of publishing, whatsoever each one likes, without any hindrance, is not in itself an advantage over which society can wisely rejoice. On the contrary, it is the fountainhead and origin of many evils. Liberty is a power perfecting man, and hence should have truth and goodness for its object. But the character of goodness and truth cannot be changed at option. These remain ever one and the same and are no less unchangeable than nature itself. If the mind assents to false opinions, and the will chooses and follows after what is wrong, neither can attain its native fulness, but both must fall from their native dignity into an abyss of corruption. Whatever, therefore, is opposed to virtue and truth may not rightly be brought temptingly before the eye of man, much less sanctioned by the favor and protection of the law. A well-spent life is the only way to heaven, whither all are bound, and on this account the State is acting against the laws and dictates of nature whenever it permits the license of opinion and of action to lead minds astray from truth and souls away from the practice of virtue. To exclude the Church, founded by God Himself, from life, from laws, from the education of youth, from domestic society, is a grave and fatal error. A State from which religion is banished can never be well regulated; and already perhaps more than is desirable is known of the nature and tendency of the so-called civil philosophy of life and morals. The Church of Christ is the true and sole teacher of virtue and guardian of morals. She it is who preserves in their purity the principles from which duties flow, and, by setting forth most urgent reasons for

virtuous life, bids us not only to turn away from wicked deeds, but even to curb all movements of the mind that are opposed to reason, even though they be not carried out in action.

33. To wish the Church to be subject to the civil power in the exercise of her duty is a great folly and a sheer injustice. Whenever this is the case, order is disturbed, for things natural are put above things supernatural; the many benefits which the Church, if free to act, would confer on society are either prevented or at least lessened in number; and a way is prepared for enmities and contentions between the two powers. The issue of events has taught us only too frequently how evil results to both powers in such cases.

34. Doctrines such as these, which cannot be approved by human reason, and most seriously affect the whole civil order, Our predecessors the Roman Pontiffs (well aware of what their Apostolic office required of them) have never allowed to pass uncondemned. Thus, Gregory XVI in his Encyclical Letter *Mirari vos,* dated August 15, 1832, inveighed with weighty words against the sophisms which even at his time were being publicly inculcated—namely, that no preference should be shown for any particular form of worship; that it is right for individuals to form their own personal judgments about religion; that each man's conscience is his sole and all-sufficing guide; and that it is lawful for every man to publish his own views, whatever they may be, and even to conspire against the State. On the question of the separation of Church and State, the same Pontiff writes as follows: "Nor can We hope for happier results either for religion or for the civil government from the wishes of those who desire that the Church be separated from the State, and the concord between the secular and ecclesiastical authority be dissolved. It is clear that these men, who yearn for a shameless liberty, live in dread of an agreement which has always been fraught with good, and advantageous alike to sacred and civil interests." To the like effect, also, as occasion presented itself, did Pius IX brand publicly many false opinions which

were gaining ground, and afterwards ordered them to be condensed in summary form in order that in this sea of error Catholics might have a light which they might safely follow.[5]

35. From these pronouncements of the Popes it is evident that the origin of public power is to be sought for in God Himself, and not in the multitude, and that it is repugnant to reason to allow free scope for sedition. Again, that it is not lawful for the State, any more than for the individual, either to disregard all religious duties or to hold in equal favor different kinds of religion; that the unrestrained freedom of thinking and of openly making known one's thoughts is not inherent in the rights of citizens and is by no means to be reckoned worthy of favor and support. In like manner it is to be understood that the Church no less than the State itself is a society perfect in its own nature and its own right, and that those who exercise sovereignty ought not so to act as to compel the Church to become subservient or subject to them, or to hamper her liberty in the management of her own affairs, or to despoil her in any way of the other privileges conferred upon her by Jesus Christ. In matters, however, of mixed jurisdiction, it is in the highest degree consonant to nature, as also to the designs of God, that so far from one of the powers separating itself from the other, or still less coming into conflict with it, complete harmony, such as is suited to the end for which each power exists, should be preserved between them.

5. Pope Pius IX, encyclical *Quanta cura* (December 8, 1864): *Syllabus*. It will suffice to indicate a few of them. Proposition 19: The Church is not a true, perfect, and wholly independent society, possessing in its own unchanging rights conferred upon it by its divine Founder; but it is for the civil power to determine what are the rights of the Church, and the limits within which it may use them. Proposition 29: The State, as the origin and source of all rights, enjoys a right that is unlimited. Proposition 55: The Church must be separated from the Stare and the State from the Church. Proposition 79: It is unsure that the civil liberty of every form of worship, and the full power given to all of openly and publicly manifesting whatsoever opinions and thoughts, lead to the more ready corruption of the minds and morals of the people, and to the spread of the plague of religious indifference.

36. This, then, is the teaching of the Catholic Church concerning the constitution and government of the State. By the words and decrees just cited, if judged dispassionately, no one of the several forms of government is in itself condemned, inasmuch as none of them contains anything contrary to Catholic doctrine, and all of them are capable, if wisely and justly managed, to insure the welfare of the State. Neither is it blameworthy in itself, in any manner, for the people to have a share greater or less in the government: for at certain times, and under certain laws, such participation may not only be of benefit to the citizens but may even be of obligation. Nor is there any reason why anyone should accuse the Church of being wanting in gentleness of action or largeness of view, or of being opposed to real and lawful liberty. The Church, indeed, deems it unlawful to place the various forms of divine worship on the same footing as the true religion, but does not, on that account, condemn those rulers who, for the sake of securing some great good or of hindering some great evil, allow patiently custom or usage to be a kind of sanction for each kind of religion having its place in the State. And, in fact, the Church is wont to take earnest heed that no one shall be forced to embrace the Catholic faith against his will, for, as St. Augustine wisely reminds us, "Man cannot believe otherwise than of his own will."

37. In the same way the Church cannot approve of that liberty which begets a contempt of the most sacred laws of God, and casts off the obedience due to lawful authority, for this is not liberty so much as license, and is most correctly styled by St. Augustine the "liberty of self ruin," and by the Apostle St. Peter the "cloak of malice" (1 Pet. 2:16). Indeed, since it is opposed to reason, it is a true slavery, "for whosoever committeth sin is the slave of sin" (John 8:34). On the other hand, that liberty is truly genuine, and to be sought after, which in regard to the individual does not allow men to be the slaves of error and of passion, the worst of all masters; which, too, in public

administration guides the citizens in wisdom and provides for them increased means of well-being; and which, further, protects the State from foreign interference.

38. This honorable liberty, alone worthy of human beings, the Church approves most highly and has never slackened her endeavor to preserve, strong and unchanged, among nations. And, in truth, whatever in the State is of chief avail for the common welfare; whatever has been usefully established to curb the license of rulers who are opposed to the true interests of the people, or to keep in check the leading authorities from unwarrantably interfering in municipal or family affairs; whatever tends to uphold the honor, manhood, and equal rights of individual citizens—of all these things, as the monuments of past ages bear witness, the Catholic Church has always been the originator, the promoter, or the guardian. Ever, therefore, consistent with herself, while on the one hand she rejects that exorbitant liberty which in individuals and in nations ends in license or in thralldom, on the other hand, she willingly and most gladly welcomes whatever improvements the age brings forth, if these really secure the prosperity of life here below, which is, as it were, a stage in the journey to the life that will know no ending.

39. Therefore, when it is said that the Church is hostile to modern political regimes and that she repudiates the discoveries of modern research, the charge is a ridiculous and groundless calumny. Wild opinions she does repudiate, wicked and seditious projects she does condemn, together with that attitude of mind which points to the beginning of a willful departure from God. But, as all truth must necessarily proceed from God, the Church recognizes in all truth that is reached by research a trace of the divine intelligence. And as all truth in the natural order is powerless to destroy belief in the teachings of revelation, but can do much to confirm it, and as every newly discovered truth may serve to further the knowledge or the praise of God, it follows that whatsoever spreads the range of knowledge will

always be willingly and even joyfully welcomed by the Church. She will always encourage and promote, as she does in other branches of knowledge, all study occupied with the investigation of nature. In these pursuits, should the human intellect discover anything not known before, the Church makes no opposition. She never objects to search being made for things that minister to the refinements and comforts of life. So far, indeed, from opposing these she is now, as she ever has been, hostile alone to indolence and sloth, and earnestly wishes that the talents of men may bear more and more abundant fruit by cultivation and exercise. Moreover, she gives encouragement to every kind of art and handicraft, and through her influence, directing all strivings after progress toward virtue and salvation, she labors to prevent man's intellect and industry from turning him away from God and from heavenly things.

40. All this, though so reasonable and full of counsel, finds little favor nowadays when States not only refuse to conform to the rules of Christian wisdom, but seem even anxious to recede from them further and further on each successive day. Nevertheless, since truth when brought to light is wont, of its own nature, to spread itself far and wide, and gradually take possession of the minds of men, We, moved by the great and holy duty of Our Apostolic mission to all nations, speak, as We are bound to do, with freedom. Our eyes are not closed to the spirit of the times. We repudiate not the assured and useful improvements of our age, but devoutly wish affairs of State to take a safer course than they are now taking, and to rest on a more firm foundation without injury to the true freedom of the people; for the best parent and guardian of liberty amongst men is truth. "The truth shall make you free" (John 8:32).

41. If in the difficult times in which Our lot is cast, Catholics will give ear to Us, as it behooves them to do, they will readily see what are the duties of each one in matters of opinion as well as action. As regards opinion, whatever the Roman Pontiffs have hitherto taught,

or shall hereafter teach, must be held with a firm grasp of mind, and, so often as occasion requires, must be openly professed.

42. Especially with reference to the so-called "liberties" which are so greatly coveted in these days, all must stand by the judgment of the Apostolic See, and have the same mind. Let no man be deceived by the honest outward appearance of these liberties, but let each one reflect whence these have had their origin, and by what efforts they are everywhere upheld and promoted. Experience has made Us well acquainted with their results to the State, since everywhere they have borne fruits which the good and wise bitterly deplore. If there really exist anywhere, or if we in imagination conceive, a State, waging wanton and tyrannical war against Christianity, and if we compare with it the modern form of government just described, this latter may seem the more endurable of the two. Yet, undoubtedly, the principles on which such a government is grounded are, as We have said, of a nature which no one can approve.

43. Secondly, action may relate to private and domestic matters, or to matters public. As to private affairs, the first duty is to conform life and conduct to the Gospel precepts, and to refuse to shrink from this duty when Christian virtue demands some sacrifice slightly more difficult to make. All, moreover, are bound to love the Church as their common mother, to obey her laws, promote her honor, defend her rights, and to endeavor to make her respected and loved by those over whom they have authority. It is also of great moment to the public welfare to take a prudent part in the business of municipal administration, and to endeavor above all to introduce effectual measures, so that, as becomes a Christian people, public provision may be made for the instruction of youth in religion and true morality. Upon these things the well-being of every State greatly depends.

44. Furthermore, it is in general fitting and salutary that Catholics should extend their efforts beyond this restricted sphere and give their attention to national politics. We say "in general" because these

Our precepts are addressed to all nations. However, it may in some places be true that, for most urgent and just reasons, it is by no means expedient for Catholics to engage in public affairs or to take an active part in politics. Nevertheless, as We have laid down, to take no share in public matters would be as wrong as to have no concern for, or to bestow no labor upon, the common good, and the more so because Catholics are admonished, by the very doctrines which they profess, to be upright and faithful in the discharge of duty, while, if they hold aloof, men whose principles offer but small guarantee for the welfare of the State will the more readily seize the reins of government. This would tend also to the injury of the Christian religion, forasmuch as those would come into power who are badly disposed toward the Church, and those who are willing to befriend her would be deprived of all influence.

45. It follows clearly, therefore, that Catholics have just reasons for taking part in the conduct of public affairs. For in so doing they assume not nor should they assume the responsibility of approving what is blameworthy in the actual methods of government, but seek to turn these very methods, so far as is possible, to the genuine and true public good, and to use their best endeavors at the same time to infuse, as it were, into all the veins of the State the healthy sap and blood of Christian wisdom and virtue. The morals and ambitions of the heathens differed widely from those of the Gospel, yet Christians were to be seen living undefiled everywhere in the midst of pagan superstition, and, while always true to themselves, coming to the front boldly wherever an opening was presented. Models of loyalty to their rulers, submissive, so far as was permitted, to the sovereign power, they shed around them on every side a halo of sanctity; they strove to be helpful to their brethren, and to attract others to the wisdom of Jesus Christ, yet were bravely ready to withdraw from public life, nay, even to lay down their life, if they could not without loss of virtue retain honors, dignities, and offices. For this reason, Christian ways

and manners speedily found their way not only into private houses but into the camp, the senate, and even into the imperial palaces. "We are but of yesterday," wrote Tertullian, "yet we swarm in all your institutions, we crowd your cities, islands, villages, towns, assemblies, the army itself, your wards and corporations, the palace, the senate, and the law courts."[6] So that the Christian faith, when once it became lawful to make public profession of the Gospel, appeared in most of the cities of Europe, not like an infant crying in its cradle, but already grown up and full of vigor.

46. In these Our days it is well to revive these examples of Our forefathers. First and foremost, it is the duty of all Catholics worthy of the name and wishful to be known as most loving children of the Church, to reject without swerving whatever is inconsistent with so fair a title; to make use of popular institutions, so far as can honestly be done, for the advancement of truth and righteousness; to strive that liberty of action shall not transgress the bounds marked out by nature and the law of God; to endeavor to bring back all civil society to the pattern and form of Christianity which We have described. It is barely possible to lay down any fixed method by which such purposes are to be attained, because the means adopted must suit places and times widely differing from one another. Nevertheless, above all things, unity of aim must be preserved, and similarity must be sought after in all plans of action. Both these objects will be carried into effect without fail if all will follow the guidance of the Apostolic See as their rule of life and obey the bishops whom the Holy Spirit has placed to rule the Church of God (Acts 20:28). The defense of Catholicism, indeed, necessarily demands that in the profession of doctrines taught by the Church all shall be of one mind and all steadfast in believing; and care must be taken never to connive, in any way, at false opinions, never to withstand them less strenuously than truth

6. *Apologia*, 27 (*PL* 1:525).

allows. In mere matters of opinion, it is permissible to discuss things with moderation, with a desire of searching into the truth, without unjust suspicion or angry recriminations.

47. Hence, lest concord be broken by rash charges, let this be understood by all, that the integrity of Catholic faith cannot be reconciled with opinions verging on naturalism or rationalism, the essence of which is utterly to do away with Christian institutions and to install in society the supremacy of man to the exclusion of God. Further, it is unlawful to follow one line of conduct in private life and another in public, respecting privately the authority of the Church, but publicly rejecting it; for this would amount to joining together good and evil, and to putting man in conflict with himself; whereas he ought always to be consistent, and never in the least point nor in any condition of life to swerve from Christian virtue.

48. But in matters merely political, as, for instance, the best form of government, and this or that system of administration, a difference of opinion is lawful. Those, therefore, whose piety is in other respects known, and whose minds are ready to accept in all obedience the decrees of the Apostolic See, cannot in justice be accounted as bad men because they disagree as to subjects We have mentioned; and still graver wrong will be done them, if—as We have more than once perceived with regret—they are accused of violating, or of wavering in, the Catholic faith.

49. Let this be well borne in mind by all who are in the habit of publishing their opinions, and above all by journalists. In the endeavor to secure interests of the highest order there is no room for internal strife or party rivalries; since all should aim with one mind and purpose to make safe that which is the common object of all—the maintenance of religion and of the State. If, therefore, there have hitherto been dissensions, let them henceforth be gladly buried in oblivion. If rash or injurious acts have been committed, whoever may have been at fault, let mutual charity make amends, and let the past

be redeemed by a special submission of all to the Apostolic See. In this way Catholics will attain two most excellent results: They will become helpers to the Church in preserving and propagating Christian wisdom, and they will confer the greatest benefit on civil society, the safety of which is exceedingly imperiled by evil teachings and bad passions.

50. This, Venerable Brethren, is what We have thought it Our duty to expound to all nations of the Catholic world touching the Christian constitution of States and the duties of individual citizens. It behooves Us now with earnest prayer to implore the protection of heaven, beseeching God, who alone can enlighten the minds of men and move their will, to bring about those happy ends for which We yearn and strive, for His greater glory and the general salvation of mankind. As a happy augury of the divine benefits, and in token of Our paternal benevolence, to you, Venerable Brothers, and to the clergy and to the whole people committed to your charge and vigilance, We grant lovingly in the Lord the Apostolic Benediction.

Given at St. Peter's, in Rome, the first day of November, 1885, the seventh year of Our pontificate.

LEO PP. XIII

ENCYCLICAL LETTER
QUOD MULTUM
OF THE SUPREME PONTIFF
LEO XIII

TO THE BISHOPS OF HUNGARY ON THE LIBERTY OF THE CHURCH

Venerable Brothers, Greetings and Apostolic Benediction

1. We have long and ardently desired an opportunity to address you with an apostolic letter. Just as We have addressed the bishops of many other nations, We desire to inform you of Our plans, which concern the prosperity of the Christian cause and the salvation of the Hungarian nation. These days present Us with an excellent opportunity, since Hungary is celebrating the liberation, two centuries ago, of Budapest. That victory will stand out forever in the memory of the Hungarian people. It was granted to your ancestors, because of their strength and perseverance, to recapture their capital city, which for a century and a half had been occupied by their enemies. That the grace and memory of this divine blessing might remain, Pope Innocent XI justly decreed a celebration throughout all Christendom in honor of St. Stephen, the first of your apostolic kings, on the second day of September, the anniversary of this great event. Moreover, it is well-known that the Apostolic See took a significant part in the almost spontaneous victory three years before over the same foe at Vienna. This victory, rightly attributed in great part to the ap-

ostolic efforts of Pope Innocent, began the decline of the influence of the Mohammedans in Europe. Besides, even before that age and under similar circumstances, Our predecessors assisted the Hungarian forces with counsel, aid, money, and treaties. From Callistus III to Innocent XI, many Roman Pontiffs are recorded whose names deserve to be honored for their activity in such affairs. Let Clement VIII serve as an example. When Stregan and Vincentgraz were liberated from the domination of the Turks, the highest councils of the kingdom decreed that public thanks be given to him for he alone had come to their aid opportunely at a time when the situation was almost beyond hope. Therefore, just as the Apostolic See never failed the people of Hungary whenever they had to fight the enemies of religion and Christian morality, so now, when happy memories inspire the people, We gladly join you in sharing their joy. Taking into account the differing conditions of time, We desire to confirm the people in their profession of the Catholic faith and also to assist them in warding off common dangers. In this way We shall serve the public good.

Stephen

2. Hungary herself knows that no gift of God either to individuals or to nations is greater than to receive by His grace the Catholic faith, and having received it, to keep it with perseverance. This gift contains an abundance of other gifts by means of which individual persons receive both eternal happiness in heaven and greatness and prosperity for their state on earth. When Stephen first clearly grasped this truth, he asked God for nothing more vehemently, indeed he labored for nothing more energetically and consistently, than to obtain the Catholic faith for his whole kingdom and to establish it on a firm foundation from the very beginning. Therefore, very early he began a change of studies and offices among the Roman bishops, the kings, and the people of Hungary which future ages did not abolish. Stephen founded and built a kingdom, but received his crown only from

the Roman Pontiff, for he wanted to offer his kingdom to the Apostolic See. He established many Episcopal Sees, endowing munificently, and founding piously. Accompanying these many good works was the good pleasure and indulgence of the Apostolic See in many matters altogether singular. From his faith and piety, this holy king drew the light of counsel and the best norms for ruling his kingdom. He acquired his strength from diligence in prayer, by which he put down the evil plots of public enemies and returned as victor from the attacks of his foes. Thus, under the auspices of religion, your state was born. Under the same guardian and leader, you have come at quick march not only to maturity, but also to the strength of empire and the glory of your name. Hungary has kept holy and inviolate the faith received from her king and parent as an inheritance, and this despite the great difficulties of the times, when neighboring nations were drawn from the bosom of the Church by pernicious error. Faith, obedience and devotion to the Apostolic See have remained constant in kings, bishops, and all the people. In turn We see the predilection and paternal benevolence of the Roman Pontiffs for the Hungarian people confirmed by many testimonies. Today after many centuries and many events, the original intimate friendship remains, by the blessing of God. The virtues of your ancestors are by no means lacking in their descendants. There are many laudable and fruitful labors of the episcopate: relief in calamities, zealous defense of the rights of the Church, and your constant and courageous determination to preserve the Catholic faith.

Current Evils

3. When We recall these things, Our soul is filled with joy. To you and to the people of Hungary, We gladly pay the tribute of praise for things well done. But We cannot remain silent. Everyone knows how inimical to virtue these times are and how the Church is attacked. We have much to fear amid such dangers, lest a shaken faith languish

even where it has taken strong and deep roots. It is enough to recall rationalism and naturalism, those deadly sources of evil whose teachings are everywhere freely distributed. We must then add the many allurements to corruption: the opposition to or open defection from the Church by public officials, the bold obstinacy of secret societies, here and there a curriculum for the education of youth without regard for God. And if ever, then surely now is the time to realize not only how appropriate, but entirely necessary the Catholic religion is for public safety and tranquility. Daily experience proves to what lengths they who fear no authority nor have ever restrained their passions will go to undermine the State. Indeed, everyone knows what they intend, what means they employ, and with what perseverance they labor. The mightiest empires and the most flourishing states are compelled to contend almost every hour with such societies of men, joined together in unity of intention and likeness of deeds. Thus, the public safety is always in danger. Against such audacity of evil men, a good plan has been perfected in some places, that the authority of magistrates and the force of laws be well prepared.

Effective Means of Restraining Socialism

4. Nevertheless, to restrain the danger of socialism, there is only one genuinely effective means, in the absence of which the fear of punishment has little weight to discourage offenders. It is that citizens should be thoroughly educated in religion and restrained by respect for and love of the Church. For the Church as parent and teacher is the holy guardian of religion, moral integrity, and virtue. All who follow the precepts of the Gospel religiously and entirely are, by this very fact, far from the suspicion of socialism. For religion commands us to worship and fear God and to submit to and obey legitimate authority. It forbids anyone to act seditiously and demands for everyone the security of his possessions and rights. It furthermore commands those who have wealth to come graciously to the aid of the poor. Re-

ligion aids the needy with all the works of charity and consoles those who suffer loss, enkindling in them the hope of the greatest eternal blessings which will be in proportion to the labor endured and the length of that labor. Therefore, those who rule the states will do nothing wiser and more opportune than to recognize that religion influences the people despite all obstacles and recalls them to virtue and uprightness of character through her teachings. To distrust the Church or hold it suspect is, in the first place, unjust, and in the second, profits no one except the enemies of civil discipline and those bent on destruction.

Keep Religion Flourishing

5. By the blessing of God, great civil unrest and the gathering of fearsome mobs, which have occurred elsewhere, have been spared the people of Hungary. But threatening dangers force all of us to strive by daily zeal to assure that the name of religion flourishes there and that honor endures in its Christian institutions. For this reason, the Church should enjoy full and integral freedom in the whole kingdom of Hungary as it did in former times, and this for the common good. As for Us, We are most anxious that those things which conflict with the rights of the Church, diminish its liberty of action, and impede the profession of the faith be removed from the laws. To attain this end, both We and you must constantly labor, as far as We legally can and as so many illustrious men have already done. Meanwhile, as long as these laws remain, it is your duty to see to it that they injure the common security as little as possible and to admonish the citizens what they have to do in this matter. We shall mention some statutes which seem more injurious than others.

6. To embrace religion is a most serious duty, which is nor to be restricted by age. No age is unfit for the kingdom of God. As everyone knows this, so he ought to act without delay, for from the will to act is born the right to act for everyone, which cannot be violated

without the greatest injury. Therefore, if pastors of souls are forced to make a choice in the matter, they must choose to endure the penalties prescribed by civil law rather than provoke the wrath of an avenging God.

Marriage

7. You must labor, Venerable Brothers, that Catholic teaching about the sanctity, oneness, and perpetuity of matrimony takes firm root in souls. Remind the faithful frequently that the marriage of Christians is subject solely to ecclesiastical authority. Remind them also what the Church thinks and teaches concerning so-called civil marriage and with what mind and heart Catholic people should obey such laws. Further remind them that even for the gravest of reasons it is not permitted to enter into marriage with Christians who are not Catholics; those who do so without the authority and indulgence of the Church sin before God and the Church. Since these issues are so vital, all who have a concern in this matter should most diligently see to it, as far as they can, that no one sins here for any reason. For in this especially, obedience to the Church is necessarily bound to the public interest. This is the reason why the beginnings and best principles of civil life depend in great part on domestic society, so that the peace and prosperity of the state result in large part from marriage. Nor can marriage succeed except under the care of God and the Church. Deprived of such care and entered upon contrary to the will of God, matrimony is reduced to the service of various passions, is deprived of necessary heavenly aids, and is despoiled of that common life which is of greatest concern to man, i.e., religion. Of necessity it produces bitter fruit, to the great harm of the family and of the State. For this reason, We must commend those Catholic men who, when the legislative assembly of Hungary was asked two years ago whether it would consider the marriage of Christians with Jews valid, rejected the proposal unanimously and freely and succeeded in hav-

ing the old marriage law retained. Their vote received the approval of the vast majority of people from all parts of Hungary, proving with admirable testimony that the people thought and felt as they did. May there be like consent and similar constancy whenever the Catholic cause is in controversy, for then victory will be at hand. At least civil life will be more vigorous and fruitful when languor and sloth have been banished, for these are the means by which the enemies of the Christian name certainly wish to stupefy all Catholic virtue.

Catholic Education of Youth

8. Nor will less profit accrue to the State if the education of youth is wisely and rightly provided for from the beginning. Such are the times and customs that too many people with too much effort strive to keep studious youth away from the vigilance of the Church and the salutary virtue of religion. Schools called neuter, mixed, and lay are popular and sought out here and there, doubtless with the intention that the students grow up ignorant of all things holy and of all religious concerns. Since this evil is more widespread and greater than its remedies, we see a progeny growing up uninterested in spiritual goods, without religion and often impious. Keep so great a calamity out of Hungary with all your energy! The education of youth from childhood in Christian habits and Christian wisdom is today of the greatest possible concern not only to the Church, but also to the State. All who are truly wise understand this. That is why We see many Catholic men in many places who are deeply concerned about the proper upbringing of youth devoting special and constant effort to this matter, undismayed by the greatness of the labor or by the cost. We also know of many in Hungary who are working toward the same goal with similar proposals. Permit Us nevertheless to rouse your episcopal zeal even more. In this grave situation, We desire that in the public education of youth, that part be reserved to the Church which has been divinely assigned to it. All We can do is to exhort

you to deal vigorously with this matter. Meanwhile continue to admonish fathers again and again not to permit their children to study and learn so as to threaten injury to their Catholic faith. At the same time see to it that the schools which are under your or the clergy's direction be commendable for their soundness of doctrine and the uprightness of their teachers. This is to be understood not only of primary schools, but also of those of higher learning.

Centers of Study

9. With God-fearing generosity, and especially with the liberal contributions of your kings and bishops, many noble institutions devoted to the study of letters have been established. The memory of Cardinal Pazmany, Archbishop of Esztergom, is still alive among you, not only as the founder of the Catholic University at Budapest, but also as its generous patron. It is inspiring to recall that he undertook so great a work out of the pure and sincere motive of advancing the Catholic religion. King Ferdinand II confirmed this when he said of its purpose that the truth of the Catholic religion would remain unshaken where it flourished; where weakened, it would be strengthened, and divine worship would be propagated everywhere. We realize how diligently you have labored to ensure that these excellent centers of study retain their original nature, the kind that their founders intended, namely that they remain Catholic institutions. Their household, administration, and faculty are entirely under the control of the Church and the bishops. Therefore, We exhort you to continue to encourage this noble and excellent venture. And you will succeed because of the goodness of the Apostolic King and the prudent men in charge of the government; also, what has been given to non-Catholic communities will not be denied to the Catholic Church. If the tenor of the times demands that some new institutions are to be founded or old ones expanded, We have no doubt that you will imitate the example of your fathers and their devotion to religion. In fact, We have re-

ceived reports that you are already planning a school for the training of teachers; this is an excellent plan, one worthy of your wisdom and virtue. That you may accomplish it quickly with the Lord's help is Our prayer and exhortation.

Education of Priests

10. If the education of all youth in general contributes a great deal to the true welfare of the State, this is much more true of the education of those aiming at ordination. To this matter you must give special attention; it should occupy the greater portion of your vigils and labors, since the youths destined for orders are the hope and, as it were, the incomplete form of future priests. You surely know how much the reputation of the Church and the eternal salvation of her people depend on priests. In the education of clerics, two elements are absolutely necessary: learning for the development of the mind and virtue for the perfection of the spirit. To the ordinary humanistic subjects in which youths are educated must be added Sacred and Canonical studies. Care must be taken that their content is sound and everywhere pure, in full harmony with the documents of the Church and eloquent, so that the priest may be able to exhort...even those who contradict. Holiness of life, without which knowledge puffs up and does not edify, consists not only in good and honorable habits, but also in that group of sacerdotal virtues which makes good priests exemplars of Jesus Christ, the eternal High Priest. For this purpose, there are sacred seminaries. You have some for youths preparing for the priesthood and others for the education of seminarians, all of them well-founded. Choose teachers and spiritual directors for these institutions thoughtfully. They should be men of sound doctrine and good morals, men to whom you can confidently entrust a matter of such great importance. Choose rectors and spiritual guides who are outstanding in prudence, counsel, and experience. The common life and discipline should be so arranged by your authority that not only

will the students never offend against piety, but that there will be an abundance of all aids which nourish piety. The students should thus be encouraged to make daily progress in acquiring the sacerdotal virtues. Your industrious and diligent labors in the education of priests will bear much desirable fruit, making your episcopal office easier to administer and producing a richer profit for all.

Assistance for Priests

11. But it is necessary that your paternal care extend further, namely to the assistance of priests in the exercise of their duties. Skillfully and sweetly, as becomes your love, see to it that they are not exposed to worldly temptations and that they are not led by selfish desires or concern for secular affairs. See to it that they excel in virtue, providing an example of deeds well-done. Further, see to it that they never fail in their devotion to prayer and that they approach the sacred mysteries spotlessly. When supported and strengthened by these defenses, they will gladly fulfil their daily sacred duties and fittingly turn to the studious cultivation of the spirits of their people, especially by the ministry of word and sacraments. But to renew the strength of soul which human weakness does not allow to flourish constantly, nothing seems more effective than that they retire from time to time to meditation, devoting all of their time solely to God and themselves. This is the custom in other places and has proven very successful. Furthermore, you will easily and spontaneously get to know the talents and the habits of individual priests as you go about administering your dioceses. You will also learn what you have to do by way of prohibition in this matter, and what evils have to be eradicated. To do this and to save ecclesiastical discipline from violation, you must use the just severity of canon law where necessary. All must understand that both the priesthood and the various grades of dignity are no more than a reward for useful labors. For this reason, they are reserved for those who have served the Church, who have labored in

the care of souls, and who are distinguished for their learning and the holiness of their lives.

Concern for the Faithful

12. When the clergy is distinguished by these virtues, the people will profit in no small measure, since they love the Church, are very devoted to the ancestral religion, and easily and willingly submit to the directives of their pastors. However. you must never fail to make sure that the integrity of Catholic doctrine is preserved in the people and that evangelical discipline is retained in their actions, life and character. Let frequent sacred retreats for the care of souls be undertaken. To direct this work, choose men of tried virtue, animated by the spirit of Christ, and inflamed with love of neighbor. Well-written pamphlets to guard against errors or to extirpate them should be widely disseminated. They must be in accord with the truth and encourage virtue. Some societies have already taken up this laudable proposal, with fruitful results. We wish therefore that their number increase and that their success continue from day to day. Another thing We wish all of you to do, but especially those of you who excel in learning, dignity, and authority, is that in both private and public life, you be solicitous for the good name of religion. Let the cause of the Church be more vigorously prosecuted under your leadership. Let all present and future institutions founded to promote the Catholic cause be willingly aided and increased. In like manner you must oppose certain false opinions, perversely proposed to safeguard each one's dignity, but which are entirely contrary to the precepts and faith of Christian customs and which open the door to many pernicious and criminal acts. Finally, you must assiduously and vehemently oppose improper organizations, particularly those which We have mentioned in our encyclicals to other places, whose contagion must be averted by every means. In this matter, We desire that you exercise care in proportion to their number, power, and resources.

13. Urged by Our love, this is what We have to prescribe for you, Venerable Brethren, and which We trust will be accepted by the whole nation of Hungary with prompt obedience. The fact that your forefathers triumphed so magnificently over bitter foes at Budapest was not solely due to their warlike fortitude, but also to the strength of religion. Just as in the beginning religion gave birth to the strength and authority of a great empire, so it also promises for the future prosperity at home and glory abroad. All of these things, whether they are for your honor or for your advantage, We desire for you, and We pray that you obtain them with the assistance and under the patronage of the Blessed Virgin, Mother of God. The kingdom of Hungary has been consecrated to her and received its name from her. For the same reason We earnestly ask the aid of St. Stephen, who has blessed your kingdom with every kind of gift for its glory and growth. We have the certain hope that he will look down from heaven and guard you with his strong patronage.

14. Relying on this hope, Venerable Brothers, We impart to you individually, to the clergy, and to all your people, as a sign of heavenly gifts and a proof of Our paternal good will, Our Apostolic Benediction.

Given at Rome at St. Peter's, the twenty-second day of August, 1886, in the ninth year of Our Pontificate.

LEO PP. XIII

ENCYCLICAL LETTER

IN PLURIMIS

OF THE SUPREME PONTIFF

LEO XIII

TO THE BISHOPS OF BRAZIL
ON THE ABOLITION OF SLAVERY

1. Amid the many and great demonstrations of affection which from almost all the peoples of the earth have come to Us, and are still coming to Us, in congratulation upon the happy attainment of the fiftieth anniversary of Our priesthood, there is one which moves Us in a quite special way. We mean one which comes from Brazil, where, upon the occasion of this happy event, large numbers of those who in that vast empire groan beneath the yoke of slavery, have been legally set free. And this work, so full of the spirit of Christian mercy, has been offered up in cooperation with the clergy, by charitable members of the laity of both sexes, to God, the Author and Giver of all good things, in testimony of their gratitude for the favor of the health and the years which have been granted to Us. But this was especially acceptable and sweet to Us because it lent confirmation to the belief, which is so welcome to Us, that the great majority of the people of Brazil desire to see the cruelty of slavery ended and rooted out from the land. This popular feeling has been strongly seconded by the emperor and his august daughter, and also by the ministers, by means of various laws which, with this end in view, have been introduced

and sanctioned. We told the Brazilian ambassador last January what a consolation these things were to Us, and We also assured him that We would address letters to the bishops of Brazil in behalf of these unhappy slaves.

2. We, indeed, to all men are the Vicar of Christ, the Son of God, who so loved the human race that not only did He not refuse, taking our nature to Himself, to live among men, but delighted in bearing the name of the Son of Man, openly proclaiming that He had come upon earth "to preach deliverance to the captives" (Isa. 61:1; Luke 4:19) in order that, rescuing mankind from the worst slavery, which is the slavery of sin, "he might re-establish all things that are in heaven and on earth" (Eph. 1:10), and so bring back all the children of Adam from the depths of the ruin of the common fall to their original dignity. The words of St. Gregory the Great are very applicable here: "Since our Redeemer, the Author of all life, deigned to take human flesh, that by the power of His Godhood the chains by which we were held in bondage being broken, He might restore us to our first state of liberty, it is most fitting that men by the concession of manumission should restore to the freedom in which they were born those whom nature sent free into the world, but who have been condemned to the yoke of slavery by the law of nations."[1] It is right, therefore, and obviously in keeping with Our apostolic office, that We should favor and advance by every means in Our power whatever helps to secure for men, whether as individuals or as communities, safeguards against the many miseries, which, like the fruits of an evil tree, have sprung from the sin of our first parents; and such safeguards, of whatever kind they may be, help not only to promote civilization and the amenities of life, but lead on to that universal restitution of all things which our Redeemer Jesus Christ contemplated and desired.

---

1. *Epist.*, lib. 6, epist. 12 (*PL* 77:803c–804a).

3. In the presence of so much suffering, the condition of slavery, in which a considerable part of the great human family has been sunk in squalor and affliction now for many centuries, is deeply to be deplored; for the system is one which is wholly opposed to that which was originally ordained by God and by nature. The Supreme Author of all things so decreed that man should exercise a sort of royal dominion over beasts and cattle and fish and fowl, but never that men should exercise a like dominion over their fellow men. As St. Augustine puts it: "Having created man a reasonable being, and after His own likeness, God wished that he should rule only over the brute creation; that he should be the master, not of men, but of beasts." From this it follows that "the state of slavery is rightly regarded as a penalty upon the sinner; thus, the word slave does not occur in the Bible until the just man Noe branded with it the sin of his son. It was sin, therefore, which deserved this name; it was not natural."[2]

4. From the first sin came all evils, and specially this perversity that there were men who, forgetful of the original brotherhood of the race, instead of seeking, as they should naturally have done, to promote mutual kindness and mutual respect, following their evil desires began to think of other men as their inferiors, and to hold them as cattle born for the yoke. In this way, through an absolute forgetfulness of our common nature, and of human dignity, and the likeness of God stamped upon us all, it came to pass that in the contentions and wars which then broke out, those who were the stronger reduced the conquered into slavery; so that mankind, though of the same race, became divided into two sections, the conquered slaves and their victorious masters. The history of the ancient world presents us with this miserable spectacle down to the time of the coming of our Lord, when the calamity of slavery had fallen heavily upon all the peoples, and the number of freemen had become so reduced that

2. *De civ. Dei*, 19, 15 (*PL* 41:643).

the poet was able to put this atrocious phrase into the mouth of Caesar: "The human race exists for the sake of a few."[3]

5. The system flourished even among the most civilized peoples, among the Greeks and among the Romans, with whom the few imposed their will upon the many; and this power was exercised so unjustly and with such haughtiness that a crowd of slaves was regarded merely as so many chattels—not as persons, but as things. They were held to be outside the sphere of law, and without even the claim to retain and enjoy life. "Slaves are in the power of their masters, and this power is derived from the law of nations; for we find that among all nations masters have the power of life and death over their slaves, and whatever a slave earns belongs to his master."[4] Owing to this state of moral confusion it became lawful for men to sell their slaves, to give them in exchange, to dispose of them by will, to beat them, to kill them, to abuse them by forcing them to serve for the gratification of evil passions and cruel superstitions; these things could be done, legally, with impunity, and in the light of heaven. Even those who were wisest in the pagan world, illustrious philosophers and learned jurisconsults, outraging the common feeling of mankind, succeeded in persuading themselves and others that slavery was simply a necessary condition of nature. Nor did they hesitate to assert that the slave class was very inferior to the freemen both in intelligence and perfection of bodily development, and therefore that slaves, as things wanting in reason and sense, ought in all things to be the instruments of the will, however rash and unworthy, of their masters. Such inhuman and wicked doctrines are to be specially detested; for, when once they are accepted, there is no form of oppression so wicked but that it will defend itself beneath some color of legality and justice.

---

3. Lucan, *Pharsalia*, 5, 343.
4. Justinian, *Institutiones*, I, t. 8, n. 1; in *Corpus juris civilis*, 4th ed. (Berlin: Weidmann, 1886), vol. 1, p. 3.

History is full of examples showing what a seedbed of crime, what a pest and calamity, this system has been for states. Hatreds are excited in the breasts of the slaves, and the masters are kept in a state of suspicion and perpetual dread; the slaves prepare to avenge themselves with the torches of the incendiary, and the masters continue the task of oppression with greater cruelty. States are disturbed alternately by the number of the slaves and by the violence of the masters, and so are easily overthrown; hence, in a word, come riots and seditions, pillage and fire.

6. The greater part of humanity were toiling in this abyss of misery and were the more to be pitied because they were sunk in the darkness of superstition, when in the fulness of time and by the designs of God, light shone down upon the world, and the merits of Christ the Redeemer were poured out upon mankind. By that means they were lifted out of the slough and the distress of slavery and recalled and brought back from the terrible bondage of sin to their high dignity as the sons of God. Thus, the Apostles, in the early days of the Church, among other precepts for a devout life taught and laid down the doctrine which more than once occurs in the Epistles of St. Paul addressed to those newly baptized: "For you are all the children of God by faith, in Jesus Christ. For as many of you as have been baptized in Christ, have put on Christ. There is neither Jew, nor Greek; there is neither bond, nor free; there is neither male nor female. For you are all one in Christ Jesus" (Gal. 3:26–28). "Where there is neither Gentile nor Jew, circumcision nor uncircumcision, barbarian nor Scythian, bond nor free. But Christ is all and in all" (Col. 3:11). "For in one Spirit were we all baptized into one body, whether Jews or Gentiles, whether bond or free; and in one Spirit we have all been made to drink" (1 Cor. 12:13). Golden words, indeed, noble and wholesome lessons, whereby its old dignity is given back and with increase to the human race, and men of whatever land or tongue of class are bound together and joined in the strong bonds of

brotherly kinship. Those things St. Paul, with that Christian charity with which he was filled, learned from the very heart of Him who, with much surpassing goodness, gave Himself to be the brother of us all, and in His own person, without omitting or excepting anyone, so ennobled men that they might become participators in the divine nature. Through this Christian charity, the various races of men were drawn together under the divine guidance in such a wonderful way that they blossomed into a new state of hope and public happiness; as with the progress of time and events and the constant labor of the Church the various nations were able to gather together, Christian and free, organized anew after the manner of a family.

7. From the beginning, the Church spared no pains to make the Christian people, in a matter of such high importance, accept and firmly hold the true teachings of Christ and the Apostles. And now through the new Adam, who is Christ, there is established a brotherly union between man and man, and people and people; just as in the order of nature they all have a common origin, so in the order which is above nature they all have one and the same origin in salvation and faith; all alike are called to be the adopted sons of God and the Father, who has paid the selfsame ransom for us all; we are all members of the same body, all are allowed to partake of the same divine banquet, and offered to us all are the blessings of divine grace and of eternal life. Having established these principles as beginnings and foundations, the Church, like a tender mother, went on to try to find some alleviation for the sorrows and the disgrace of the life of the slave; with this end in view she clearly defined and strongly enforced the rights and mutual duties of masters and slaves as they are laid down in the letters of the Apostles. It was in these words that the Princes of the Apostles admonished the slaves they had admitted to the fold of Christ. "Servants, be subject to your masters with all fear, not only to the good and gentle, but also to the forward" (1 Pet. 2:18). "Servants, be obedient to them that are your lords according to the

flesh, with fear and trembling in the simplicity of your heart, as to Christ. Not serving to the eye, but as the servants of Christ, doing the will of God from the heart. With a good will serving as to the Lord, and nor to men. Knowing that whatsoever good thing any man shall do, the same shall he receive from the Lord, whether he be bond or free" (Eph. 6:5–8). St. Paul says the same to Timothy: "Whosoever are servants under the yoke, let them count their masters worthy of all honor; lest the name of the Lord and his doctrine be blasphemed. But they that have believing masters, let them not despise them because they are brethren, but serve them the rather, because they are faithful and beloved, who are partakers of the benefit. These things teach and exhort" (1 Tim. 6:1–2). In like manner he commanded Titus to teach servants "to be obedient to their masters, in all things pleasing, not gainsaying. Not defrauding, but in all things showing good fidelity, that they may adorn the doctrine of God our Savior in all things" (Titus 2:9–10).

8. Those first disciples of the Christian faith very well understood that this brotherly equality of all men in Christ ought in no way to diminish or detract from the respect, honor, faithfulness, and other duties due to those placed above them. From this many good results followed, so that duties became at once more certain of being performed, and lighter and pleasanter to do, and at the same time more fruitful in obtaining the glory of heaven. Thus, they treated their masters with reverence and honor as men clothed in the authority of Him from whom comes all power. Among these disciples, the motive of action was not the fear of punishment or any enlightened prudence or the promptings of utility, but a consciousness of duty and the force of charity. On the other hand, masters were wisely counseled by the Apostle to treat their slaves with consideration in return for their services: "And you, masters, do the same things unto them, forbearing threatenings; knowing that the Lord both of them and you is in heaven, and there is not respect of persons with Him" (Eph. 6:9).

They were also told to remember that the slave had no reason to regret his lot, seeing that he is "the freeman of the Lord," nor the freeman, seeing that he is "the bondman of Christ" (1 Cor. 7:22), to feel proud and to give his commands with haughtiness. It was impressed upon masters that they ought to recognize in their slaves their fellow men, and respect them accordingly, recognizing that by nature they were not different from themselves, that by religion and in relation to the majesty of their common Lord all were equal. These precepts, so well calculated to introduce harmony among the various parts of domestic society, were practised by the Apostles themselves. Especially remarkable is the case of St. Paul when he exerted himself in behalf of Onesimus, the fugitive of Philemon, with whom, when he returned him to his master, he sent this loving recommendation: "And do thou receive him as my own heart, not now as a servant, but instead of a servant a most dear brother.... And if he have wronged thee in anything, or is in thy debt, put that to my account" (Philem. 1:12, 18).

9. Whoever compare the pagan and the Christian attitude toward slavery will easily come to the conclusion that the one was marked by great cruelty and wickedness, and the other by great gentleness and humanity, nor will it be possible to deprive the Church of the credit due to her as the instrument of this happy change. And this becomes still more apparent when we consider carefully how tenderly and with what prudence the Church has cut out and destroyed this dreadful curse of slavery. She has deprecated any precipitate action in securing the manumission and liberation of the slaves, because that would have entailed tumults and wrought injury, as well to the slaves themselves as to the commonwealth, but with singular wisdom she has seen that the minds of the slaves should be instructed through her discipline in the Christian faith, and with baptism should acquire habits suitable to the Christian life. Therefore, when, amid the slave multitude whom she has numbered among her children, some, led astray by some hope of liberty, have had recourse to violence and

sedition, the Church has always condemned these unlawful efforts and opposed them, and through her ministers has applied the remedy of patience. She taught the slaves to feel that, by virtue of the light of holy faith, and the character they received from Christ, they enjoyed a dignity which placed them above their heathen lords, but that they were bound the more strictly by the Author and Founder of their faith Himself never to set themselves against these, or even to be wanting in the reverence and obedience due to them. Knowing themselves as the chosen ones of the Kingdom of God, and endowed with the freedom of His children, and called to the good things that are not of this life, they were able to work on without being cast down by the sorrows and troubles of this passing world, but with eyes and hearts turned to heaven were consoled and strengthened in their holy resolutions. St. Peter was addressing himself specially to slaves when he wrote: "For this is thankworthy, if for conscience towards God a man endure sorrows, suffering wrongfully. For unto this you are called; because Christ also suffered for us, leaving you an example that you should follow his steps" (1 Pet. 2:19–21).

10. The credit for this solicitude joined with moderation, which in such a wonderful way adorns the divine powers of the Church, is increased by the marvelous and unconquerable courage with which she was able to inspire and sustain so many poor slaves. It was a wonderful sight to behold those who, in their obedience and the patience with which they submitted to every task, were such an example to their masters, refusing to let themselves be persuaded to prefer the wicked commands of those above them to the holy law of God, and even giving up their lives in the most cruel tortures with unconquered hearts and unclouded brows. The pages of Eusebius keep alive for us the memory of the unshaken constancy of the virgin Potamiana, who, rather than consent to gratify the lusts of her master, fearlessly accepted death, and sealed her faithfulness to Jesus Christ with her blood. Many other admirable examples abound of slaves, who, for

their souls' sake and to keep their faith with God, have resisted their masters to the death. History has no case to show of Christian slaves for any other cause setting themselves in opposition to their masters of joining in conspiracies against the State. Thence, peace and quiet times having been restored to the Church, the holy Fathers made a wise and admirable exposition of the apostolic precepts concerning the fraternal unanimity which should exist between Christians, and with a like charity extended it to the advantage of slaves, striving to point out that the rights of masters extended lawfully indeed over the works of their slaves, but that their power did not extend to using horrible cruelties against their persons. St. Chrysostom stands pre-eminent among the Greeks, who often treats of this subject, and affirms with exulting mind and tongue that slavery, in the old meaning of the word, had at that time disappeared through the beneficence of the Christian faith, so that it both seemed, and was, a word without any meaning among the disciples of the Lord. For Christ indeed (so he sums up his argument), when in His great mercy to us He wiped away the sin contracted by our birth, at the same time healed the manifold corruptions of human society; so that, as death itself by His means has laid aside its terrors and become a peaceful passing away to a happy life, so also has slavery been banished. Do not, then, call any Christian man a slave, unless, indeed, he is in bondage again to sin; they are altogether brethren who are born again and received in Christ Jesus. Our advantages flow from the new birth and adoption into the household of God, not from the eminence of our race; our dignity arises from the praise of our truth, not of our blood. But in order that that kind of evangelical brotherhood may have more fruit, it is necessary that in the actions of our ordinary life there should appear a willing interchange of kindnesses and good offices, so that slaves should be esteemed of nearly equal account with the rest of our household and friends, and that the master of the house should supply them, not only with what is necessary for their life and food, but also all necessary safeguards of religious training. Finally, from the marked address of Paul to Philemon, bidding grace and peace "to the church which is in thy house" (Philem. 1:2), the precept should be held in respect equally by Christian masters and servants, that they who have an intercommunion of faith should also have an intercommunion of charity.[5]

11. Of the Latin authors, we worthily and justly call to mind St. Ambrose, who so earnestly inquired into all that was necessary in this cause, and so clearly ascribes what is due to each kind of man according to the laws of Christianity, that no one has ever achieved it better, whose sentiments, it is unnecessary to say, fully and perfectly coincide with those of St. Chrysostom.[6] These things were, as is evident, most justly and usefully laid down; but more, the chief point is that they have been observed wholly and religiously from the earliest times wherever the profession of the Christian faith has flourished. Unless this had been the case, that excellent defender of religion, Lactantius, could not have maintained it so confidently, as though a witness of it. "Should anyone say: Are there not among you some poor, some rich, some slaves, some who are masters; is there no difference between different persons? I answer: There is none, nor is there any other cause why we call each other by the name of brother than that we consider ourselves to be equals; first, when we measure all human things, not by the body but by the spirit, although their corporal condition may be different from ours, yet in spirit they are not slaves to us, but we esteem and call them brethren, fellow workers in religion."[7]

---

5. St. John Chrysostom, *Hom. in Lazar.* (*PG* 58:1039); *Hom.* 19 *in 1 ad Cor.* (*PG* 61:157–158); *Hom.* 1 *in ad Phil.* (PG 62:705).
6. *De Jacob et de vita beata*, c. 3 (*PL* 14:633a–636a); *De patr. Joseph*, c. 4 (*PL* 16:680c–682b); *Exhort. Virgin.*, c. 1. (*PL* 16:351a–352b).
7. *Divin. Instit.*, V, 16 (*PL* 6:599a–600a).

12. The care of the Church extended to the protection of slaves, and without interruption tended carefully to one object, that they should finally be restored to freedom, which would greatly conduce to their eternal welfare. That the event happily responded to these efforts, the annals of sacred antiquity afford abundant proof. Noble matrons, rendered illustrious by the praises of St. Jerome, themselves afforded great aid in carrying this matter into effect; so that as Salvian relates, in Christian families, even though not very rich, it often happened that the slaves were freed by a generous manumission. But, also, St. Clement long before praised that excellent work of charity by which some Christians became slaves, by an exchange of persons, because they could in no other way liberate those who were in bondage. Wherefore, in addition to the fact that the act of manumission began to take place in churches as an act of piety, the Church ordered it to be proposed to the faithful when about to make their wills, as a work very pleasing to God and of great merit and value with Him. Therefore, those precepts of manumission to the heir were introduced with the words, "for the love of God, for the welfare or benefit of my soul."[8] Neither was anything grudged as the price of the captives, gifts dedicated to God were sold, consecrated gold and silver melted down, the ornaments and gifts of the basilicas alienated, as, indeed, was done more than once by Ambrose, Augustine, Hilary, Eligius, Patrick, and many other holy men.

13. Moreover, the Roman Pontiffs, who have always acted, as history truly relates, as the protectors of the weak and helpers of the oppressed, have done their best for slaves. St. Gregory himself set at liberty as many as possible, and in the Roman Council of 597 desired those to receive their freedom who were anxious to enter the monastic state. Hadrian I maintained that slaves could freely enter into matrimony even without their masters' consent. It was clearly ordered by

8. St. Clement of Rome, *Ep. ad Cor.*, I, 55 (PG 1:319a).

Alexander III in the year 1167 to the Moorish King of Valencia that he should not make a slave of any Christian, because no one was a slave by the law of nature, all men having been made free by God. Innocent III, in the year 1190, at the prayer of its founders, John de Matha and Felix of Valois, approved and established the Order of the Most Holy Trinity for Redeeming Christians who had fallen into the power of the Turks. At a later date, Honorius III, and, afterwards, Gregory IX, duly approved the Order of St. Mary of Help, founded for a similar purpose, which Peter Nolasco had established, and which included the severe rule that its religious should give themselves up as slaves in the place of Christians taken captive by tyrants, if it should be necessary in order to redeem them. The same St. Gregory passed a decree, which was a far greater support of liberty, that it was unlawful to sell slaves to the Church, and he further added an exhortation to the faithful that, as a punishment for their faults, they should give their slaves to God and His saints as an act of expiation.

14. There are also many other good deeds of the Church in the same behalf. For she, indeed, was accustomed by severe penalties to defend slaves from the savage anger and cruel injuries of their masters. To those upon whom the hand of violence had rested, she was accustomed to open her sacred temples as places of refuge to receive the freemen into her good faith, and to restrain those by censure who dared by evil inducements to lead a man back again into slavery. In the same way she was still more favorable to the freedom of the slaves whom, by any means she held as her own, according to times and places; when she laid down either that those should be released by the bishops from every bond of slavery who had shown themselves during a certain time of trial of praiseworthy honesty of life, or when she easily permitted the bishops of their own will to declare those belonging to them free. It must also be ascribed to the compassion and virtue of the Church that somewhat of the pressure of civil law upon slaves was remitted, and, as far as it was brought about, that the

milder alleviations of Gregory the Great, having been incorporated in the written law of nations, became of force. That, however, was done principally by the agency of Charlemagne, who included them in his *Capitularia*, as Gratian afterwards did in his *Decretum*.[9] Finally, monuments, laws, institutions, through a continuous series of ages, teach and splendidly demonstrate the great love of the Church toward slaves, whose miserable condition she never left destitute of protection, and always to the best of her power alleviated. Therefore, sufficient praise or thanks can never be returned to the Catholic Church, the banisher of slavery and causer of true liberty, fraternity, and equality among men, since she has merited it by the prosperity of nations, through the very great beneficence of Christ our Redeemer.

15. Toward the end of the fifteenth century, at which time the base stain of slavery having been nearly blotted out from among Christian nations, States were anxious to stand firmly in evangelical liberty, and also to increase their empire, this Apostolic See took the greatest care that the evil germs of such depravity should nowhere revive. She therefore directed her provident vigilance to the newly discovered regions of Africa, Asia, and America; for a report had reached her that the leaders of those expeditions, Christians though they were, were wickedly making use of their arms and ingenuity for establishing and imposing slavery on these innocent nations. Indeed, since the crude nature of the soil which they had to overcome, nor less the wealth of metals which had to be extracted by digging, required very hard work, unjust and inhuman plans were entered into. For a certain traffic was begun, slaves being transported for that purpose from Ethiopia, which, at that time, under the name of *La tratta dei Negri*, too much occupied those colonies. An oppression of the indigenous inhabitants (who are collectively called Indians), much the same as slavery, followed with a like maltreatment.

---

9. Gratian, *Decretum*, I, d. 54; ed. E. Friedberg, vol. 1, cols. 206–214.

16. When Pius II had become assured of these matters without delay, on October 7, 1462, he gave a letter to the bishop of the place in which he reproved and condemned such wickedness. Sometime afterwards, Leo X lent, as far as he could, his good offices and authority to the kings of both Portugal and Spain, who took care to radically extirpate that abuse, opposed alike to religion, humanity, and justice. Nevertheless, that evil having grown strong, remained there, its impure cause, the unquenchable desire of gain, remaining. Then Paul III, anxious with a fatherly love as to the condition of the Indians and of the Moorish slaves, came to this last determination, that in open day, and, as it were, in the sight of all nations, he declared that they all had a just and natural right of a threefold character, namely, that each one of them was master of his own person, that they could live together under their own laws, and that they could acquire and hold property for themselves. More than this, having sent letters to the Cardinal Archbishop of Toledo, he pronounced an interdict and deprival of sacraments against those who acted contrary to the aforesaid decree, reserving to the Roman Pontiff the power of absolving them.[10]

17. With the same forethought and constancy, other Pontiffs at a later period, as Urban VIII, Benedict XIV, and Pius VII, showed themselves strong asserters of liberty for the Indians and Moors and those who were even as yet not instructed in the Christian faith. The last, moreover, at the Council of the confederated Princes of Europe, held at Vienna, called their attention in common to this point, that that traffic in Negroes, of which We have spoken before, and which had now ceased in many places, should be thoroughly rooted out. Gregory XVI also severely censured those neglecting the duties of humanity and the laws, and restored the decrees and statutory penalties of the Apostolic See, and left no means untried that foreign

10. Paul III, *Veritas ipsa* (June 2, 1537).

nations, also, following the kindliness of the Europeans, should cease from and abhor the disgrace and brutality of slavery.[11] But it has turned out most fortunately for Us that We have received the congratulations of the chief princes and rulers of public affairs for having obtained, thanks to Our constant pleadings, some satisfaction for the long-continued and most just complaints of nature and religion.

18. We have, however, in Our mind, in a matter of the same kind, another care which gives Us no light anxiety and presses upon Our solicitude. This shameful trading in men has, indeed, ceased to take place by sea, but on land is carried on to too great an extent and too barbarously, and that especially in some parts of Africa. For it having been perversely laid down by the Mohammedans that Ethiopians and men of similar nations are very little superior to brute beasts, it is easy to see and shudder at the perfidy and cruelty of man. Suddenly, like plunderers making an attack, they invade the tribes of Ethiopians, fearing no such thing; they rush into their villages, houses, and huts; they lay waste, destroy, and seize everything; they lead away from thence the men, women, and children, easily captured and bound, so that they may drag them away by force for their shameful traffic. These hateful expeditions are made into Egypt, Zanzibar, and partly also into the Sudan, as though so many stations. Men bound with chains are forced to take long journeys, ill supplied with food, under the frequent use of the lash; those who are too weak to undergo this are killed; those who are strong enough go like a flock with a crowd of others to be sold and to be passed over to a brutal and shameless purchaser. But whoever is thus sold and given up is exposed to what is a miserable rending asunder of wives, children, and parents, and is driven by him into whose power he falls into a hard and indescribable slavery; nor can he refuse to conform to the religious rites of Mahomet. These things We have received not long since with the

11. Gregory XVI, *In supremo apostolatus fastigio* (December 3, 1837).

greatest bitterness of feeling from some who have been eyewitnesses, though tearful ones, of that kind of infamy and misery; with these, moreover, what has been related lately by the explorers in equatorial Africa entirely coincides. It is indeed manifest, by their testimony and word, that each year four hundred thousand Africans are usually thus sold like cattle, about half of whom, wearied out by the roughness of the tracks, fall down and perish there, so that, sad to relate, those traveling through such places see the pathway strewn with the remains of bones.

19. Who would not be moved by the thought of such miseries. We, indeed, who are holding the place of Christ, the loving Liberator and Redeemer of all mankind, and who so rejoice in the many and glorious good deeds of the Church to all who are afflicted, can scarcely express how great is Our commiseration for those unhappy nations, with what fulness of charity We open Our arms to them, how ardently We desire to be able to afford them every alleviation and support, with the hope, that, having cast off the slavery of superstition as well as the slavery of man, they may at length serve the one true God under the gentle yoke of Christ, partakers with Us of the divine inheritance. Would that all who hold high positions in authority and power, or who desire the rights of nations and of humanity to be held sacred, or who earnestly devote themselves to the interests of the Catholic religion, would all, everywhere acting on Our exhortations and wishes, strive together to repress, forbid, and put an end to that kind of traffic, than which nothing is more base and wicked.

20. In the meantime, while by a more strenuous application of ingenuity and labor new roads are being made, and new commercial enterprises undertaken in the lands of Africa, let apostolic men endeavor to find out how they can best secure the safety and liberty of slaves. They will obtain success in this matter in no other way than if, strengthened by divine grace, they give themselves up to spreading our most holy faith and daily caring for it, whose distinguishing fruit

is that it wonderfully flavors and develops the liberty "with which Christ made us free" (Gal. 4:31). We therefore advise them to look, as if into a mirror of apostolic virtue, at the life and works of St. Peter Claver, to whom We have lately added a crown of glory.[12] Let them look at him who for fully forty years gave himself up to minister with the greatest constancy in his labors, to a most miserable assembly of Moorish slaves; truly he ought to be called the apostle of those whose constant servant he professed himself and gave himself up to be. If they endeavor to take to themselves and reflect the charity and patience of such a man, they will shine indeed as worthy ministers of salvation, authors of consolation, messengers of peace, who, by God's help, may turn solicitude, desolation, and fierceness into the most joyful fertility of religion and civilization.

21. And now, Venerable Brethren, Our thoughts and letters desire to turn to you that We may again announce to you and again share with you the exceeding joy which We feel on account of the determinations which have been publicly entered into in that empire with regard to slavery. If, indeed, it seemed to Us a good, happy, and propitious event, that it was provided and insisted upon by law that whoever were still in the condition of slaves ought to be admitted to the status and rights of free men, so also it conforms and increases Our hope of future acts which will be the cause of joy, both in civil and religious matters. Thus, the name of the Empire of Brazil will be justly held in honor and praise among the most civilized nations, and the name of its august emperor will likewise be esteemed, whose excellent speech is on record, that he desired nothing more ardently than that every vestige of slavery should be speedily obliterated from

12. St. Peter Claver (1551–1654), joined the Society of Jesus in 1602; in 1610, he went to Cartagena, then the main slave market of the New World, and for forty-four years devoted himself to missionary work. He had declared his intention to remain "the slave of the Negroes" for his entire life and, in point of fact, is said to have baptized over three hundred thousand of them. He was canonized by Pope Leo XIII on January 15, 1888. (EDITOR)

his territories. But, truly, until those precepts of the laws are carried into effect, earnestly endeavor, We beseech you, by all means, and press on as much as possible the accomplishment of this affair, which no light difficulties hinder. Through your means let it be brought to pass that masters and slaves may mutually agree with the highest goodwill and best good faith, nor let there be any transgression of clemency or justice, but, whatever things have to be carried out, let all be done lawfully, temperately, and in a Christian manner. It is, however, chiefly to be wished that this may be prosperously accomplished, which all desire, that slavery may be banished and blotted out without any injury to divine or human rights, with no political agitation, and so with the solid benefit of the slaves themselves, for whose sake it is undertaken.

22. To each one of these, whether they have already been made free or are about to become so, We address with a pastoral intention and fatherly mind a few salutary cautions culled from the words of the great Apostle of the Gentiles. Let them, then, endeavor piously and constantly to retain grateful memory and feeling towards those by whose council and exertion they were set at liberty. Let them never show themselves unworthy of so great a gift nor ever confound liberty with license; but let them use it as becomes well-ordered citizens for the industry of an active life, for the benefit and advantage both of their family and of the State. To respect and increase the dignity of their princes, to obey the magistrates, to be obedient to the laws, these and similar duties let them diligently fulfil, under the influence, not so much of fear as of religion; let them also restrain and keep in subjection envy of another's wealth or position, which unfortunately daily distresses so many of those in inferior positions, and present so many incitements of rebellion against security of order and peace. Content with their state and lot, let them think nothing dearer, let them desire nothing more ardently than the good things of the heavenly kingdom by whose grace they have been brought to the light

and redeemed by Christ; let them feel piously towards God who is their Lord and Liberator; let them love Him with all their power; let them keep His commandments with all their might; let them rejoice in being sons of His spouse, the Holy Church; let them labor to be as good as possible, and as much as they can let them carefully return His love. Do you also, Venerable Brethren, be constant in showing and urging on the freedmen these same doctrines; that, that which is Our chief prayer, and at the same time ought to be yours and that of all good people, religion, amongst the first, may ever feel that she has gained the most ample fruits of that liberty which has been obtained wherever that empire extends.

23. But that that may happily take place, We beg and implore the full grace of God and motherly aid of the Immaculate Virgin. As a foretaste of heavenly gifts and witness of Our fatherly good will towards you, Venerable Brethren, your clergy, and all your people, We lovingly impart the apostolic blessing.

Given at St. Peter's, in Rome, the fifth day of May, 1888, the eleventh of Our Pontificate.

LEO PP. XIII

ENCYCLICAL LETTER
LIBERTAS
OF THE SUPREME PONTIFF
LEO XIII

TO THE PATRIARCHS, PRIMATES, ARCHBISHOPS, AND BISHOPS OF THE CATHOLIC WORLD IN GRACE AND COMMUNION WITH THE APOSTOLIC SEE ON THE NATURE OF HUMAN LIBERTY

1. Liberty, the highest of natural endowments, being the portion only of intellectual or rational natures, confers on man this dignity—that he is "in the hand of his counsel" (Eccl. 15:14) and has power over his actions. But the manner in which such dignity is exercised is of the greatest moment, inasmuch as on the use that is made of liberty the highest good and the greatest evil alike depend. Man, indeed, is free to obey his reason, to seek moral good, and to strive unswervingly after his last end. Yet he is free also to turn aside to all other things; and, in pursuing the empty semblance of good, to disturb rightful order and to fall headlong into the destruction which he has voluntarily chosen. The Redeemer of mankind, Jesus Christ, having restored and exalted the original dignity of nature, vouchsafed special assistance to the will of man; and by the gifts of His grace here, and the promise of heavenly bliss hereafter, He raised it to a nobler state. In like manner, this great gift of nature has ever been, and always will be, deservingly cherished by the Catholic Church, for to her alone has

been committed the charge of handing down to all ages the benefits purchased for us by Jesus Christ. Yet there are many who imagine that the Church is hostile to human liberty. Having a false and absurd notion as to what liberty is, either they pervert the very idea of freedom, or they extend it at their pleasure to many things in respect of which man cannot rightly be regarded as free.

2. We have on other occasions, and especially in Our Encyclical Letter *Immortale Dei*, in treating of the so-called *modern liberties*, distinguished between their good and evil elements; and We have shown that whatsoever is good in those liberties is as ancient as truth itself, and that the Church has always most willingly approved and practiced that good. But whatsoever has been added as new is, to tell the plain truth, of a vitiated kind, the fruit of the disorders of the age, and of an insatiate longing after novelties. Seeing, however, that many cling so obstinately to their own opinion in this matter as to imagine these modern liberties, cankered as they are, to be the greatest glory of our age, and the very basis of civil life, without which no perfect government can be conceived, We feel it a pressing duty, for the sake of the common good, to treat separately of this subject.

3. It is with *moral* liberty, whether in individuals or in communities, that We proceed at once to deal. But, first of all, it will be well to speak briefly of *natural* liberty; for, though it is distinct and separate from moral liberty, natural freedom is the fountainhead from which liberty of whatsoever kind flows, *sua vi suaque sponte*. The unanimous consent and judgment of men, which is the trusty voice of nature, recognizes this natural liberty in those only who are endowed with intelligence or reason; and it is by his use of this that man is rightly regarded as responsible for his actions. For while other animate creatures follow their senses, seeking good and avoiding evil only by instinct, man has reason to guide him in each and every act of his life. Reason sees that whatever things that are held to be good upon earth may exist or may not, and discerning that none of them

is of necessity for us, it leaves the will free to choose what it pleases. But man can judge of this contingency, as We say, only because he has a soul that is simple, spiritual, and intellectual—a soul, therefore, which is not produced by matter, and does not depend on matter for its existence; but which is created immediately by God, and, far surpassing the condition of things material, has a life and action of its own so that, knowing the unchangeable and necessary reasons of what is true and good, it sees that no particular kind of good is necessary to us. When, therefore, it is established that man's soul is immortal and endowed with reason and not bound up with things material, the foundation of natural liberty is at once most firmly laid.

4. As the Catholic Church declares in the strongest terms the simplicity, spirituality, and immortality of the soul, so with unequaled constancy and publicity she ever also asserts its freedom. These truths she has always taught, and has sustained them as a dogma of faith, and whenever heretics or innovators have attacked the liberty of man, the Church has defended it and protected this noble possession from destruction. History bears witness to the energy with which she met the fury of the Manichaeans and others like them; and the earnestness with which in later years she defended human liberty at the Council of Trent, and against the followers of Jansenius, is known to all. At no time, and in no place, has she held truce with *fatalism*.

5. Liberty, then, as We have said, belongs only to those who have the gift of reason or intelligence. Considered as to its nature, it is the faculty of choosing means fitted for the end proposed, for he is master of his actions who can choose one thing out of many. Now, since everything chosen as a means is viewed as good or useful, and since good, as such, is the proper object of our desire, it follows that freedom of choice is a property of the will, or, rather, is identical with the will in so far as it has in its action the faculty of choice. But the will cannot proceed to act until it is enlightened by the knowledge

possessed by the intellect. In other words, the good wished by the will is necessarily good in so far as it is known by the intellect; and this the more, because in all voluntary acts choice is subsequent to a judgment upon the truth of the good presented, declaring to which good preference should be given. No sensible man can doubt that judgment is an act of reason, not of the will. The end, or object, both of the rational will and of its liberty is that good only which is in conformity with reason.

6. Since, however, both these faculties are imperfect, it is possible, as is often seen, that the reason should propose something which is not really good, but which has the appearance of good, and that the will should choose accordingly. For as the possibility of error, and actual error, are defects of the mind and attest its imperfection, so the pursuit of what has a false appearance of good, though a proof of our freedom, just as a disease is a proof of our vitality, implies defect in human liberty. The will also, simply because of its dependence on the reason, no sooner desires anything contrary thereto than it abuses its freedom of choice and corrupts its very essence. Thus it is that the infinitely perfect God, although supremely free, because of the supremacy of His intellect and of His essential goodness, nevertheless cannot choose evil; neither can the angels and saints, who enjoy the beatific vision. St. Augustine and others urged most admirably against the Pelagians that, if the possibility of deflection from good belonged to the essence or perfection of liberty, then God, Jesus Christ, and the angels and saints, who have not this power, would have no liberty at all, or would have less liberty than man has in his state of pilgrimage and imperfection. This subject is often discussed by the Angelic Doctor in his demonstration that the possibility of sinning is not freedom, but slavery. It will suffice to quote his subtle commentary on the words of our Lord: "Whosoever committeth sin is the slave of sin" (John 8:34). "Everything," he says, "is that which belongs to it naturally. When, therefore, it acts through a power outside

itself, it does not act of itself, but through another, that is, as a slave. But man is by nature rational. When, therefore, he acts according to reason, he acts of himself and according to his free will; and this is liberty. Whereas, when he sins, he acts in opposition to reason, is moved by another, and is the victim of foreign misapprehensions. Therefore, 'Whosoever committeth sin is the slave of sin.'"[1] Even the heathen philosophers clearly recognized this truth, especially they who held that the wise man alone is free; and by the term "wise man" was meant, as is well known, the man trained to live in accordance with his nature, that is, in justice and virtue.

7. Such, then, being the condition of human liberty, it necessarily stands in need of light and strength to direct its actions to good and to restrain them from evil. Without this, the freedom of our will would be our ruin. First of all, there must be *law*; that is, a fixed rule of teaching what is to be done and what is to be left undone. This rule cannot affect the lower animals in any true sense, since they act of necessity, following their natural instinct, and cannot of themselves act in any other way. On the other hand, as was said above, he who is free can either act or not act, can do this or do that, as he pleases, because his judgment precedes his choice. And his judgment not only decides what is right or wrong of its own nature, but also what is practically good and therefore to be chosen, and what is practically evil and therefore to be avoided. In other words, the reason prescribes to the will what it should seek after or shun, in order to the eventual attainment of man's last end, for the sake of which all his actions ought to be performed. This ordination of *reason* is called law. In man's free will, therefore, or in the moral necessity of our voluntary acts being in accordance with reason, lies the very root of the necessity of law. Nothing more foolish can be uttered or conceived than the notion that, because man is free by nature, he is therefore exempt from law.

1. St. Thomas Aquinas, *On the Gospel of St. John*, c. 8, lect. 4, n. 3.

Were this the case, it would follow that to become free we must be deprived of reason; whereas the truth is that we are bound to submit to law precisely because we are free by our very nature. For law is the guide of man's actions; it turns him toward good by its rewards, and deters him from evil by its punishments.

8. Foremost in this office comes the *natural law*, which is written and engraved in the mind of every man; and this is nothing but our reason, commanding us to do right and forbidding sin. Nevertheless, all prescriptions of human reason can have force of law only inasmuch as they are the voice and the interpreters of some higher power on which our reason and liberty necessarily depend. For since the force of law consists in the imposing of obligations and the granting of rights, authority is the one and only foundation of all law—the power, that is, of fixing duties and defining rights, as also of assigning the necessary sanctions of reward and chastisement to each and all of its commands. But all this, clearly, cannot be found in man, if, as his own supreme legislator, he is to be the rule of his own actions. It follows, therefore, that the law of nature is the same thing as the *eternal law*, implanted in rational creatures, and inclining them *to their right action and end*; and can be nothing else but the eternal reason of God, the Creator and Ruler of all the world. To this rule of action and restraint of evil, God has vouchsafed to give special and most suitable aids for strengthening and ordering the human will. The first and most excellent of these is the power of His divine *grace*, whereby the mind can be enlightened and the will wholesomely invigorated and moved to the constant pursuit of moral good, so that the use of our inborn liberty becomes at once less difficult and less dangerous. Not that the divine assistance hinders in any way the free movement of our will; just the contrary, for grace works inwardly in man and in harmony with his natural inclinations, since it flows from the very Creator of his mind and will, by whom all things are moved in conformity with their nature. As the Angelic Doctor points out, it

is because divine grace comes from the Author of nature that it is so admirably adapted to be the safeguard of all natures, and to maintain the character, efficiency, and operations of each.

9. What has been said of the liberty of individuals is no less applicable to them when considered as bound together in civil society. For what reason and the natural law do for individuals, that *human law*, promulgated for their good, does for the citizens of States. Of the laws enacted by men, some are concerned with what is good or bad by its very nature; and they command men to follow after what is right and to shun what is wrong, adding at the same time a suitable sanction. But such laws by no means derive their origin from civil society, because, just as civil society did not create human nature, so neither can it be said to be the author of the good which befits human nature, or of the evil which is contrary to it. Laws come before men live together in society, and have their origin in the natural, and consequently in the eternal, law. The precepts, therefore, of the natural law, contained bodily in the laws of men, have not merely the force of human law, but they possess that higher and more august sanction which belongs to the law of nature and the eternal law. And within the sphere of this kind of laws the duty of the civil legislator is, mainly, to keep the community in obedience by the adoption of a common discipline and by putting restraint upon refractory and viciously inclined men, so that, deterred from evil, they may turn to what is good, or at any rate may avoid causing trouble and disturbance to the State. Now, there are other enactments of the civil authority which do not follow directly, but somewhat remotely, from the natural law, and decide many points which the law of nature treats only in a general and indefinite way. For instance, though nature commands all to contribute to the public peace and prosperity, whatever belongs to the manner, and circumstances, and conditions under which such service is to be rendered must be determined by the wisdom of men and not by nature herself. It is in the constitution of these particular rules of

life, suggested by reason and prudence, and put forth by competent authority, that human law, properly so called, consists, binding all citizens to work together for the attainment of the common end proposed to the community, and forbidding them to depart from this end, and, in so far as human law is in conformity with the dictates of nature, leading to what is good, and deterring from evil.

10. From this it is manifest that the eternal law of God is the sole standard and rule of human liberty, not only in each individual man, but also in the community and civil society which men constitute when united. Therefore, the true liberty of human society does not consist in every man doing what he pleases, for this would simply end in turmoil and confusion, and bring on the overthrow of the State; but rather in this: that through the injunctions of the civil law all may more easily conform to the prescriptions of the eternal law. Likewise, the liberty of those who are in authority does not consist in the power to lay unreasonable and capricious commands upon their subjects, which would equally be criminal and would lead to the ruin of the commonwealth; but the binding force of human laws is in this: that they are to be regarded as applications of the eternal law and incapable of sanctioning anything which is not contained in the eternal law, as in the principle of all law. Thus, St. Augustine most wisely says: "I think that you can see, at the same time, that there is nothing just and lawful in that temporal law, unless what men have gathered from this eternal law."[2] If, then, by anyone in authority, something be sanctioned out of conformity with the principles of right reason, and consequently hurtful to the commonwealth, such an enactment can have no binding force of law, as being no rule of justice, but certain to lead men away from that good which is the very end of civil society.

11. Therefore, the nature of human liberty, however it be considered, whether in individuals or in society, whether in those who

---

2. Augustine, *De libero arbitrio*, I, 6, 15 (*PL* 32:1229).

command or in those who obey, supposes the necessity of obedience to some supreme and eternal law, which is no other than the authority of God, commanding good and forbidding evil. And so far from this most just authority of God over men diminishing, or even destroying their liberty, it protects and perfects it, for the real perfection of all creatures is found in the prosecution and attainment of their respective ends; but the supreme end to which human liberty must aspire is God.

12. These precepts of the truest and highest teaching, made known to us by the light of reason itself, the Church, instructed by the example and doctrine of her divine Author, has ever propagated and asserted; for she has ever made them the measure of her office and of her teaching to the Christian nations. As to morals, the laws of the Gospel not only immeasurably surpass the wisdom of the heathen, but are an invitation and an introduction to a state of holiness unknown to the ancients; and, bringing man nearer to God, they make him at once the possessor of a more perfect liberty. Thus, the powerful influence of the Church has ever been manifested in the custody and protection of the civil and political liberty of the people. The enumeration of its merits in this respect does not belong to our present purpose. It is sufficient to recall the fact that slavery, that old reproach of the heathen nations, was mainly abolished by the beneficent efforts of the Church. The impartiality of law and the true brotherhood of man were first asserted by Jesus Christ; and His Apostles re-echoed His voice when they declared that in future there was to be neither Jew, nor Gentile, nor barbarian, nor Scythian, but all were brothers in Christ. So powerful, so conspicuous, in this respect is the influence of the Church that experience abundantly testifies how savage customs are no longer possible in any land where she has once set her foot; but that gentleness speedily takes the place of cruelty, and the light of truth quickly dispels the darkness of barbarism. Nor has the Church been less lavish in the benefits she has conferred on

civilized nations in every age, either by resisting the tyranny of the wicked or by protecting the innocent and helpless from injury or, finally, by using her influence in the support of any form of government which commended itself to the citizens at home because of its justice, or was feared by their enemies without because of its power.

13. Moreover, the highest duty is to respect authority, and obediently to submit to just law; and by this the members of a community are effectually protected from the wrongdoing of evil men. Lawful power is from God, "and whosoever resisteth authority resisteth the ordinance of God" (Rom. 13:2); wherefore, obedience is greatly ennobled when subjected to an authority which is the most just and supreme of all. But where the power to command is wanting, or where a law is enacted contrary to reason, or to the eternal law, or to some ordinance of God, obedience is unlawful, lest, while obeying man, we become disobedient to God. Thus, an effectual barrier being opposed to tyranny, the authority in the State will not have all its own way, but the interests and rights of all will be safeguarded—the rights of individuals, of domestic society, and of all the members of the commonwealth; all being free to live according to law and right reason; and in this, as We have shown, true liberty really consists.

14. If when men discuss the question of liberty, they were careful to grasp its true and legitimate meaning, such as reason and reasoning have just explained, they would never venture to affix such a calumny on the Church as to assert that she is the foe of individual and public liberty. But many there are who follow in the footsteps of Lucifer, and adopt as their own his rebellious cry, "I will not serve"; and consequently substitute for true liberty what is sheer and most foolish license. Such, for instance, are the men belonging to that widely spread and powerful organization, who, usurping the name of liberty, style themselves liberals.

15. What *naturalists* or *rationalists* aim at in philosophy, that the supporters of *liberalism*, carrying out the principles laid down

by naturalism, are attempting in the domain of morality and politics. The fundamental doctrine of rationalism is the supremacy of the human reason, which, refusing due submission to the divine and eternal reason, proclaims its own independence, and constitutes itself the supreme principle and source and judge of truth. Hence, these followers of liberalism deny the existence of any divine authority to which obedience is due, and proclaim that every man is the law to himself; from which arises that ethical system which they style *independent* morality, and which, under the guise of liberty, exonerates man from any obedience to the commands of God, and substitutes a boundless license. The end of all this it is not difficult to foresee, especially when society is in question. For when once man is firmly persuaded that he is subject to no one, it follows that the efficient cause of the unity of civil society is not to be sought in any principle external to man, or superior to him, but simply in the free will of individuals; that the authority in the State comes from the people only; and that, just as every man's individual reason is his only rule of life, so the collective reason of the community should be the supreme guide in the management of all public affairs. Hence the doctrine of the supremacy of the greater number, and that all right and all duty reside in the majority. But, from what has been said, it is clear that all this is in contradiction to reason. To refuse any bond of union between man and civil society, on the one hand, and God the Creator and consequently the supreme Lawgiver, on the other, is plainly repugnant to the nature, not only of man, but of all created things; for, of necessity, all effects must in some proper way be connected with their cause; and it belongs to the perfection of every nature to contain itself within that sphere and grade which the order of nature has assigned to it, namely, that the lower should be subject and obedient to the higher.

16. Moreover, besides this, a doctrine of such character is most hurtful both to individuals and to the State. For once ascribe to

human reason the only authority to decide what is true and what is good, and the real distinction between good and evil is destroyed; honor and dishonor differ not in their nature, but in the opinion and judgment of each one; pleasure is the measure of what is lawful; and, given a code of morality which can have little or no power to restrain or quiet the unruly propensities of man, a way is naturally opened to universal corruption. With reference also to public affairs: authority is severed from the true and natural principle whence it derives all its efficacy for the common good; and the law determining what it is right to do and avoid doing is at the mercy of a majority. Now, this is simply a road leading straight to tyranny. The empire of God over man and civil society once repudiated, it follows that religion, as a public institution, can have no claim to exist, and that everything that belongs to religion will be treated with complete indifference. Furthermore, with ambitious designs on sovereignty, tumult and sedition will be common amongst the people; and when duty and conscience cease to appeal to them, there will be nothing to hold them back but force, which of itself alone is powerless to keep their covetousness in check. Of this we have almost daily evidence in the conflict with *socialists* and members of other seditious societies, who labor unceasingly to bring about revolution. It is for those, then, who are capable of forming a just estimate of things to decide whether such doctrines promote that true liberty which alone is worthy of man, or rather pervert and destroy it.

17. There are, indeed, some adherents of liberalism who do not subscribe to these opinions, which we have seen to be fearful in their enormity, openly opposed to the truth, and the cause of most terrible evils. Indeed, very many amongst them, compelled by the force of truth, do not hesitate to admit that such liberty is vicious, nay, is simple license, whenever intemperate in its claims, to the neglect of truth and justice; and therefore they would have liberty ruled and directed by right reason, and consequently subject to the natural law

and to the divine eternal law. But here they think they may stop, holding that man as a free being is bound by no law of God except such as He makes known to us through our natural reason. In this they are plainly inconsistent. For if—as they must admit, and no one can rightly deny—the will of the divine Lawgiver is to be obeyed, because every man is under the power of God, and tends toward Him as his end, it follows that no one can assign limits to His legislative authority without failing in the obedience which is due. Indeed, if the human mind be so presumptuous as to define the nature and extent of God's rights and its own duties, reverence for the divine law will be apparent rather than real, and arbitrary judgment will prevail over the authority and providence of God. Man must, therefore, take his standard of a loyal and religious life from the eternal law; and from all and every one of those laws which God, in His infinite wisdom and power, has been pleased to enact, and to make known to us by such clear and unmistakable signs as to leave no room for doubt. And the more so because laws of this kind have the same origin, the same Author, as the eternal law, are absolutely in accordance with right reason, and perfect the natural law. These laws it is that embody the government of God, who graciously guides and directs the intellect and the will of man lest these fall into error. Let, then, that continue to remain in a holy and inviolable union which neither can nor should be separated; and in all things—for this is the dictate of right reason itself—let God be dutifully and obediently served.

18. There are others, somewhat more moderate though not more consistent, who affirm that the morality of individuals is to be guided by the divine law, but not the morality of the State, for that in public affairs the commands of God may be passed over, and may be entirely disregarded in the framing of laws. Hence follows the fatal theory of the need of separation between Church and State. But the absurdity of such a position is manifest. Nature herself proclaims the necessity of the State providing means and opportunities whereby the

community may be enabled to live properly, that is to say, according to the laws of God. For since God is the source of all goodness and justice, it is absolutely ridiculous that the State should pay no attention to these laws or render them abortive by contrary enactment. Besides, those who are in authority owe it to the commonwealth not only to provide for its external well-being and the conveniences of life, but still more to consult the welfare of men's souls in the wisdom of their legislation. But, for the increase of such benefits, nothing more suitable can be conceived than the laws which have God for their author; and, therefore, they who in their government of the State take no account of these laws abuse political power by causing it to deviate from its proper end and from what nature itself prescribes. And, what is still more important, and what We have more than once pointed out, although the civil authority has not the same proximate end as the spiritual, nor proceeds on the same lines, nevertheless in the exercise of their separate powers they must occasionally meet. For their subjects are the same, and not infrequently they deal with the same objects, though in different ways. Whenever this occurs, since a state of conflict is absurd and manifestly repugnant to the most wise ordinance of God, there must necessarily exist some order or mode of procedure to remove the occasions of difference and contention, and to secure harmony in all things. This harmony has been not inaptly compared to that which exists between the body and the soul for the well-being of both one and the other, the separation of which brings irremediable harm to the body, since it extinguishes its very life.

19. To make this more evident, the growth of liberty ascribed to our age must be considered apart in its various details. And, first, let us examine that liberty in individuals which is so opposed to the virtue of religion, namely, the *liberty of worship*, as it is called. This is based on the principle that every man is free to profess as he may choose any religion or none.

20. But, assuredly, of all the duties which man has to fulfil, that, without doubt, is the chiefest and holiest which commands him to worship God with devotion and piety. This follows of necessity from the truth that we are ever in the power of God, are ever guided by His will and providence, and, having come forth from Him, must return to Him. Add to which, no true virtue can exist without religion, for moral virtue is concerned with those things which lead to God as man's supreme and ultimate good; and therefore religion, which (as St. Thomas says) "performs those actions which are directly and immediately ordained for the divine honor,"[3] rules and tempers all virtues. And if it be asked which of the many conflicting religions it is necessary to adopt, reason and the natural law unhesitatingly tell us to practice that one which God enjoins, and which men can easily recognize by certain exterior notes, whereby divine providence has willed that it should be distinguished, because, in a matter of such moment, the most terrible loss would be the consequence of error. Wherefore, when a liberty such as We have described is offered to man, the power is given him to pervert or abandon with impunity the most sacred of duties, and to exchange the unchangeable good for evil; which, as We have said, is no liberty, but its degradation, and the abject submission of the soul to sin.

21. This kind of liberty, if considered in relation to the State, clearly implies that there is no reason why the State should offer any homage to God, or should desire any public recognition of Him; that no one form of worship is to be preferred to another, but that all stand on an equal footing, no account being taken of the religion of the people, even if they profess the Catholic faith. But, to justify this, it must needs be taken as true that the State has no duties toward God, or that such duties, if they exist, can be abandoned with impunity, both of which assertions are manifestly false. For it cannot be

3. *Summa theologiae* II-II, q. 81, a. 6.

doubted but that, by the will of God, men are united in civil society; whether its component parts be considered; or its form, which implies authority; or the object of its existence; or the abundance of the vast services which it renders to man. God it is who has made man for society, and has placed him in the company of others like himself, so that what was wanting to his nature, and beyond his attainment if left to his own resources, he might obtain by association with others. Wherefore, civil society must acknowledge God as its Founder and Parent, and must obey and reverence His power and authority. Justice therefore forbids, and reason itself forbids, the State to be godless; or to adopt a line of action which would end in godlessness—namely, to treat the various religions (as they call them) alike, and to bestow upon them promiscuously equal rights and privileges. Since, then, the profession of one religion is necessary in the State, that religion must be professed which alone is true, and which can be recognized without difficulty, especially in Catholic States, because the marks of truth are, as it were, engraven upon it. This religion, therefore, the rulers of the State must preserve and protect, if they would provide—as they should do—with prudence and usefulness for the good of the community. For public authority exists for the welfare of those whom it governs; and, although its proximate end is to lead men to the prosperity found in this life, yet, in so doing, it ought not to diminish, but rather to increase, man's capability of attaining to the supreme good in which his everlasting happiness consists: which never can be attained if religion be disregarded.

22. All this, however, We have explained more fully elsewhere. We now only wish to add the remark that liberty of so false a nature is greatly hurtful to the true liberty of both rulers and their subjects. Religion, of its essence, is wonderfully helpful to the State. For since it derives the prime origin of all power directly from God Himself, with grave authority it charges rulers to be mindful of their duty, to govern without injustice or severity, to rule their people kindly and

with almost paternal charity; it admonishes subjects to be obedient to lawful authority, as to the ministers of God; and it binds them to their rulers, not merely by obedience, but by reverence and affection, forbidding all seditious and venturesome enterprises calculated to disturb public order and tranquility, and cause greater restrictions to be put upon the liberty of the people. We need not mention how greatly religion conduces to pure morals and pure morals to liberty. Reason shows, and history confirms the fact, that the higher the morality of States, the greater are the liberty and wealth and power which they enjoy.

23. We must now consider briefly *liberty of speech*, and liberty of the press. It is hardly necessary to say that there can be no such right as this, if it be not used in moderation, and if it pass beyond the bounds and end of all true liberty. For a right is a moral power which—as We have before said and must again and again repeat—it is absurd to suppose that nature has accorded indifferently to truth and falsehood, to justice and injustice. Men have a right freely and prudently to propagate throughout the State what things so ever are true and honorable, so that as many as possible may possess them; but lying opinions, than which no mental plague is greater, and vices which corrupt the heart and moral life should be diligently repressed by public authority, lest they insidiously work the ruin of the State. The excesses of an unbridled intellect, which unfailingly end in the oppression of the untutored multitude, are no less rightly controlled by the authority of the law than are the injuries inflicted by violence upon the weak. And this all the more surely, because by far the greater part of the community is either absolutely unable, or able only with great difficulty, to escape from illusions and deceitful subtleties, especially such as flatter the passions. If unbridled license of speech and of writing be granted to all, nothing will remain sacred and inviolate; even the highest and truest mandates of natures, justly held to be the common and noblest heritage of the human race, will not

be spared. Thus, truth being gradually obscured by darkness, pernicious and manifold error, as too often happens, will easily prevail. Thus, too, license will gain what liberty loses; for liberty will ever be more free and secure in proportion as license is kept in fuller restraint. In regard, however, to all matter of opinion which God leaves to man's free discussion, full liberty of thought and of speech is naturally within the right of everyone; for such liberty never leads men to suppress the truth, but often to discover it and make it known.

24. A like judgment must be passed upon what is called *liberty of teaching*. There can be no doubt that truth alone should imbue the minds of men, for in it are found the well-being, the end, and the perfection of every intelligent nature; and therefore nothing but truth should be taught both to the ignorant and to the educated, so as to bring knowledge to those who have it not, and to preserve it in those who possess it. For this reason it is plainly the duty of all who teach to banish error from the mind, and by sure safeguards to close the entry to all false convictions. From this it follows, as is evident, that the liberty of which We have been speaking is greatly opposed to reason, and tends absolutely to pervert men's minds, in as much as it claims for itself the right of teaching whatever it pleases—a liberty which the State cannot grant without failing in its duty. And the more so because the authority of teachers has great weight with their hearers, who can rarely decide for themselves as to the truth or falsehood of the instruction given to them.

25. Wherefore, this liberty, also, in order that it may deserve the name, must be kept within certain limits, lest the office of teaching be turned with impunity into an instrument of corruption. Now, truth, which should be the only subject matter of those who teach, is of two kinds: natural and supernatural. Of natural truths, such as the principles of nature and whatever is derived from them immediately by our reason, there is a kind of common patrimony in the human race. On this, as on a firm basis, morality, justice, religion, and the very

bonds of human society rest; and to allow people to go unharmed who violate or destroy it would be most impious, most foolish, and most inhuman.

26. But with no less religious care must we preserve that great and sacred treasure of the truths which God Himself has taught us. By many and convincing arguments, often used by defenders of Christianity, certain leading truths have been laid down: namely, that some things have been revealed by God; that the only-begotten Son of God was made flesh to bear witness to the truth; that a perfect society was founded by Him—the Church, namely, of which He is the head, and with which He has promised to abide till the end of the world. To this society He entrusted all the truths which He had taught, in order that it might keep and guard them and with lawful authority explain them; and at the same time He commanded all nations to hear the voice of the Church, as if it were His own, threatening those who would nor hear it with everlasting perdition. Thus, it is manifest that man's best and surest teacher is God, the Source and Principle of all truth; and the only-begotten Son, who is in the bosom of the Father, the Way, the Truth, and the Life, the true Light which enlightens every man, and to whose teaching all must submit: "And they shall all be taught of God" (John 6:45).

27. In faith and in the teaching of morality, God Himself made the Church a partaker of His divine authority, and through His heavenly gift she cannot be deceived. She is therefore the greatest and most reliable teacher of mankind, and in her swells an inviolable right to teach them. Sustained by the truth received from her divine Founder, the Church has ever sought to fulfil holily the mission entrusted to her by God; unconquered by the difficulties on all sides surrounding her, she has never ceased to assert her liberty of teaching, and in this way the wretched superstition of paganism being dispelled, the wide world was renewed unto Christian wisdom. Now, reason itself clearly teaches that the truths of divine revelation and those of

nature cannot really be opposed to one another, and that whatever is at variance with them must necessarily be false. Therefore, the divine teaching of the Church, so far from being an obstacle to the pursuit of learning and the progress of science, or in any way retarding the advance of civilization, in reality brings to them the sure guidance of shining light. And for the same reason it is of no small advantage for the perfecting of human liberty, since our Savior Jesus Christ has said that by truth is man made free: "You shall know the truth, and the truth shall make you free" (John 8:32). Therefore, there is no reason why genuine liberty should grow indignant, or true science feel aggrieved, at having to bear the just and necessary restraint of laws by which, in the judgment of the Church and of reason itself, human teaching has to be controlled.

28. The Church, indeed—as facts have everywhere proved—looks chiefly and above all to the defense of the Christian faith, while careful at the same time to foster and promote every kind of human learning. For learning is in itself good, and praiseworthy, and desirable; and further, all erudition which is the outgrowth of sound reason, and in conformity with the truth of things, serves not a little to confirm what we believe on the authority of God. The Church, truly, to our great benefit, has carefully preserved the monuments of ancient wisdom, has opened everywhere homes of science, and has urged on intellectual progress by fostering most diligently the arts by which the culture of our age is so much advanced. Lastly, we must not forget that a vast field lies freely open to man's industry and genius, containing all those things which have no necessary connection with Christian faith and morals, or as to which the Church, exercising no authority, leaves the judgment of the learned free and unconstrained.

29. From all this may be understood the nature and character of that liberty which the followers of liberalism so eagerly advocate and proclaim. On the one hand, they demand for themselves and for the State a license which opens the way to every perversity of opinion;

and on the other, they hamper the Church in diverse ways, restricting her liberty within narrowest limits, although from her teaching not only is there nothing to be feared, but in every respect very much to be gained.

30. Another liberty is widely advocated, namely, *liberty of conscience.* If by this is meant that everyone may, as he chooses, worship God or not, it is sufficiently refuted by the arguments already adduced. But it may also be taken to mean that every man in the State may follow the will of God and, from a consciousness of duty and free from every obstacle, obey His commands. This, indeed, is true liberty, a liberty worthy of the sons of God, which nobly maintains the dignity of man and is stronger than all violence or wrong—a liberty which the Church has always desired and held most dear. This is the kind of liberty the Apostles claimed for themselves with intrepid constancy, which the apologists of Christianity confirmed by their writings, and which the martyrs in vast numbers consecrated by their blood. And deservedly so; for this Christian liberty bears witness to the absolute and most just dominion of God over man, and to the chief and supreme duty of man toward God. It has nothing in common with a seditious and rebellious mind; and in no title derogates from obedience to public authority; for the right to command and to require obedience exists only so far as it is in accordance with the authority of God, and is within the measure that He has laid down. But when anything is commanded which is plainly at variance with the will of God, there is a wide departure from this divinely constituted order, and at the same time a direct conflict with divine authority; therefore, it is right not to obey.

31. By the patrons of liberalism, however, who make the State absolute and omnipotent, and proclaim that man should live altogether independently of God, the liberty of which We speak, which goes hand in hand with virtue and religion, is not admitted; and whatever is done for its preservation is accounted an injury and an offense

against the State. Indeed, if what they say were really true, there would be no tyranny, no matter how monstrous, which we should not be bound to endure and submit to.

32. The Church most earnestly desires that the Christian teaching, of which We have given an outline, should penetrate every rank of society in reality and in practice; for it would be of the greatest efficacy in healing the evils of our day, which are neither few nor slight, and are the offspring in great part of the false liberty which is so much extolled, and in which the germs of safety and glory were supposed to be contained. The hope has been disappointed by the result. The fruit, instead of being sweet and wholesome, has proved cankered and bitter. If, then, a remedy is desired, let it be sought for in a restoration of sound doctrine, from which alone the preservation of order and, as a consequence, the defense of true liberty can be confidently expected.

33. Yet, with the discernment of a true mother, the Church weighs the great burden of human weakness, and well knows the course down which the minds and actions of men are in this our age being borne. For this reason, while not conceding any right to anything save what is true and honest, she does not forbid public authority to tolerate what is at variance with truth and justice, for the sake of avoiding some greater evil, or of obtaining or preserving some greater good. God Himself in His providence, though infinitely good and powerful, permits evil to exist in the world, partly that greater good may not be impeded, and partly that greater evil may not ensue. In the government of States it is not forbidden to imitate the Ruler of the world; and, as the authority of man is powerless to prevent every evil, it has (as St. Augustine says) to overlook and leave unpunished many things which are punished, and rightly, by divine providence.[4] But if, in such circumstances, for the sake of the common good (and

4. Augustine, *De libero arbitrio*, I, 6, 14 (*PL* 32:1228).

this is the only legitimate reason), human law may or even should tolerate evil, it may not and should not approve or desire evil for its own sake; for evil of itself, being a privation of good, is opposed to the common welfare which every legislator is bound to desire and defend to the best of his ability. In this, human law must endeavor to imitate God, who, as St. Thomas teaches, in allowing evil to exist in the world, "neither wills evil to be done, nor wills it not to be done, but wills only to permit it to be done; and this is good."[5] This saying of the Angelic Doctor contains briefly the whole doctrine of the permission of evil.

34. But, to judge aright, we must acknowledge that, the more a State is driven to tolerate evil, the further is it from perfection; and that the tolerance of evil which is dictated by political prudence should be strictly confined to the limits which its justifying cause, the public welfare, requires. Wherefore, if such tolerance would be injurious to the public welfare, and entail greater evils on the State, it would not be lawful; for in such case the motive of good is wanting. And although in the extraordinary condition of these times the Church usually acquiesces in certain modern liberties, not because she prefers them in themselves, but because she judges it expedient to permit them, she would in happier times exercise her own liberty; and, by persuasion, exhortation, and entreaty would endeavor, as she is bound, to fulfil the duty assigned to her by God of providing for the eternal salvation of mankind. One thing, however, remains always true—that the liberty which is claimed for all to do all things is not, as We have often said, of itself desirable, inasmuch as it is contrary to reason that error and truth should have equal rights.

35. And as to *tolerance*, it is surprising how far removed from the equity and prudence of the Church are those who profess what is called liberalism. For in allowing that boundless license of which We

5. *Summa theologiae* I, q. 19, a. 9, ad 3.

have spoken, they exceed all limits, and end at last by making no apparent distinction between truth and error, honesty and dishonesty. And because the Church, the pillar and ground of truth, and the unerring teacher of morals, is forced utterly to reprobate and condemn tolerance of such an abandoned and criminal character, they calumniate her as being wanting in patience and gentleness, and thus fail to see that, in so doing, they impute to her as a fault what is in reality a matter for commendation. But, in spite of all this show of tolerance, it very often happens that, while they profess themselves ready to lavish liberty on all in the greatest profusion, they are utterly intolerant toward the Catholic Church, by refusing to allow her the liberty of being herself free.

36. And now to reduce for clearness' sake to its principal heads all that has been set forth with its immediate conclusions, the summing up in this briefly: that man, by a necessity of his nature, is wholly subject to the most faithful and ever-enduring power of God; and that, as a consequence, any liberty, except that which consists in submission to God and in subjection to His will, is unintelligible. To deny the existence of this authority in God, or to refuse to submit to it, means to act, not as a free man, but as one who treasonably abuses his liberty; and in such a disposition of mind the chief and deadly vice of liberalism essentially consists. The form, however, of the sin is manifold; for in more ways and degrees than one can the will depart from the obedience which is due to God or to those who share the divine power.

37. For to reject the supreme authority to God, and to cast off all obedience to Him in public matters, or even in private and domestic affairs, is the greatest perversion of liberty and the worst kind of liberalism; and what We have said must be understood to apply to this alone in its fullest sense.

38. Next comes the system of those who admit indeed the duty of submitting to God, the Creator and Ruler of the world, inasmuch as all nature is dependent on His will, but who boldly reject all laws of

faith and morals which are above natural reason, but are revealed by the authority of God; or who at least impudently assert that there is no reason why regard should be paid to these laws, at any rate publicly, by the State. How mistaken these men also are, and how inconsistent, we have seen above. From this teaching, as from its source and principle, flows that fatal principle of the separation of Church and State; whereas it is, on the contrary, clear that the two powers, though dissimilar in functions and unequal in degree, ought nevertheless to live in concord, by harmony in their action and the faithful discharge of their respective duties.

39. But this teaching is understood in two ways. Many wish the State to be separated from the Church wholly and entirely, so that with regard to every right of human society, in institutions, customs, and laws, the offices of State, and the education of youth, they would pay no more regard to the Church than if she did not exist; and, at most, would allow the citizens individually to attend to their religion in private if so minded. Against such as these, all the arguments by which We disprove the principle of separation of Church and State are conclusive; with this super-added, that it is absurd the citizen should respect the Church, while the State may hold her in contempt.

40. Others oppose not the existence of the Church, nor indeed could they; yet they despoil her of the nature and rights of a perfect society, and maintain that it does not belong to her to legislate, to judge, or to punish, but only to exhort, to advise, and to rule her subjects in accordance with their own consent and will. By such opinion they pervert the nature of this divine society, and attenuate and narrow its authority, its office of teacher, and its whole efficiency; and at the same time they aggrandize the power of the civil government to such extent as to subject the Church of God to the empire and sway of the State, like any voluntary association of citizens. To refute completely such teaching, the arguments often used by the defenders of Christianity, and set forth by Us, especially in the Encyclical Letter

Immortale Dei, are of great avail; for by those arguments it is proved that, by a divine provision, all the rights which essentially belong to a society that is legitimate, supreme, and perfect in all its parts exist in the Church.

41. Lastly, there remain those who, while they do not approve the separation of Church and State, think nevertheless that the Church ought to adapt herself to the times and conform to what is required by the modern system of government. Such an opinion is sound, if it is to be understood of some equitable adjustment consistent with truth and justice; in so far, namely, that the Church, in the hope of some great good, may show herself indulgent, and may conform to the times in so far as her sacred office permits. But it is not so in regard to practices and doctrines which a perversion of morals and a warped judgment have unlawfully introduced. Religion, truth, and justice must ever be maintained; and, as God has entrusted these great and sacred matters to her office as to dissemble in regard to what is false or unjust, or to connive at what is hurtful to religion.

42. From what has been said it follows that it is quite unlawful to demand, to defend, or to grant unconditional freedom of thought, of speech, or writing, or of worship, as if these were so many rights given by nature to man. For if nature had really granted them, it would be lawful to refuse obedience to God, and there would be no restraint on human liberty. It likewise follows that freedom in these things may be tolerated wherever there is just cause, but only with such moderation as will prevent its degenerating into license and excess. And, where such liberties are in use, men should employ them in doing good, and should estimate them as the Church does; for liberty is to be regarded as legitimate in so far only as it affords greater facility for doing good, but no farther.

43. Whenever there exists, or there is reason to fear, an unjust oppression of the people on the one hand, or a deprivation of the liberty of the Church on the other, it is lawful to seek for such a change

of government as will bring about due liberty of action. In such case, an excessive and vicious liberty is not sought, but only some relief, for the common welfare, in order that, while license for evil is allowed by the State, the power of doing good may not be hindered.

44. Again, it is not of itself wrong to prefer a democratic form of government, if only the Catholic doctrine be maintained as to the origin and exercise of power. Of the various forms of government, the Church does not reject any that are fitted to procure the welfare of the subject; she wishes only—and this nature itself requires—that they should be constituted without involving wrong to anyone, and especially without violating the rights of the Church.

45. Unless it be otherwise determined, by reason of some exceptional condition of things, it is expedient to take part in the administration of public affairs. And the Church approves of everyone devoting his services to the common good, and doing all that he can for the defense, preservation, and prosperity of his country.

46. Neither does the Church condemn those who, if it can be done without violation of justice, wish to make their country independent of any foreign or despotic power. Nor does she blame those who wish to assign to the State the power of self-government, and to its citizens the greatest possible measure of prosperity. The Church has always most faithfully fostered civil liberty, and this was seen especially in Italy, in the municipal prosperity, and wealth, and glory which were obtained at a time when the salutary power of the Church has spread, without opposition, to all parts of the State.

47. These things, Venerable Brothers, which, under the guidance of faith and reason, in the discharge of Our Apostolic office, We have now delivered to you, We hope, especially by your cooperation with Us, will be useful unto very many. In lowliness of heart We raise Our eyes in supplication to God, and earnestly beseech Him to shed mercifully the light of His wisdom and of His counsel upon men, so that, strengthened by these heavenly gifts, they may in matters of such

moment discern what is true, and may afterwards, in public and private at all times and with unshaken constancy, live in accordance with the truth. As a pledge of these heavenly gifts, and in witness of Our good will to you, Venerable Brothers, and to the clergy and people committed to each of you, We most lovingly grant in the Lord the Apostolic Benediction.

Given at St. Peter's, in Rome, the twentieth day of June 1888, the tenth year of Our Pontificate.

LEO PP. XIII

ENCYCLICAL LETTER

SAPIENTIAE CHRISTIANAE

OF THE SUPREME PONTIFF

LEO XIII

TO THE PATRIARCHS, PRIMATES, ARCHBISHOPS, AND BISHOPS OF THE CATHOLIC WORLD IN GRACE AND COMMUNION WITH THE APOSTOLIC SEE ON CHRISTIANS AS CITIZENS

1. From day to day it becomes more and more evident how needful it is that the principles of Christian wisdom should ever be borne in mind, and that the life, the morals, and the institutions of nations should be wholly conformed to them. For when these principles have been disregarded, evils so vast have accrued that no right-minded man can face the trials of the time being without grave anxiety or consider the future without alarm. Progress, not inconsiderable indeed, has been made towards securing the well-being of the body and of material things, but the material world, with the possession of wealth, power, and resources, although it may well procure comforts and increase the enjoyment of life, is incapable of satisfying our soul created for higher and more glorious things. To contemplate God, and to tend to Him, is the supreme law of the life of man. For we were created in the divine image and likeness, and are impelled, by our very nature, to the enjoyment of our Creator. But not by bodily motion or effort do we make advance toward God, but through acts

of the soul, that is, through knowledge and love. For indeed, God is the first and supreme truth, and the mind alone feeds on truth. God is perfect holiness and the sovereign good, to which only the will can desire and attain, when virtue is its guide.

2. But what applies to individual men applies equally to society—domestic alike and civil. Nature did not form society in order that man should seek in it his last end, but in order that in it and through it he should find suitable aids whereby to attain to his own perfection. If, then, a political government strives after external advantages only, and the achievement of a cultured and prosperous life; if, in administering public affairs, it is wont to put God aside, and show no solicitude for the upholding of moral law, it deflects woefully from its right course and from the injunctions of nature; nor should it be accounted as a society or a community of men, but only as the deceitful imitation or appearance of a society.

3. As to what We have called the goods of the soul, which consist chiefly in the practice of the true religion and in the unswerving observance of the Christian precepts, We see them daily losing esteem among men, either by reason of forgetfulness or disregard, in such wise that all that is gained for the well-being of the body seems to be lost for that of the soul. A striking proof of the lessening and weakening of the Christian faith is seen in the insults too often done to the Catholic Church, openly and publicly—insults, indeed, which an age cherishing religion would not have tolerated. For these reasons, an incredible multitude of men is in danger of not achieving salvation; and even nations and empires themselves cannot long remain unharmed, since, when Christian institutions and morality decline, the main foundation of human society goes together with them. Force alone will remain to preserve public tranquility and order. But force is very feeble when the bulwark of religion has been removed, and, being more apt to beget slavery than obedience, it bears within itself the germs of ever-increasing troubles. The present century has

encountered memorable disasters, and it is not certain that some equally terrible are not impending. The very times in which we live are warning us to seek remedies there where alone they are to be found—namely, by re-establishing in the family circle and throughout the whole range of society the doctrines and practices of the Christian religion. In this lies the sole means of freeing us from the ills now weighing us down, of forestalling the dangers now threatening the world. For the accomplishment of this end, Venerable Brethren, We must bring to bear all the activity and diligence that lie within Our power. Although we have already, under other circumstances, and whenever occasion required, treated of these matters, We deem it expedient in this letter to define more in detail the duties of Catholics, inasmuch as these would, if strictly observed, wonderfully contribute to the good of the commonwealth. We have fallen upon times when a violent and well-nigh daily battle is being fought about matters of highest moment, a battle in which it is hard not to be sometimes deceived, not to go astray and, for many, not to lose heart. It behooves us, Venerable Brethren, to warn, instruct, and exhort each of the faithful with an earnestness befitting the occasion: that none may abandon the way of truth (Tobit 1:2).

4. It cannot be doubted that duties more numerous and of greater moment devolve on Catholics than upon such as are either not sufficiently enlightened in relation to the Catholic faith, or who are entirely unacquainted with its doctrines. Considering that forthwith upon salvation being brought out for mankind, Jesus Christ laid upon His Apostles the injunction to "preach the Gospel to every creature," He imposed, it is evident, upon all men the duty of learning thoroughly and believing what they were taught. This duty is intimately bound up with the gaining of eternal salvation: "He that believeth and is baptized shall be saved; but he that believeth not, shall be condemned" (Mark 16:16). But the man who has embraced the Christian faith, as in duty bound, is by that very fact a subject of the Church as

one of the children born of her and becomes a member of that greatest and holiest body, which it is the special charge of the Roman Pontiff to rule with supreme power, under its invisible head, Jesus Christ.

5. Now, if the natural law enjoins us to love devotedly and to defend the country in which we had birth, and in which we were brought up, so that every good citizen hesitates not to face death for his native land, very much more is it the urgent duty of Christians to be ever quickened by like feelings toward the Church. For the Church is the holy City of the living God, born of God Himself, and by Him built up and established. Upon this earth, indeed, she accomplishes her pilgrimage, but by instructing and guiding men she summons them to eternal happiness. We are bound, then, to love dearly the country whence we have received the means of enjoyment this mortal life affords, but we have a much more urgent obligation to love, with ardent love, the Church to which we owe the life of the soul, a life that will endure forever. For fitting it is to prefer the good of the soul to the well-being of the body, inasmuch as duties toward God are of a far more hallowed character than those toward men.

6. Moreover, if we would judge aright, the supernatural love for the Church and the natural love of our own country proceed from the same eternal principle, since God Himself is their Author and originating Cause. Consequently, it follows that between the duties they respectively enjoin, neither can come into collision with the other. We can, certainly, and should love ourselves, bear ourselves kindly toward our fellow men, nourish affection for the State and the governing powers; but at the same time we can and must cherish toward the Church a feeling of filial piety, and love God with the deepest love of which we are capable. The order of precedence of these duties is, however, at times, either under stress of public calamities, or through the perverse will of men, inverted. For instances occur where the State seems to require from men as subjects one thing, and religion, from men as Christians, quite another; and this in reality

without any other ground than that the rulers of the State either hold the sacred power of the Church of no account or endeavor to subject it to their own will. Hence arises a conflict, and an occasion, through such conflict, of virtue being put to the proof. The two powers are confronted and urge their behests in a contrary sense; to obey both is wholly impossible. No man can serve two masters (Matt. 6:24), for to please the one amounts to condemning the other.

7. As to which should be preferred, no one ought to balance for an instant. It is a high crime indeed to withdraw allegiance from God in order to please men, an act of consummate wickedness to break the laws of Jesus Christ, in order to yield obedience to earthly rulers, or, under pretext of keeping the civil law, to ignore the rights of the Church; "we ought to obey God rather than men" (Acts 5:29). This answer, which of old Peter and the other Apostles were used to give the civil authorities who enjoined unrighteous things, we must, in like circumstances, give always and without hesitation. No better citizen is there, whether in time of peace or war, than the Christian who is mindful of his duty; but such a one should be ready to suffer all things, even death itself, rather than abandon the cause of God or of the Church.

8. Hence, they who blame, and call by the name of sedition, this steadfastness of attitude in the choice of duty have not rightly apprehended the force and nature of true law. We are speaking of matters widely known, and which We have before now more than once fully explained. Law is of its very essence a mandate of right reason, proclaimed by a properly constituted authority, for the common good. But true and legitimate authority is void of sanction, unless it proceed from God, the supreme Ruler and Lord of all. The Almighty alone can commit power to a man over his fellow men[1]; nor may

1. Note the extreme importance of this principle; it justifies the doctrine according to which the only conceivable foundation of political authority must be divine in origin. (EDITOR)

that be accounted as right reason which is in disaccord with truth and with divine reason; nor that held to be true good which is repugnant to the supreme and unchangeable good, or that wrests aside and draws away the wills of men from the charity of God.

9. Hallowed, therefore, in the minds of Christians is the very idea of public authority, in which they recognize some likeness and symbol as it were of the divine Majesty, even when it is exercised by one unworthy. A just and due reverence to the laws abides in them, not from force and threats, but from a consciousness of duty; "for God hath not given us the spirit of fear" (2 Tim. 1:7).

10. But, if the laws of the State are manifestly at variance with the divine law, containing enactments hurtful to the Church, or conveying injunctions adverse to the duties imposed by religion, or if they violate in the person of the supreme Pontiff the authority of Jesus Christ, then, truly, to resist becomes a positive duty, to obey, a crime; a crime, moreover, combined with misdemeanor against the State itself, inasmuch as every offense leveled against religion is also a sin against the State. Here anew it becomes evident how unjust is the reproach of sedition; for the obedience due to rulers and legislators is not refused, but there is a deviation from their will in those precepts only which they have no power to enjoin. Commands that are issued adversely to the honor due to God, and hence are beyond the scope of justice, must be looked upon as anything rather than laws. You are fully aware, Venerable Brothers, that this is the very contention of the Apostle St. Paul, who, in writing to Titus, after reminding Christians that they are "to be subject to princes and powers, and to obey at a word," at once adds: "And to be ready to every good work" (Titus 3:1). Thereby he openly declares that, if laws of men contain injunctions contrary to the eternal law of God, it is right not to obey them. In like manner, the Prince of the Apostles gave this courageous and sublime answer to those who would have deprived him of the liberty of preaching the Gospel: "If it be just in the sight of God to hear you

rather than God, judge ye, for we cannot but speak the things which we have seen and heard" (Acts 4:19–20).

11. Wherefore, to love both countries, that of earth below and that of heaven above, yet in such mode that the love of our heavenly surpass the love of our earthly home, and that human laws be never set above the divine law, is the essential duty of Christians, and the fountainhead, so to say, from which all other duties spring. The Redeemer of mankind of Himself has said: "For this was I born, and for this came I into the world, that I should give testimony to the truth" (John 18:37). In like manner: "I am come to cast fire upon earth, and what will I but that it be kindled?" (Luke 12:49). In the knowledge of this truth, which constitutes the highest perfection of the mind; in divine charity which, in like manner, completes the will, all Christian life and liberty abide. This noble patrimony of truth and charity entrusted by Jesus Christ to the Church she defends and maintains ever with untiring endeavor and watchfulness.

12. But with what bitterness and in how many guises war has been waged against the Church it would be ill-timed now to urge. From the fact that it has been vouchsafed to human reason to snatch from nature, through the investigations of science, many of her treasured secrets and to apply them befittingly to the diverse requirements of life, men have become possessed with so arrogant a sense of their own powers as already to consider themselves able to banish from social life the authority and empire of God. Led away by this delusion, they make over to human nature the dominion of which they think God has been despoiled; from nature, they maintain, we must seek the principle and rule of all truth; from nature, they aver, alone spring, and to it should be referred, all the duties that religious feeling prompts. Hence, they deny all revelation from on high, and all fealty due to the Christian teaching of morals as well as all obedience to the Church, and they go so far as to deny her power of making laws and exercising every other kind of right, even disallowing the Church any

place among the civil institutions of the commonweal. These men aspire unjustly, and with their might strive, to gain control over public affairs and lay hands on the rudder of the State, in order that the legislation may the more easily be adapted to these principles, and the morals of the people influenced in accordance with them. Whence it comes to pass that in many countries Catholicism is either openly assailed or else secretly interfered with, full impunity being granted to the most pernicious doctrines, while the public profession of Christian truth is shackled oftentimes with manifold constraints.

13. Under such evil circumstances therefore, each one is bound in conscience to watch over himself, taking all means possible to preserve the faith inviolate in the depths of his soul, avoiding all risks, and arming himself on all occasions, especially against the various specious sophisms rife among non-believers. In order to safeguard this virtue of faith in its integrity, We declare it to be very profitable and consistent with the requirements of the time, that each one, according to the measure of his capacity and intelligence, should make a deep study of Christian doctrine, and imbue his mind with as perfect a knowledge as may be of those matters that are interwoven with religion and lie within the range of reason. And as it is necessary that faith should not only abide untarnished in the soul, but should grow with ever painstaking increase, the suppliant and humble entreaty of the Apostles ought constantly to be addressed to God: "Increase our faith" (Luke 17:5).

14. But in this same matter, touching Christian faith, there are other duties whose exact and religious observance, necessary at all times in the interests of eternal salvation, become more especially so in these our days. Amid such reckless and widespread folly of opinion, it is, as We have said, the office of the Church to undertake the defense of truth and uproot errors from the mind, and this charge has to be at all times sacredly observed by her, seeing that the honor of God and the salvation of men are confided to her keeping.

But, when necessity compels, not those only who are invested with power of rule are bound to safeguard the integrity of faith, but, as St. Thomas maintains: "Each one is under obligation to show forth his faith, either to instruct and encourage others of the faithful, or to repel the attacks of unbelievers."[2] To recoil before an enemy, or to keep silence when from all sides such clamors are raised against truth, is the part of a man either devoid of character or who entertains doubt as to the truth of what he professes to believe. In both cases such mode of behaving is base and is insulting to God, and both are incompatible with the salvation of mankind. This kind of conduct is profitable only to the enemies of the faith, for nothing emboldens the wicked so greatly as the lack of courage on the part of the good. Moreover, want of vigor on the part of Christians is so much the more blameworthy, as not seldom little would be needed on their part to bring to naught false charges and refute erroneous opinions, and by always exerting themselves more strenuously they might reckon upon being successful. After all, no one can be prevented from putting forth that strength of soul which is the characteristic of true Christians, and very frequently by such display of courage our enemies lose heart and their designs are thwarted. Christians are, moreover, born for combat, whereof the greater the vehemence, the more assured, God aiding, the triumph: "Have confidence; I have overcome the world" (John 16:33). Nor is there any ground for alleging that Jesus Christ, the Guardian and Champion of the Church, needs not in any manner the help of men. Power certainly is not wanting to Him, but in His loving kindness He would assign to us a share in obtaining and applying the fruits of salvation procured through His grace.

15. The chief elements of this duty consist in professing openly and unflinchingly the Catholic doctrine and in propagating it to the

2. *Summa theologiae* II-II, q. 3, a. 2, ad 2.

utmost of our power. For as is often said, with the greatest truth, there is nothing so hurtful to Christian wisdom as that it should not be known, since it possesses, when loyally received, inherent power to drive away error. So soon as Catholic truth is apprehended by a simple and unprejudiced soul, reason yields assent. Now, faith, as a virtue, is a great boon of divine grace and goodness; nevertheless, the objects themselves to which faith is to be applied are scarcely known in any other way than through the hearing. "How shall they believe Him of whom they have not heard? And how shall they hear without a preacher? Faith then cometh by hearing, and hearing by the word of Christ" (Rom. 10:14, 17). Since, then, faith is necessary for salvation, it follows that the word of Christ must be preached. The office, indeed, of preaching, that is, of teaching, lies by divine right in the province of the pastors, namely, of the bishops whom "the Holy Spirit has placed to rule the Church of God" (Acts 20:28). It belongs, above all, to the Roman Pontiff, vicar of Jesus Christ, established as head of the universal Church, teacher of all that pertains to morals and faith.

16. No one, however, must entertain the notion that private individuals are prevented from taking some active part in this duty of teaching, especially those on whom God has bestowed gifts of mind with the strong wish of rendering themselves useful. These, so often as circumstances demand, may take upon themselves, not, indeed, the office of the pastor, but the task of communicating to others what they have themselves received, becoming, as it were, living echoes of their masters in the faith. Such co-operation on the part of the laity has seemed to the Fathers of the Vatican Council so opportune and fruitful of good that they thought well to invite it. "All faithful Christians, but those chiefly who are in a prominent position, or engaged in teaching, we entreat, by the compassion of Jesus Christ, and enjoin by the authority of the same God and Savior, that they bring aid to ward off and eliminate these errors from holy Church, and contribute their zealous help in spreading abroad the light of undefiled

faith."[3] Let each one, therefore, bear in mind that he both can and should, so far as may be, preach the Catholic faith by the authority of his example, and by open and constant profession of the obligations it imposes. In respect, consequently, to the duties that bind us to God and the Church, it should be borne earnestly in mind that in propagating Christian truth and warding off errors the zeal of the laity should, as far as possible, be brought actively into play.

17. The faithful would not, however, so completely and advantageously satisfy these duties as is fitting they should were they to enter the field as isolated champions of the faith. Jesus Christ, indeed, has clearly intimated that the hostility and hatred of men, which He first and foremost experienced, would be shown in like degree toward the work founded by Him, so that many would be barred from profiting by the salvation for which all are indebted to His loving kindness. Wherefore, He willed not only to train disciples in His doctrine, but to unite them into one society, and closely conjoin them in one body, "which is the Church" (Col. 1:24), whereof He would be the head. The life of Jesus Christ pervades, therefore, the entire framework of this body, cherishes and nourishes its every member, uniting each with each, and making all work together to the same end, albeit the action of each be not the same (cf. Rom. 12:4–5). Hence it follows that not only is the Church a perfect society far excelling every other, but it is enjoined by her Founder that for the salvation of mankind she is to contend "as an army drawn up in battle array" (Cant. 6:9). The organization and constitution of Christian society can in no wise be changed, neither can any one of its members live as he may choose, nor elect that mode of fighting which best pleases him. For, in effect, he scatters and gathers not who gathers not with the Church and with Jesus Christ, and all who fight not jointly with him and with the Church are in very truth contending against God (cf. Luke 11:22).

3. Constitution *Dei Filius*, at end.

18. To bring about such a union of minds and uniformity of action—not without reason so greatly feared by the enemies of Catholicism—the main point is that a perfect harmony of opinion should prevail; in which intent we find Paul the Apostle exhorting the Corinthians with earnest zeal and solemn weight of words: "Now I beseech you, brethren, by the name of our Lord Jesus Christ, that you all speak the same thing, and that there be no schisms among you: but that you be perfectly in the same mind, and in the same judgment" (1 Cor. 1:10).

19. The wisdom of this precept is readily apprehended. In truth, thought is the principle of action, and hence there cannot exist agreement of will, or similarity of action, if people all think differently one from the other.

20. In the case of those who profess to take reason as their sole guide, there would hardly be found, if, indeed, there ever could be found, unity of doctrine. Indeed, the art of knowing things as they really are is exceedingly difficult; moreover, the mind of man is by nature feeble and drawn this way and that by a variety of opinions, and not seldom led astray by impressions coming from without; and, furthermore, the influence of the passions oftentimes takes away, or certainly at least diminishes, the capacity for grasping the truth. On this account, in controlling State affairs means are often used to keep those together by force who cannot agree in their way of thinking.

21. It happens far otherwise with Christians; they receive their rule of faith from the Church, by whose authority and under whose guidance they are conscious that they have beyond question attained to truth. Consequently, as the Church is one, because Jesus Christ is one, so throughout the whole Christian world there is, and ought to be, but one doctrine: "One Lord, one faith" (Eph. 4:5); "but having the same spirit of faith" (2 Cor. 4:13), they possess the saving principle whence proceed spontaneously one and the same will in all, and one and the same tenor of action.

22. Now, as the Apostle Paul urges, this unanimity ought to be perfect. Christian faith reposes not on human but on divine authority, for what God has revealed "we believe not on account of the intrinsic evidence of the truth perceived by the natural light of our reason, but on account of the authority of God revealing, who cannot be deceived nor Himself deceive."[4] It follows as a consequence that whatever things are manifestly revealed by God we must receive with a similar and equal assent. To refuse to believe any one of them is equivalent to rejecting them all, for those at once destroy the very groundwork of faith who deny that God has spoken to men, or who bring into doubt His infinite truth and wisdom. To determine, however, which are the doctrines divinely revealed belongs to the teaching Church, to whom God has entrusted the safekeeping and interpretation of His utterances. But the supreme teacher in the Church is the Roman Pontiff. Union of minds, therefore, requires, together with a perfect accord in the one faith, complete submission and obedience of will to the Church and to the Roman Pontiff, as to God Himself. This obedience should, however, be perfect, because it is enjoined by faith itself, and has this in common with faith, that it cannot be given in shreds; nay, were it not absolute and perfect in every particular, it might wear the name of obedience, but its essence would disappear. Christian usage attaches such value to this perfection of obedience that it has been, and will ever be, accounted the distinguishing mark by which we are able to recognize Catholics. Admirably does the following passage from St. Thomas Aquinas set before us the right view: "The formal object of faith is primary truth, as it is shown forth in the holy Scriptures, and in the teaching of the Church, which proceeds from the fountainhead of truth. It follows, therefore, that he who does not adhere, as to an infallible divine rule, to the teaching of the Church, which proceeds from the primary truth manifested

4. *Constitution Dei Filius*, c. 3.

in the holy Scriptures, possesses not the habit of faith; but matters of faith he holds otherwise than true faith. Now, it is evident that he who clings to the doctrines of the Church as to an infallible rule yields his assent to everything the Church teaches; but otherwise, if with reference to what the Church teaches he holds what he likes but does not hold what he does not like, he adheres not to the teaching of the Church as to an infallible rule, but to his own will."[5]

23. The faith of the whole Church should be one, according to the precept: "Let all speak the same thing, and let there be no schisms among you" (1 Cor. 1:10); and this cannot be observed save on condition that questions which arise touching faith should be determined by him who presides over the whole Church, whose sentence must consequently be accepted without wavering. And hence to the sole authority of the supreme Pontiff does it pertain to publish a new revision of the symbol, as also to decree all other matters that concern the universal Church."[6]

24. In defining the limits of the obedience owed to the pastors of souls, but most of all to the authority of the Roman Pontiff, it must not be supposed that it is only to be yielded in relation to dogmas of which the obstinate denial cannot be disjoined from the crime of heresy. Nay, further, it is not enough sincerely and firmly to assent to doctrines which, though not defined by any solemn pronouncement of the Church, are by her proposed to belief, as divinely revealed, in her common and universal teaching, and which the Vatican Council declared are to be believed "with Catholic and divine faith."[7] But this likewise must be reckoned amongst the duties of Christians, that they allow themselves to be ruled and directed by the authority and leadership of bishops, and, above all, of the Apostolic See. And how fitting

5. *Summa theologiae* II-II, q. 5, a. 3.
6. Ibid., q. 1, a. 10.
7. Vatican Council, Constitution *De fide catholica*, c. 3, "De fide." Cf. H. Denziger, *Enchiridion Symbolorium*, 11th ed. (Freiburg i. Br., 1911), p. 476.

it is that this should be so anyone can easily perceive. For the things contained in the divine oracles have reference to God in part, and in part to man, and to whatever is necessary for the attainment of his eternal salvation. Now, both these, that is to say, what we are bound to believe and what we are obliged to do, are laid down, as we have stated, by the Church using her divine right, and in the Church by the supreme Pontiff. Wherefore it belongs to the Pope to judge authoritatively what things the sacred oracles contain, as well as what doctrines are in harmony, and what in disagreement, with them; and also, for the same reason, to show forth what things are to be accepted as right, and what to be rejected as worthless; what it is necessary to do and what to avoid doing, in order to attain eternal salvation. For otherwise, there would be no sure interpreter of the commands of God, nor would there be any safe guide showing man the way he should live.

25. In addition to what has been laid down, it is necessary to enter more fully into the nature of the Church. She is not an association of Christians brought together by chance, but is a divinely established and admirably constituted society, having for its direct and proximate purpose to lead the world to peace and holiness. And since the Church alone has, through the grace of God, received the means necessary to realize such end, she has her fixed laws, special spheres of action, and a certain method, fixed and conformable to her nature, of governing Christian peoples. But the exercise of such governing power is difficult, and leaves room for numberless conflicts, inasmuch as the Church rules peoples scattered through every portion of the earth, differing in race and customs, who, living under the sway of the laws of their respective countries, owe obedience alike to the civil and religious authorities. The duties enjoined are incumbent on the same persons, as already stated, and between them there exists neither contradiction nor confusion; for some of these duties have relation to the prosperity of the State, others refer to the general good of the Church, and both have as their object to train men to perfection.

26. The tracing out of these rights and duties being thus set forth, it is plainly evident that the governing powers are wholly free to carry out the business of the State; and this not only not against the wish of the Church, but manifestly with her cooperation, inasmuch as she strongly urges to the practice of piety, which implies right feeling towards God, and by that very fact inspires a right-mindedness toward the rulers in the State. The spiritual power, however, has a far loftier purpose, the Church directing her aim to govern the minds of men in the defending of the "kingdom of God, and His justice" (Matt. 6:33), a task she is wholly bent upon accomplishing.

27. No one can, however, without risk to faith, foster any doubt as to the Church alone having been invested with such power of governing souls as to exclude altogether the civil authority. In truth, it was not to Caesar but to Peter that Jesus Christ entrusted the keys of the kingdom of Heaven. From this doctrine touching the relations of politics and religion originate important consequences which we cannot pass over in silence.

28. A notable difference exists between every kind of civil rule and that of the kingdom of Christ. If this latter bear a certain likeness and character to a civil kingdom, it is distinguished from it by its origin, principle, and essence. The Church, therefore, possesses the right to exist and to protect herself by institutions and laws in accordance with her nature. And since she not only is a perfect society in herself, but superior to every other society of human growth, she resolutely refuses, promoted alike by right and by duty, to link herself to any mere party and to subject herself to the fleeting exigencies of politics. On like grounds, the Church, the guardian always of her own right and most observant of that of others, holds that it is not her province to decide which is the best amongst many diverse forms of government and the civil institutions of Christian States, and amid the various kinds of State rule she does not disapprove of any, provided the respect due to religion and the observance of good

morals be upheld. By such standard of conduct should the thoughts and mode of acting of every Catholic be directed.

29. There is no doubt that in the sphere of politics ample matter may exist for legitimate difference of opinion, and that, the single reserve being made of the rights of justice and truth, all may strive to bring into actual working the ideas believed likely to be more conducive than others to the general welfare. But to attempt to involve the Church in party strife and seek to bring her support to bear against those who take opposite views is only worthy of partisans. Religion should, on the contrary, be accounted by everyone as holy and inviolate; nay, in the public order itself of States—which cannot be severed from the laws influencing morals and from religious duties—it is always urgent, and indeed the main preoccupation, to take thought how best to consult the interests of Catholicism. Wherever these appear by reason of the efforts of adversaries to be in danger, all differences of opinion among Catholics should forthwith cease, so that, like thoughts and counsels prevailing, they may hasten to the aid of religion, the general and supreme good, to which all else should be referred. We think it well to treat this matter somewhat more in detail.

30. The Church alike and the State, doubtless, both possess individual sovereignty; hence, in the carrying out of public affairs, neither obeys the other within the limits to which each is restricted by its constitution. It does not hence follow, however, that Church and State are in any manner severed, and still less antagonistic. Nature, in fact, has given us not only physical existence, but moral life likewise. Hence, from the tranquility of public order, which is the immediate purpose of civil society, man expects to derive his well-being, and still more the sheltering care necessary to his moral life, which consists exclusively in the knowledge and practice of virtue. He wishes, moreover, at the same time, as in duty bound, to find in the Church the aids necessary to his religious perfection, in the knowledge and practice of the true religion; of that religion which is the

queen of virtues, because in binding these to God it completes them all and perfects them. Therefore, they who are engaged in framing constitutions and in enacting laws should bear in mind the moral and religious nature of man, and take care to help him, but in a right and orderly way, to gain perfection, neither enjoining nor forbidding anything save what is reasonably consistent with civil as well as with religious requirements. On this very account, the Church cannot stand by, indifferent as to the import and significance of laws enacted by the State; not insofar, indeed, as they refer to the State, but in so far as, passing beyond their due limits, they trench upon the rights of the Church.

31. From God has the duty been assigned to the Church not only to interpose resistance, if at any time the State rule should run counter to religion, but, further, to make a strong endeavor that the power of the Gospel may pervade the law and institutions of the nations. Inasmuch as the destiny of the State depends mainly on the disposition of those who are at the head of affairs, it follows that the Church cannot give countenance or favor to those whom she knows to be imbued with a spirit of hostility to her; who refuse openly to respect her rights; who make it their aim and purpose to tear asunder the alliance that should, by the very nature of things, connect the interests of religion with those of the State. On the contrary, she is (as she is bound to be) the upholder of those who are themselves imbued with the right way of thinking as to the relations between Church and State, and who strive to make them work in perfect accord for the common good. These precepts contain the abiding principle by which every Catholic should shape his conduct in regard to public life. In short, where the Church does not forbid taking part in public affairs, it is fit and proper to give support to men of acknowledged worth, and who pledge themselves to deserve well in the Catholic cause, and on no account may it be allowed to prefer to them any such individuals as are hostile to religion.

32. Whence it appears how urgent is the duty to maintain perfect union of minds, especially at these our times, when the Christian name is assailed with designs so concerted and subtle. All who have it at heart to attach themselves earnestly to the Church, which is "the pillar and ground of the truth" (1 Tim. 3:15), will easily steer clear of masters who are "lying and promising them liberty, when they themselves are slaves of corruption" (2 Pet. 2:1, 19). Nay, more, having made themselves sharers in the divine virtue which resides in the Church, they will triumph over the craft of their adversaries by wisdom, and over their violence by courage. This is not now the time and place to inquire whether and how far the inertness and internal dissensions of Catholics have contributed to the present condition of things; but it is certain at least that the perverse-minded would exhibit less boldness, and would not have brought about such an accumulation of ills, if the faith "which worketh by charity" (Gal. 5:6) had been generally more energetic and lively in the souls of men, and had there not been so universal a drifting away from the divinely established rule of morality throughout Christianity. May at least the lessons afforded by the memory of the past have the good result of leading to a wiser mode of acting in the future.

33. As to those who mean to take part in public affairs, they should avoid with the very utmost care two criminal excesses: so-called prudence and false courage. Some there are, indeed, who maintain that it is not opportune boldly to attack evil-doing in its might and when in the ascendant, lest, as they say, opposition should exasperate minds already hostile. These make it a matter of guesswork as to whether they are for the Church or against her, since on the one hand they give themselves out as professing the Catholic faith, and yet wish that the Church should allow certain opinions, at variance with her teaching, to be spread abroad with impunity. They moan over the loss of faith and the perversion of morals, yet trouble themselves not to bring any remedy; nay, not seldom, even add to the

intensity of the mischief through too much forbearance or harmful dissembling. These same individuals would not have anyone entertain a doubt as to their good will towards the Holy See; yet they have always a something by way of reproach against the supreme Pontiff.

34. The prudence of men of this cast is of that kind which is termed by the Apostle Paul "wisdom of the flesh" and "death" of the soul, "because it is not subject to the law of God, neither can it be" (cf. Rom. 8:6–7). Nothing is less calculated to emend such ills than prudence of this kind. For the enemies of the Church have for their object—and they hesitate not to proclaim it, and many among them boast of it—to destroy outright, if possible, the Catholic religion, which alone is the true religion. With such a purpose in hand, they shrink from nothing, for they are fully conscious that the more faint-hearted those who withstand them become, the more easy will it be to work out their wicked will. Therefore, they who cherish the "prudence of the flesh" and who pretend to be unaware that every Christian ought to be a valiant soldier of Christ; they who would fain obtain the rewards owing to conquerors, while they are leading the lives of cowards, untouched in the fight, are so far from thwarting the onward march of the evil—disposed that, on the contrary, they even help it forward.

35. On the other hand, not a few, impelled by a false zeal, or—what is more blameworthy still—affecting sentiments which their conduct belies, take upon themselves to act a part which does not belong to them. They would fain see the Church's mode of action influenced by their ideas and their judgment to such an extent that everything done otherwise they take ill or accept with repugnance. Some, yet again, expend their energies in fruitless contention, being worthy of blame equally with the former. To act in such manner is nor to follow lawful authority but to forestall it, and, unauthorized, assume the duties of the spiritual rulers, to the great detriment of the order which God established in His Church to be observed forever,

and which He does not permit to be violated with impunity by anyone, whoever he may be.

36. Honor, then, to those who shrink not from entering the arena as often as need calls, believing and being convinced that the violence of injustice will be brought to an end and finally give way to the sanctity of right and religion! They truly seem invested with the dignity of time-honored virtue, since they are struggling to defend religion, and chiefly against the faction banded together to attack Christianity with extreme daring and without tiring, and to pursue with incessant hostility the sovereign Pontiff, fallen into their power. But men of this high character maintain without wavering the love of obedience, nor are they wont to undertake anything upon their own authority. Now, since a like resolve to obey, combined with constancy and sturdy courage, is needful, so that whatever trials the pressure of events may bring about, they may be "deficient in nothing" (James 1:4), We greatly desire to fix deep in the minds of each one that which Paul calls the "wisdom of the spirit" (Rom. 8:6), for in controlling human actions this wisdom follows the excellent rule of moderation, with the happy result that no one either timidly despairs through lack of courage or presumes overmuch from want to prudence. There is, however, a difference between the political prudence that relates to the general good and that which concerns the good of individuals. This latter is shown forth in the case of private persons who obey the prompting of right reason in the direction of their own conduct; while the former is the characteristic of those who are set over others, and chiefly of rulers of the State, whose duty it is to exercise the power of command, so that the political prudence of private individuals would seem to consist wholly in carrying out faithfully the orders issued by lawful authority.[8]

8. "Prudence proceeds from reason, and to reason it specially pertains to guide and govern. Whence it follows that, in so much as anyone takes part in the control and government of affairs, in so far ought he to be gifted with reason

37. The like disposition and the same order should prevail in the Christian society by so much the more that the political prudence of the Pontiff embraces diverse and multiform things, for it is his charge not only to rule the Church, but generally so to regulate the actions of Christian citizens that these may be in apt conformity to their hope of gaining eternal salvation. Whence it is clear that, in addition to the complete accordance of thought and deed, the faithful should follow the practical political wisdom of the ecclesiastical authority. Now, the administration of Christian affairs immediately under the Roman Pontiff appertains to the bishops, who, although they attain not to the summit of pontifical power, are nevertheless truly princes in the ecclesiastical hierarchy; and as each one of them administers a particular church, they are "as master-workers...in the spiritual edifice,"[9] and they have members of the clergy to share their duties and carry out their decisions. Everyone has to regulate his mode of conduct according to this constitution of the Church, which it is not in the power of any man to change. Consequently, just as in the exercise of their episcopal authority the bishops ought to be united with the Apostolic See so should the members of the clergy and the laity live in close union with their bishops. Among the prelates, indeed, one or other there may be affording scope to criticism either in regard to personal conduct or in reference to opinions by him entertained about points of doctrine; but no private person may arrogate

and prudence. But it is evident that the subject, so far as subject, and the servant ought neither to control nor govern, but rather to be controlled and governed. Prudence, then, is not the special virtue of the servant, so far as servant, nor of the subject, so far as subject. But because any man, on account of his character of a reasonable being, may have some share in the government on account of the rational choice which he exercises, it is fitting that in such proportion he should possess the virtue of prudence. Whence it manifestly results that prudence exists in the ruler as the art of building exists in the architect, whereas prudence exists in the subject as the art of building exists in the hand of the workman employed in the construction." *Summa theologiae* II-II, q. 47, a. 12. St. Thomas Aquinas refers to Aristotle, *Ethic. Nic.*, VI, 8, 1141b21–29.

9. Thomas Aquinas, *Quaestiones quodlibetales* I, q. 7, a. 2.

to himself the office of judge which Christ our Lord has bestowed on that one alone whom He placed in charge of His lambs and of His sheep. Let everyone bear in mind that most wise teaching of Gregory the Great: "Subjects should be admonished not rashly to judge their prelates, even if they chance to see them acting in a blameworthy manner, lest, justly reproving what is wrong, they be led by pride into greater wrong. They are to be warned against the danger of setting themselves up in audacious opposition to the superiors whose shortcomings they may notice. Should, therefore, the superiors really have committed grievous sins, their inferiors, penetrated with the fear of God, ought not to refuse them respectful submission. The actions of superiors should not be smitten by the sword of the word, even when they are rightly judged to have deserved censure."[10]

38. However, all endeavors will avail but little unless our life be regulated conformably with the discipline of the Christian virtues. Let us call to mind what holy Scripture records concerning the Jewish nation: "As long as they sinned not in the sight of their God, it was well with them: for their God hateth iniquity. And even...when they had revolted from the way that God had given them to walk therein, they were destroyed in battles by many nations" (Jud. 5:21–22). Now, the nation of the Jews bore an inchoate semblance to the Christian people, and the vicissitudes of their history in olden times have often foreshadowed the truth that was to come, saving that God in His goodness has enriched and loaded us with far greater benefits, and on this account the sins of Christians are much greater, and bear the stamp of more shameful and criminal ingratitude.

39. The Church, it is certain, at no time and in no particular is deserted by God; hence, there is no reason why she should be alarmed at the wickedness of men; but in the case of nations falling away from Christian virtue there is not a like ground of assurance, "for sin maketh

10. *Regina pastorales*, III, 4 (*PL* 77:55).

nations miserable" (Prov. 14:34). If every bygone age has experienced the force of this truth, wherefore should not our own? There are, in truth, very many signs which proclaim that just punishments are already menacing, and the condition of modern States tends to confirm this belief, since we perceive many of them in sad plight from internal disorders, and not one entirely exempt. But, should those leagued together in wickedness hurry onward in the road they have boldly chosen, should they increase in influence and power in proportion as they make headway in their evil purposes and crafty schemes, there will be ground to fear lest the very foundations nature has laid for States to rest upon be utterly destroyed. Nor can such misgivings be removed by any mere human effort, especially as a vast number of men, having rejected the Christian faith, are on that account justly incurring the penalty of their pride, since blinded by their passions they search in vain for truth, laying hold on the false for the true, and thinking themselves wise when they call "evil good, and good evil," and "put darkness in the place of light, and light in the place of darkness" (Isa. 5:20). It is therefore necessary that God come to the rescue, and that, mindful of His mercy, He turn an eye of compassion on human society.

40. Hence, We renew the urgent entreaty We have already made, to redouble zeal and perseverance, when addressing humble supplications to our merciful God, so that the virtues whereby a Christian life is perfected may be reawakened. It is, however, urgent before all, that charity, which is the main foundation of the Christian life, and apart from which the other virtues exist not or remain barren, should be quickened and maintained. Therefore is it that the Apostle Paul, after having exhorted the Colossians to flee all vice and cultivate all virtue, adds: "Above all things, have charity, which is the bond of perfection" (Col. 3:14). Yea, truly, charity is the bond of perfection, for it binds intimately to God those whom it has embraced and with loving tenderness, causes them to draw their life from God, to act with God,

to refer all to God. Howbeit, the love of God should not be severed from the love of our neighbor, since men have a share in the infinite goodness of God and bear in themselves the impress of His image and likeness. "This commandment we have from God, that he who loveth God, love also his brother" (1 John 4:21). "If any man say I love God, and he hateth his brother, he is a liar" (1 John 4:20). And this commandment concerning charity its divine proclaimer styled new, not in the sense that a previous law, or even nature itself, had not enjoined that men should love one another, but because the Christian precept of loving each other in that manner was truly new, and quite unheard of in the memory of man. For that love with which Jesus Christ is beloved by His Father and with which He Himself loves men, He obtained for His disciples and followers that they might be of one heart and of one mind in Him by charity, as He Himself and His Father are one by their nature.

41. No one is unaware how deeply and from the very beginning the import of that precept has been implanted in the breast of Christians, and what abundant fruits of concord, mutual benevolence, piety, patience, and fortitude it has produced. Why, then, should we not devote ourselves to imitate the examples set by our fathers? The very times in which we live should afford sufficient motives for the practice of charity. Since impious men are bent on giving fresh impulse to their hatred against Jesus Christ, Christians should be quickened anew in piety; and charity, which is the inspirer of lofty deeds, should be imbued with new life. Let dissensions therefore, if there be any, wholly cease; let those strifes which waste the strength of those engaged in the fight, without any advantage resulting to religion, be scattered to the winds; let all minds be united in faith and all hearts in charity, so that, as it behooves, life may be spent in the practice of the love of God and the love of men.

42. This is a suitable moment for us to exhort especially heads of families to govern their households according to these precepts,

and to be solicitous without failing for the right training of their children. The family may be regarded as the cradle of civil society, and it is in great measure within the circle of family life that the destiny of the States is fostered. Whence it is that they who would break away from Christian discipline are working to corrupt family life, and to destroy it utterly, root and branch. From such an unholy purpose they allow not themselves to be turned aside by the reflection that it cannot, even in any degree, be carried out without inflicting cruel outrage on the parents. These hold from nature their right of training the children to whom they have given birth, with the obligation super-added of shaping and directing the education of their little ones to the end for which God vouchsafed the privilege of transmitting the gift of life. It is, then, incumbent on parents to strain every nerve to ward off such an outrage, and to strive manfully to have and to hold exclusive authority to direct the education of their offspring, as is fitting, in a Christian manner, and first and foremost to keep them away from schools where there is risk of their drinking in the poison of impiety. Where the right education of youth is concerned, no amount of trouble or labor can be undertaken, how greatsoever, but that even greater still may not be called for. In this regard, indeed, there are to be found in many countries Catholics worthy of general admiration, who incur considerable outlay and bestow much zeal in founding schools for the education of youth. It is highly desirable that such noble example may be generously followed, where time and circumstances demand, yet all should be intimately persuaded that the minds of children are most influenced by the training they receive at home. If in their early years they find within the walls of their homes the rule of an upright life and the discipline of Christian virtues, the future welfare of society will in great measure be guaranteed.

43. And now We seem to have touched upon those matters which Catholics ought chiefly nowadays to follow, or mainly to avoid. It rests with you, Venerable Brothers, to take measures that Our voice may

reach everywhere, and that one and all may understand how urgent it is to reduce to practice the teachings set forth in this Our letter. The observance of these duties cannot be troublesome or onerous, for the yoke of Jesus Christ is sweet, and His burden is light. If anything, however, appear too difficult of accomplishment, you will afford aid by the authority of your example, so that each one of the faithful may make more strenuous endeavor, and display a soul unconquered by difficulties. Bring it home to their minds, as We have Ourselves oftentimes conveyed the warning, that matters of the highest moment and worthy of all honor are at stake, for the safeguarding of which every most toilsome effort should be readily endured; and that a sublime reward is in store for the labors of a Christian life. On the other hand, to refrain from doing battle for Jesus Christ amounts to fighting against Him; He Himself assures us "He will deny before His Father in heaven those who shall have refused to confess Him on earth" (Luke 9:26). As for Ourselves and you all, never assuredly, so long as life lasts, shall We allow Our authority, Our counsels, and Our solicitude to be in any wise lacking in the conflict. Nor is it to be doubted but that especial aid of the great God will be vouchsafed, so long as the struggle endures, to the flock alike and to the pastors. Sustained by this confidence, as a pledge of heavenly gifts, and of Our loving kindness in the Lord to you, Venerable Brothers, to your clergy and to all your people, We accord the Apostolic Benediction.

Given at St. Peter's, in Rome, the tenth day of January, 1890, the twelfth year of Our Pontificate.

LEO PP. XIII

ENCYCLICAL LETTER

RERUM NOVARUM

OF THE SUPREME PONTIFF

LEO XIII

TO OUR VENERABLE BRETHREN THE PATRIARCHS, PRIMATES, ARCHBISHOPS, BISHOPS, AND OTHER ORDINARIES OF PLACES HAVING PEACE AND COMMUNION WITH THE APOSTOLIC SEE

ON CAPITAL AND LABOR

1. That the spirit of revolutionary change, which has long been disturbing the nations of the world, should have passed beyond the sphere of politics and made its influence felt in the cognate sphere of practical economics is not surprising. The elements of the conflict now raging are unmistakable, in the vast expansion of industrial pursuits and the marvelous discoveries of science; in the changed relations between masters and workmen; in the enormous fortunes of some few individuals, and the utter poverty of the masses; the increased self-reliance and closer mutual combination of the working classes; as also, finally, in the prevailing moral degeneracy. The momentous gravity of the state of things now obtaining fills every mind with painful apprehension; wise men are discussing it; practical men are proposing schemes; popular meetings, legislatures, and rulers of nations are all busied with it—actually there is no question which has taken deeper hold on the public mind.

2. Therefore, Venerable Brethren, as on former occasions when it seemed opportune to refute false teaching, We have addressed you in the interests of the Church and of the common weal, and have issued letters bearing on political power, human liberty, the Christian constitution of the State, and like matters; so have We thought it expedient now to speak on the condition of the working classes. It is a subject on which We have already touched more than once, incidentally. But in the present letter, the responsibility of the apostolic office urges Us to treat the question of set purpose and in detail, in order that no misapprehension may exist as to the principles which truth and justice dictate for its settlement. The discussion is not easy, nor is it void of danger. It is no easy matter to define the relative rights and mutual duties of the rich and of the poor, of capital and of labor. And the danger lies in this, that crafty agitators are intent on making use of these differences of opinion to pervert men's judgments and to stir up the people to revolt.

3. In any case we clearly see, and on this there is general agreement, that some opportune remedy must be found quickly for the misery and wretchedness pressing so unjustly on the majority of the working class. For the ancient working-men's guilds were abolished in the last century, and no other protective organization took their place. Public institutions and the laws set aside the ancient religion. Hence, by degrees it has come to pass that working men have been surrendered, isolated and helpless, to the hardheartedness of employers and the greed of unchecked competition. The mischief has been increased by rapacious usury, which, although more than once condemned by the Church, is nevertheless, under a different guise, but with like injustice, still practiced by covetous and grasping men. To this must be added that the hiring of labor and the conduct of trade are concentrated in the hands of comparatively few; so that a small number of very rich men have been able to lay upon the teeming masses of the laboring poor a yoke little better than that of slavery itself.

4. To remedy these wrongs the socialists, working on the poor man's envy of the rich, are striving to do away with private property, and contend that individual possessions should become the common property of all, to be administered by the State or by municipal bodies. They hold that by thus transferring property from private individuals to the community, the present mischievous state of things will be set to rights, inasmuch as each citizen will then get his fair share of whatever there is to enjoy. But their contentions are so clearly powerless to end the controversy that were they carried into effect the working man himself would be among the first to suffer. They are, moreover, emphatically unjust, for they would rob the lawful possessor, distort the functions of the State, and create utter confusion in the community.

5. It is surely undeniable that, when a man engages in remunerative labor, the impelling reason and motive of his work is to obtain property, and thereafter to hold it as his very own. If one man hires out to another his strength or skill, he does so for the purpose of receiving in return what is necessary for the satisfaction of his needs; he therefore expressly intends to acquire a right full and real, not only to the remuneration, but also to the disposal of such remuneration, just as he pleases. Thus, if he lives sparingly, saves money, and, for greater security, invests his savings in land, the land, in such case, is only his wages under another form; and, consequently, a working man's little estate thus purchased should be as completely at his full disposal as are the wages he receives for his labor. But it is precisely in such power of disposal that ownership obtains, whether the property consist of land or chattels. Socialists, therefore, by endeavoring to transfer the possessions of individuals to the community at large, strike at the interests of every wage-earner, since they would deprive him of the liberty of disposing of his wages, and thereby of all hope and possibility of increasing his resources and of bettering his condition in life.

6. What is of far greater moment, however, is the fact that the remedy they propose is manifestly against justice. For every man has by nature the right to possess property as his own. This is one of the chief points of distinction between man and the animal creation, for the brute has no power of self-direction, but is governed by two main instincts, which keep his powers on the alert, impel him to develop them in a fitting manner, and stimulate and determine him to action without any power of choice. One of these instincts is self-preservation, the other the propagation of the species. Both can attain their purpose by means of things which lie within range; beyond their verge the brute creation cannot go, for they are moved to action by their senses only, and in the special direction which these suggest. But with man it is wholly different. He possesses, on the one hand, the full perfection of the animal being, and hence enjoys at least as much as the rest of the animal kind, the fruition of things material. But animal nature, however perfect, is far from representing the human being in its completeness, and is in truth but humanity's humble handmaid, made to serve and to obey. It is the mind, or reason, which is the predominant element in us who are human creatures; it is this which renders a human being human and distinguishes him essentially from the brute. And on this very account—that man alone among the animal creation is endowed with reason—it must be within his right to possess things not merely for temporary and momentary use, as other living things do, but to have and to hold them in stable and permanent possession; he must have not only things that perish in the use, but those also which, though they have been reduced into use, continue for further use in after time.

7. This becomes still more clearly evident if man's nature be considered a little more deeply. For man, fathoming by his faculty of reason matters without number, linking the future with the present, and being master of his own acts, guides his ways under the eternal law and the power of God, whose providence governs all things.

Wherefore, it is in his power to exercise his choice not only as to matters that regard his present welfare, but also about those which he deems may be for his advantage in time yet to come. Hence, man not only should possess the fruits of the earth, but also the very soil, inasmuch as from the produce of the earth he has to lay by provision for the future. Man's needs do not die out, but forever recur; although satisfied today, they demand fresh supplies for tomorrow. Nature accordingly must have given to man a source that is stable and remaining always with him, from which he might look to draw continual supplies. And this stable condition of things he finds solely in the earth and its fruits. There is no need to bring in the State. Man precedes the State, and possesses, prior to the formation of any State, the right of providing for the substance of his body.

8. The fact that God has given the earth for the use and enjoyment of the whole human race can in no way be a bar to the owning of private property. For God has granted the earth to mankind in general, not in the sense that all without distinction can deal with it as they like, but rather that no part of it was assigned to anyone in particular, and that the limits of private possession have been left to be fixed by man's own industry, and by the laws of individual races. Moreover, the earth, even though apportioned among private owners, ceases not thereby to minister to the needs of all, inasmuch as there is not one who does not sustain life from what the land produces. Those who do not possess the soil contribute their labor; hence, it may truly be said that all human subsistence is derived either from labor on one's own land, or from some toil, some calling, which is paid for either in the produce of the land itself, or in that which is exchanged for what the land brings forth.

9. Here, again, we have further proof that private ownership is in accordance with the law of nature. Truly, that which is required for the preservation of life, and for life's well-being, is produced in great abundance from the soil, but not until man has brought it into

cultivation and expended upon it his solicitude and skill. Now, when man thus turns the activity of his mind and the strength of his body toward procuring the fruits of nature, by such act he makes his own that portion of nature's field which he cultivates—that portion on which he leaves, as it were, the impress of his personality; and it cannot but be just that he should possess that portion as his very own and have a right to hold it without anyone being justified in violating that right.

10. So strong and convincing are these arguments that it seems amazing that some should now be setting up anew certain obsolete opinions in opposition to what is here laid down. They assert that it is right for private persons to have the use of the soil and its various fruits, but that it is unjust for anyone to possess outright either the land on which he has built or the estate which he has brought under cultivation. But those who deny these rights do not perceive that they are defrauding man of what his own labor has produced. For the soil which is tilled and cultivated with toil and skill utterly changes its condition; it was wild before, now it is fruitful; was barren, but now brings forth in abundance. That which has thus altered and improved the land becomes so truly part of itself as to be in great measure indistinguishable and inseparable from it. Is it just that the fruit of a man's own sweat and labor should be possessed and enjoyed by anyone else? As effects follow their cause, so is it just and right that the results of labor should belong to those who have bestowed their labor.

11. With reason, then, the common opinion of mankind, little affected by the few dissentients who have contended for the opposite view, has found in the careful study of nature, and in the laws of nature, the foundations of the division of property, and the practice of all ages has consecrated the principle of private ownership, as being pre-eminently in conformity with human nature, and as conducing in the most unmistakable manner to the peace and tranquility of

human existence. The same principle is confirmed and enforced by the civil laws—laws which, so long as they are just, derive from the law of nature their binding force. The authority of the divine law adds its sanction, forbidding us in severest terms even to covet that which is another's: "Thou shalt not covet thy neighbor's wife; nor his house, nor his field, nor his man-servant, nor his maid-servant, nor his ox, nor his ass, nor anything that is his" (Deut. 5:21).

12. The rights here spoken of, belonging to each individual man, are seen in much stronger light when considered in relation to man's social and domestic obligations. In choosing a state of life, it is indisputable that all are at full liberty to follow the counsel of Jesus Christ as to observing virginity, or to bind themselves by the marriage tie. No human law can abolish the natural and original right of marriage, nor in any way limit the chief and principal purpose of marriage ordained by God's authority from the beginning: "Increase and multiply" (Gen. 1:28). Hence we have the family, the "society" of a man's house—a society very small, one must admit, but none the less a true society, and one older than any State. Consequently, it has rights and duties peculiar to itself which are quite independent of the State.

13. That right to property, therefore, which has been proved to belong naturally to individual persons, must in like wise belong to a man in his capacity of head of a family; nay, that right is all the stronger in proportion as the human person receives a wider extension in the family group. It is a most sacred law of nature that a father should provide food and all necessaries for those whom he has begotten; and, similarly, it is natural that he should wish that his children, who carry on, so to speak, and continue his personality, should be by him provided with all that is needful to enable them to keep themselves decently from want and misery amid the uncertainties of this mortal life. Now, in no other way can a father effect this except by the ownership of productive property, which he can transmit to his children by inheritance. A family, no less than a State, is, as We

have said, a true society, governed by an authority peculiar to itself, that is to say, by the authority of the father. Provided, therefore, the limits which are prescribed by the very purposes for which it exists be not transgressed, the family has at least equal rights with the State in the choice and pursuit of the things needful to its preservation and its just liberty. We say, "at least equal rights"; for, inasmuch as the domestic household is antecedent, as well in idea as in fact, to the gathering of men into a community, the family must necessarily have rights and duties which are prior to those of the community and founded more immediately in nature. If the citizens, if the families on entering into association and fellowship, were to experience hindrance in a commonwealth instead of help and were to find their rights attacked instead of being upheld, society would rightly be an object of detestation rather than of desire.

14. The contention, then, that the civil government should at its option intrude into and exercise intimate control over the family and the household is a great and pernicious error. True, if a family finds itself in exceeding distress, utterly deprived of the counsel of friends, and without any prospect of extricating itself, it is right that extreme necessity be met by public aid, since each family is a part of the commonwealth. In like manner, if within the precincts of the household there occur grave disturbance of mutual rights, public authority should intervene to force each party to yield to the other its proper due; for this is not to deprive citizens of their rights, but justly and properly to safeguard and strengthen them. But the rulers of the commonwealth must go no further; here, nature bids them stop. Paternal authority can be neither abolished nor absorbed by the State; for it has the same source as human life itself. "The child belongs to the father," and is, as it were, the continuation of the father's personality; and speaking strictly, the child takes its place in civil society, not of its own right, but in its quality as member of the family in which it is born. And for the very reason that "the child belongs to the father,"

it is, as St. Thomas Aquinas says, "before it attains the use of free will, under the power and the charge of its parents."[1] The socialists, therefore, in setting aside the parent and setting up a State supervision, act against natural justice, and destroy the structure of the home.

15. And in addition to injustice, it is only too evident what an upset and disturbance there would be in all classes, and to how intolerable and hateful a slavery citizens would be subjected. The door would be thrown open to envy, to mutual invective, and to discord; the sources of wealth themselves would run dry, for no one would have any interest in exerting his talents or his industry; and that ideal equality about which they entertain pleasant dreams would be in reality the leveling down of all to a like condition of misery and degradation. Hence, it is clear that the main tenet of socialism, community of goods, must be utterly rejected, since it only injures those whom it would seem meant to benefit, is directly contrary to the natural rights of mankind, and would introduce confusion and disorder into the commonweal. The first and most fundamental principle, therefore, if one would undertake to alleviate the condition of the masses, must be the inviolability of private property. This being established, we proceed to show where the remedy sought for must be found.

16. We approach the subject with confidence, and in the exercise of the rights which manifestly appertain to Us, for no practical solution of this question will be found apart from the intervention of religion and of the Church. It is We who are the chief guardian of religion and the chief dispenser of what pertains to the Church; and by keeping silence we would seem to neglect the duty incumbent on us. Doubtless, this most serious question demands the attention and the efforts of others besides ourselves—to wit, of the rulers of States, of employers of labor, of the wealthy, aye, of the working classes themselves, for whom We are pleading. But We affirm without hesitation

1. *Summa theologiae* II-II, q. 10, a. 12.

that all the striving of men will be vain if they leave out the Church. It is the Church that insists, on the authority of the Gospel, upon those teachings whereby the conflict can be brought to an end, or rendered, at least, far less bitter; the Church uses her efforts not only to enlighten the mind, but to direct by her precepts the life and conduct of each and all; the Church improves and betters the condition of the working man by means of numerous organizations; does her best to enlist the services of all classes in discussing and endeavoring to further in the most practical way, the interests of the working classes; and considers that for this purpose recourse should be had, in due measure and degree, to the intervention of the law and of State authority.

17. It must be first of all recognized that the condition of things inherent in human affairs must be borne with, for it is impossible to reduce civil society to one dead level. Socialists may in that intent do their utmost, but all striving against nature is in vain. There naturally exist among mankind manifold differences of the most important kind; people differ in capacity, skill, health, strength; and unequal fortune is a necessary result of unequal condition. Such inequality is far from being disadvantageous either to individuals or to the community. Social and public life can only be maintained by means of various kinds of capacity for business and the playing of many parts; and each man, as a rule, chooses the part which suits his own peculiar domestic condition. As regards bodily labor, even had man never fallen from the state of innocence, he would not have remained wholly idle; but that which would then have been his free choice and his delight became afterwards compulsory, and the painful expiation for his disobedience. "Cursed be the earth in thy work; in thy labor thou shalt eat of it all the days of thy life" (Gen. 3:17).

18. In like manner, the other pains and hardships of life will have no end or cessation on earth; for the consequences of sin are bitter and hard to bear, and they must accompany man so long as life lasts.

To suffer and to endure, therefore, is the lot of humanity; let them strive as they may, no strength and no artifice will ever succeed in banishing from human life the ills and troubles which beset it. If any there are who pretend differently—who hold out to a hard-pressed people the boon of freedom from pain and trouble, an undisturbed repose, and constant enjoyment—they delude the people and impose upon them, and their lying promises will only one day bring forth evils worse than the present. Nothing is more useful than to look upon the world as it really is, and at the same time to seek elsewhere, as We have said, for the solace to its troubles.

19. The great mistake made in regard to the matter now under consideration is to take up with the notion that class is naturally hostile to class, and that the wealthy and the working men are intended by nature to live in mutual conflict. So irrational and so false is this view that the direct contrary is the truth. Just as the symmetry of the human frame is the result of the suitable arrangement of the different parts of the body, so in a State is it ordained by nature that these two classes should dwell in harmony and agreement, so as to maintain the balance of the body politic. Each needs the other: capital cannot do without labor, nor labor without capital. Mutual agreement results in the beauty of good order, while perpetual conflict necessarily produces confusion and savage barbarity. Now, in preventing such strife as this, and in uprooting it, the efficacy of Christian institutions is marvelous and manifold. First of all, there is no intermediary more powerful than religion (whereof the Church is the interpreter and guardian) in drawing the rich and the working class together, by reminding each of its duties to the other, and especially of the obligations of justice.

20. Of these duties, the following bind the proletarian and the worker: fully and faithfully to perform the work which has been freely and equitably agreed upon; never to injure the property, nor to outrage the person, of an employer; never to resort to violence in

defending their own cause, nor to engage in riot or disorder; and to have nothing to do with men of evil principles, who work upon the people with artful promises of great results, and excite foolish hopes which usually end in useless regrets and grievous loss. The following duties bind the wealthy owner and the employer: not to look upon their work people as their bondsmen, but to respect in every man his dignity as a person ennobled by Christian character. They are reminded that, according to natural reason and Christian philosophy, working for gain is creditable, not shameful, to a man, since it enables him to earn an honorable livelihood; but to misuse men as though they were things in the pursuit of gain, or to value them solely for their physical powers—that is truly shameful and inhuman. Again, justice demands that, in dealing with the working man, religion and the good of his soul must be kept in mind. Hence, the employer is bound to see that the worker has time for his religious duties; that he be not exposed to corrupting influences and dangerous occasions; and that he be not led away to neglect his home and family or to squander his earnings. Furthermore, the employer must never tax his work people beyond their strength or employ them in work unsuited to their sex and age. His great and principal duty is to give everyone what is just. Doubtless, before deciding whether wages are fair, many things have to be considered; but wealthy owners and all masters of labor should be mindful of this—that to exercise pressure upon the indigent and the destitute for the sake of gain, and to gather one's profit out of the need of another, is condemned by all laws, human and divine. To defraud anyone of wages that are his due is a great crime which cries to the avenging anger of Heaven. "Behold, the hire of the laborers... which by fraud has been kept back by you, crieth; and the cry of them hath entered into the ears of the Lord of Sabaoth" (James 5:4). Lastly, the rich must religiously refrain from cutting down the workmen's earnings, whether by force, by fraud, or by usurious dealing; and with all the greater reason because the laboring man is, as a rule, weak and unprotected, and because his slender means should in proportion to their scantiness be accounted sacred. Were these precepts carefully obeyed and followed out, would they not be sufficient of themselves to keep under all strife and all its causes?

21. But the Church, with Jesus Christ as her Master and Guide, aims higher still. She lays down precepts yet more perfect and tries to bind class to class in friendliness and good feeling. The things of earth cannot be understood or valued aright without taking into consideration the life to come, the life that will know no death. Exclude the idea of futurity, and forthwith the very notion of what is good and right would perish; nay, the whole scheme of the universe would become a dark and unfathomable mystery. The great truth which we learn from nature herself is also the grand Christian dogma on which religion rests as on its foundation—that, when we have given up this present life, then shall we really begin to live. God has not created us for the perishable and transitory things of earth, but for things heavenly and everlasting; He has given us this world as a place of exile, and not as our abiding place. As for riches and the other things which men call good and desirable, whether we have them in abundance, or are lacking in them—so far as eternal happiness is concerned—it makes no difference; the only important thing is to use them aright. Jesus Christ, when He redeemed us with plentiful redemption, took not away the pains and sorrows which in such large proportion are woven together in the web of our mortal life. He transformed them into motives of virtue and occasions of merit; and no man can hope for eternal reward unless he follow in the blood-stained footprints of his Savior. "If we suffer with Him, we shall also reign with Him" (2 Tim. 2:12). Christ's labors and sufferings, accepted of His own free will, have marvelously sweetened all suffering and all labor. And not only by His example, but by His grace and by the hope held forth of everlasting recompense, has He made pain and grief more easy to

endure; "for that which is at present momentary and light of our tribulation, worketh for us above measure exceedingly an eternal weight of glory" (2 Cor. 4:17).

22. Therefore, those whom fortune favors are warned that riches do not bring freedom from sorrow and are of no avail for eternal happiness, but rather are obstacles (Matt. 19:23–24); that the rich should tremble at the threatenings of Jesus Christ—threatenings so unwonted in the mouth of our Lord (Luke 6:24–25)—and that a most strict account must be given to the Supreme Judge for all we possess. The chief and most excellent rule for the right use of money is one the heathen philosophers hinted at, but which the Church has traced out clearly, and has not only made known to men's minds, but has impressed upon their lives. It rests on the principle that it is one thing to have a right to the possession of money and another to have a right to use money as one wills. Private ownership, as we have seen, is the natural right of man, and to exercise that right, especially as members of society, is not only lawful, but absolutely necessary. "It is lawful," says St. Thomas Aquinas, "for a man to hold private property; and it is also necessary for the carrying on of human existence."[2] But if the question be asked: How must one's possessions be used?—the Church replies without hesitation in the words of the same holy Doctor: "Man should not consider his material possessions as his own, but as common to all, so as to share them without hesitation when others are in need. Whence the Apostle with, 'Command the rich of this world...to offer with no stint, to apportion largely.'"[3] True, no one is commanded to distribute to others that which is required for his own needs and those of his household; nor even to give away what is reasonably required to keep up becomingly his condition in life, "for

2 *Summa theologiae* II-II, q. 66, a. 2.

3. Ibid.

4. Ibid., q. 32, a. 6.

no one ought to live other than becomingly."[4] But, when what necessity demands has been supplied, and one's standing fairly taken thought for, it becomes a duty to give to the indigent out of what remains over. "Of that which remaineth, give alms" (Luke 11:41). It is a duty, not of justice (save in extreme cases), but of Christian charity—a duty not enforced by human law. But the laws and judgments of men must yield place to the laws and judgments of Christ the true God, who in many ways urges on His followers the practice of almsgiving—"It is more blessed to give than to receive" (Acts 20:35); and who will count a kindness done or refused to the poor as done or refused to Himself—"As long as you did it to one of my least brethren you did it to me" (Matt. 25:40). To sum up, then, what has been said: Whoever has received from the divine bounty a large share of temporal blessings, whether they be external and material, or gifts of the mind, has received them for the purpose of using them for the perfecting of his own nature, and, at the same time, that he may employ them, as the steward of God's providence, for the benefit of others. "He that hath a talent," said St. Gregory the Great, "let him see that he hide it not; he that hath abundance, let him quicken himself to mercy and generosity; he that hath art and skill, let him do his best to share the use and the utility hereof with his neighbor."[5]

23. As for those who possess not the gifts of fortune, they are taught by the Church that in God's sight poverty is no disgrace, and that there is nothing to be ashamed of in earning their bread by labor. This is enforced by what we see in Christ Himself, who, "whereas He was rich, for our sakes became poor" (2 Cor. 8:9); and who, being the Son of God, and God Himself, chose to seem and to be considered the son of a carpenter—nay, did not disdain to spend a great part of His life as a carpenter Himself. "Is not this the carpenter, the son of Mary?" (Mark 6:3).

5. *Hom. in Evang.*, 9, 7 (*PL* 76:1109b).

24. From contemplation of this divine Model, it is more easy to understand that the true worth and nobility of man lie in his moral qualities, that is, in virtue; that virtue is, moreover, the common inheritance of men, equally within the reach of high and low, rich and poor; and that virtue, and virtue alone, wherever found, will be followed by the rewards of everlasting happiness. Nay, God Himself seems to incline rather to those who suffer misfortune; for Jesus Christ calls the poor "blessed" (Matt. 5:3); He lovingly invites those in labor and grief to come to Him for solace (Matt. 11:28); and He displays the tenderest charity toward the lowly and the oppressed. These reflections cannot fail to keep down the pride of the well-to-do, and to give heart to the unfortunate; to move the former to be generous and the latter to be moderate in their desires. Thus, the separation which pride would set up tends to disappear, nor will it be difficult to make rich and poor join hands in friendly concord.

25. But, if Christian precepts prevail, the respective classes will not only be united in the bonds of friendship, but also in those of brotherly love. For they will understand and feel that all men are children of the same common Father, who is God; that all have alike the same last end, which is God Himself, who alone can make either men or angels absolutely and perfectly happy; that each and all are redeemed and made sons of God, by Jesus Christ, "the first-born among many brethren"; that the blessings of nature and the gifts of grace belong to the whole human race in common, and that from none except the unworthy is withheld the inheritance of the kingdom of Heaven. "If sons, heirs also; heirs indeed of God, and co-heirs with Christ" (Rom. 8:17). Such is the scheme of duties and of rights which is shown forth to the world by the Gospel. Would it not seem that, were society penetrated with ideas like these, strife must quickly cease?

26. But the Church, not content with pointing out the remedy, also applies it. For the Church does her utmost to teach and to train

men, and to educate them and by the intermediary of her bishops and clergy diffuses her salutary teachings far and wide. She strives to influence the mind and the heart so that all may willingly yield themselves to be formed and guided by the commandments of God. It is precisely in this fundamental and momentous matter, on which everything depends, that the Church possesses a power peculiarly her own. The instruments which she employs are given to her by Jesus Christ Himself for the very purpose of reaching the hearts of men and drive their efficiency from God. They alone can reach the innermost heart and conscience and bring men to act from a motive of duty, to control their passions and appetites, to love God and their fellow men with a love that is outstanding and of the highest degree and to break down courageously every barrier which blocks the way to virtue.

27. On this subject we need but recall for one moment the examples recorded in history. Of these facts there cannot be any shadow of doubt: for instance, that civil society was renovated in every part by Christian institutions; that in the strength of that renewal the human race was lifted up to better things—nay, that it was brought back from death to life, and to so excellent a life that nothing more perfect had been known before, or will come to be known in the ages that have yet to be. Of this beneficent transformation Jesus Christ was at once the first cause and the final end; as from Him all came, so to Him was all to be brought back. For when the human race, by the light of the Gospel message, came to know the grand mystery of the Incarnation of the Word and the redemption of man, at once the life of Jesus Christ, God and Man, pervaded every race and nation, and interpenetrated them with His faith, His precepts, and His laws. And if human society is to be healed now, in no other way can it be healed save by a return to Christian life and Christian institutions. When a society is perishing, the wholesome advice to give to those who would restore it is to call it to the principles from which it sprang;

for the purpose and perfection of an association is to aim at and to attain that for which it is formed, and its efforts should be put in motion and inspired by the end and object which originally gave it being. Hence, to fall away from its primal constitution implies disease; to go back to it, recovery. And this may be asserted with utmost truth both of the whole body of the commonwealth and of that class of its citizens—by far the great majority—who get their living by their labor.

28. Neither must it be supposed that the solicitude of the Church is so preoccupied with the spiritual concerns of her children as to neglect their temporal and earthly interests. Her desire is that the poor, for example, should rise above poverty and wretchedness, and better their condition in life; and for this she makes a strong endeavor. By the fact that she calls men to virtue and forms them to its practice she promotes this in no slight degree. Christian morality, when adequately and completely practiced, leads of itself to temporal prosperity, for it merits the blessing of that God who is the source of all blessings; it powerfully restrains the greed of possession and the thirst for pleasure—twin plagues, which too often make a man who is void of self-restraint miserable in the midst of abundance (cf. 1 Tim. 6:10); it makes men supply for the lack of means through economy, teaching them to be content with frugal living, and further, keeping them out of the reach of those vices which devour not small incomes merely, but large fortunes, and dissipate many a goodly inheritance.

29. The Church, moreover, intervenes directly in behalf of the poor, by setting on foot and maintaining many associations which she knows to be efficient for the relief of poverty. Herein, again, she has always succeeded so well as to have even extorted the praise of her enemies. Such was the ardor of brotherly love among the earliest Christians that numbers of those who were in better circumstances despoiled themselves of their possessions in order to relieve their brethren; whence "neither was there anyone needy among them" (Acts 4:34). To the order of deacons, instituted in that very

intent, was committed by the Apostles the charge of the daily doles; and the Apostle Paul, though burdened with the solicitude of all the churches, hesitated not to undertake laborious journeys in order to carry the alms of the faithful to the poorer Christians. Tertullian calls these contributions, given voluntarily by Christians in their assemblies, deposits of piety, because, to cite his own words, they were employed "in feeding the needy, in burying them, in support of youths and maidens destitute of means and deprived of their parents, in the care of the aged, and the relief of the shipwrecked."[6]

30. Thus, by degrees, came into existence the patrimony which the Church has guarded with religious care as the inheritance of the poor. Nay, in order to spare them the shame of begging, the Church has provided aid for the needy. The common Mother of rich and poor has aroused everywhere the heroism of charity and has established congregations of religious and many other useful institutions for help and mercy, so that hardly any kind of suffering could exist which was not afforded relief. At the present day many there are who, like the heathen of old, seek to blame and condemn the Church for such eminent charity. They would substitute in its stead a system of relief organized by the State. But no human expedients will ever make up for the devotedness and self-sacrifice of Christian charity. Charity, as a virtue, pertains to the Church; for virtue it is not, unless it be drawn from the Most Sacred Heart of Jesus Christ; and whosoever turns his back on the Church cannot be near to Christ.

31. It cannot, however, be doubted that to attain the purpose we are treating of, not only the Church, but all human agencies, must concur. All who are concerned in the matter should be of one mind and according to their ability act together. It is with this, as with providence that governs the world; the results of causes do not usually take place save where all the causes cooperate. It is sufficient,

6. *Apologia secunda*, 39 (*Apologeticus*, c. 39; *PL* 1:533a).

therefore, to inquire what part the State should play in the work of remedy and relief.

32. By the State we here understand, not the particular form of government prevailing in this or that nation, but the State as rightly apprehended; that is to say, any government conformable in its institutions to right reason and natural law, and to those dictates of the divine wisdom which we have expounded in the encyclical *On the Christian Constitution of the State*. The foremost duty, therefore, of the rulers of the State should be to make sure that the laws and institutions, the general character and administration of the commonwealth, shall be such as of themselves to realize public well-being and private prosperity. This is the proper scope of wise statesmanship and is the work of the rulers. Now a State chiefly prospers and thrives through moral rule, well-regulated family life, respect for religion and justice, the moderation and fair imposing of public taxes, the progress of the arts and of trade, the abundant yield of the land—through everything, in fact, which makes the citizens better and happier. Hereby, then, it lies in the power of a ruler to benefit every class in the State and amongst the rest to promote to the utmost the interests of the poor; and this in virtue of his office, and without being open to suspicion of undue interference—since it is the province of the commonwealth to serve the common good. And the more that is done for the benefit of the working classes by the general laws of the country, the less need will there be to seek for special means to relieve them.

33. There is another and deeper consideration which must not be lost sight of. As regards the State, the interests of all, whether high or low, are equal. The members of the working classes are citizens by nature and by the same right as the rich; they are real parts, living the life which makes up, through the family, the body of the commonwealth; and it need hardly be said that they are in every city very largely in the majority. It would be irrational to neglect one portion of the citizens and favor another, and therefore the public

administration must duly and solicitously provide for the welfare and the comfort of the working classes; otherwise, that law of justice will be violated which ordains that each man shall have his due. To cite the wise words of St. Thomas Aquinas: "As the part and the whole are in a certain sense identical, so that which belongs to the whole in a sense belongs to the part."[7] Among the many and grave duties of rulers who would do their best for the people, the first and chief is to act with strict justice—with that justice which is called *distributive*—toward each and every class alike.

34. But although all citizens, without exception, can and ought to contribute to that common good in which individuals share so advantageously to themselves, yet it should not be supposed that all can contribute in the like way and to the same extent. No matter what changes may occur in forms of government, there will ever be differences and inequalities of condition in the State. Society cannot exist or be conceived of without them. Some there must be who devote themselves to the work of the commonwealth, who make the laws or administer justice or whose advice and authority govern the nation in times of peace and defend it in war. Such men clearly occupy the foremost place in the State, and should be held in highest estimation, for their work concerns most nearly and effectively the general interests of the community. Those who labor at a trade or calling do not promote the general welfare in such measure as this, but they benefit the nation, if less directly, in a most important manner. We have insisted, it is true, that, since the end of society is to make men better, the chief good that society can possess is virtue. Nevertheless, it is the business of a well-constituted body politic to see to the provision of those material and external helps "the use of which is necessary to virtuous action."[8] Now, for the provision of such commodities, the

7. *Summa theologiae* II-II, q. 61, a. 1, ad 2.
8. Thomas Aquinas, *On the Governance of Rulers*, 1, 15.

labor of the working class—the exercise of their skill, and the employment of their strength, in the cultivation of the land, and in the workshops of trade—is especially responsible and quite indispensable. Indeed, their cooperation is in this respect so important that it may be truly said that it is only by the labor of working men that States grow rich. Justice, therefore, demands that the interests of the working classes should be carefully watched over by the administration, so that they who contribute so largely to the advantage of the community may themselves share in the benefits which they create—that being housed, clothed, and bodily fit, they may find their life less hard and more endurable. It follows that whatever shall appear to prove conducive to the well-being of those who work should obtain favorable consideration. There is no fear that solicitude of this kind will be harmful to any interest; on the contrary, it will be to the advantage of all, for it cannot but be good for the commonwealth to shield from misery those on whom it so largely depends for the things that it needs.

35. We have said that the State must not absorb the individual or the family; both should be allowed free and untrammeled action so far as is consistent with the common good and the interest of others. Rulers should, nevertheless, anxiously safeguard the community and all its members; the community, because the conservation thereof is so emphatically the business of the supreme power, that the safety of the commonwealth is not only the first law, but it is a government's whole reason of existence; and the members, because both philosophy and the Gospel concur in laying down that the object of the government of the State should be, not the advantage of the ruler, but the benefit of those over whom he is placed. As the power to rule comes from God, and is, as it were, a participation in His, the highest of all sovereignties, it should be exercised as the power of God is exercised—with a fatherly solicitude which not only guides the whole, but reaches also individuals.

36. Whenever the general interest or any particular class suffers, or is threatened with harm, which can in no other way be met or prevented, the public authority must step in to deal with it. Now, it is to the interest of the community, as well as of the individual, that peace and good order should be maintained; that all things should be carried on in accordance with God's laws and those of nature; that the discipline of family life should be observed and that religion should be obeyed; that a high standard of morality should prevail, both in public and private life; that justice should be held sacred and that no one should injure another with impunity; that the members of the commonwealth should grow up to man's estate strong and robust, and capable, if need be, of guarding and defending their country. If by a strike of workers or concerted interruption of work there should be imminent danger of disturbance to the public peace; or if circumstances were such as that among the working class the ties of family life were relaxed; if religion were found to suffer through the workers not having time and opportunity afforded them to practice its duties; if in workshops and factories there were danger to morals through the mixing of the sexes or from other harmful occasions of evil; or if employers laid burdens upon their workmen which were unjust, or degraded them with conditions repugnant to their dignity as human beings; finally, if health were endangered by excessive labor, or by work unsuited to sex or age—in such cases, there can be no question but that, within certain limits, it would be right to invoke the aid and authority of the law. The limits must be determined by the nature of the occasion which calls for the law's interference—the principle being that the law must not undertake more, nor proceed further, than is required for the remedy of the evil or the removal of the mischief.

37. Rights must be religiously respected wherever they exist, and it is the duty of the public authority to prevent and to punish injury, and to protect everyone in the possession of his own. Still, when there is question of defending the rights of individuals, the poor and badly

off have a claim to especial consideration. The richer class have many ways of shielding themselves and stand less in need of help from the State; whereas the mass of the poor have no resources of their own to fall back upon, and must chiefly depend upon the assistance of the State. And it is for this reason that wage-earners, since they mostly belong in the mass of the needy, should be specially cared for and protected by the government.

38. Here, however, it is expedient to bring under special notice certain matters of moment. First of all, there is the duty of safeguarding private property by legal enactment and protection. Most of all it is essential, where the passion of greed is so strong, to keep the populace within the line of duty; for, if all may justly strive to better their condition, neither justice nor the common good allows any individual to seize upon that which belongs to another, or, under the futile and shallow pretext of equality, to lay violent hands on other people's possessions. Most true it is that by far the larger part of the workers prefer to better themselves by honest labor rather than by doing any wrong to others. But there are not a few who are imbued with evil principles and eager for revolutionary change, whose main purpose is to stir up disorder and incite their fellows to acts of violence. The authority of the law should intervene to put restraint upon such firebrands, to save the working classes from being led astray by their maneuvers, and to protect lawful owners from spoliation.

39. When working people have recourse to a strike and become voluntarily idle, it is frequently because the hours of labor are too long, or the work too hard, or because they consider their wages insufficient. The grave inconvenience of this not uncommon occurrence should be obviated by public remedial measures; for such paralyzing of labor not only affects the masters and their work people alike, but is extremely injurious to trade and to the general interests of the public; moreover, on such occasions, violence and disorder are generally not far distant, and thus it frequently happens that the public peace is

imperiled. The laws should forestall and prevent such troubles from arising; they should lend their influence and authority to the removal in good time of the causes which lead to conflicts between employers and employed.

40. The working man, too, has interests in which he should be protected by the State; and first of all, there are the interests of his soul. Life on earth, however good and desirable in itself, is not the final purpose for which man is created; it is only the way and the means to that attainment of truth and that love of goodness in which the full life of the soul consists. It is the soul which is made after the image and likeness of God; it is in the soul that the sovereignty resides in virtue whereof man is commanded to rule the creatures below him and to use all the earth and the ocean for his profit and advantage. "Fill the earth and subdue it; and rule over the fishes of the sea, and the fowls of the air, and all living creatures that move upon the earth" (Gen. 1:28). In this respect all men are equal; there is here no difference between rich and poor, master and servant, ruler and ruled, "for the same is Lord over all" (Rom. 10:12). No man may with impunity outrage that human dignity which God Himself treats with great reverence, nor stand in the way of that higher life which is the preparation of the eternal life of heaven. Nay, more; no man has in this matter power over himself. To consent to any treatment which is calculated to defeat the end and purpose of his being is beyond his right; he cannot give up his soul to servitude, for it is not man's own rights which are here in question, but the rights of God, the most sacred and inviolable of rights.

41. From this follows the obligation of the cessation from work and labor on Sundays and certain holy days. The rest from labor is not to be understood as mere giving way to idleness; much less must it be an occasion for spending money and for vicious indulgence, as many would have it to be; but it should be rest from labor, hallowed by religion. Rest (combined with religious observances) disposes

man to forget for a while the business of his everyday life, to turn his thoughts to things heavenly, and to the worship which he so strictly owes to the eternal Godhead. It is this, above all, which is the reason and motive of Sunday rest; a rest sanctioned by God's great law of the Ancient Covenant—"Remember thou keep holy the Sabbath day" (Exod. 20:8), and taught to the world by His own mysterious "rest" after the creation of man: "He rested on the seventh day from all His work which He had done" (Gen. 2:2).

42. If we turn not to things external and material, the first thing of all to secure is to save unfortunate working people from the cruelty of men of greed, who use human beings as mere instruments for money-making. It is neither just nor human so to grind men down with excessive labor as to stupefy their minds and wear out their bodies. Man's powers, like his general nature, are limited, and beyond these limits he cannot go. His strength is developed and increased by use and exercise, but only on condition of due intermission and proper rest. Daily labor, therefore, should be so regulated as not to be protracted over longer hours than strength admits. How many and how long the intervals of rest should be must depend on the nature of the work, on circumstances of time and place, and on the health and strength of the workman. Those who work in mines and quarries, and extract coal, stone and metals from the bowels of the earth, should have shorter hours in proportion as their labor is more severe and trying to health. Then, again, the season of the year should be taken into account; for not unfrequently a kind of labor is easy at one time which at another is intolerable or exceedingly difficult. Finally, work which is quite suitable for a strong man cannot rightly be required from a woman or a child. And, in regard to children, great care should be taken not to place them in workshops and factories until their bodies and minds are sufficiently developed. For just as very rough weather destroys the buds of spring, so does too early an experience of life's hard toil blight the young promise of a child's

faculties and render any true education impossible. Women, again, are not suited for certain occupations; a woman is by nature fitted for home-work, and it is that which is best adapted at once to preserve her modesty and to promote the good bringing up of children and the well-being of the family. As a general principle it may be laid down that a workman ought to have leisure and rest proportionate to the wear and tear of his strength, for waste of strength must be repaired by cessation from hard work.

In all agreements between masters and workers there is always the condition expressed or understood that there should be allowed proper rest for soul and body. To agree in any other sense would be against what is right and just; for it can never be just or right to require on the one side, or to promise on the other, the giving up of those duties which a man owes to his God and to himself.

43. We now approach a subject of great importance, and one in respect of which, if extremes are to be avoided, right notions are absolutely necessary. Wages, as we are told, are regulated by free consent, and therefore the employer, when he pays what was agreed upon, has done his part and seemingly is not called upon to do anything beyond. The only way, it is said, in which injustice might occur would be if the master refused to pay the whole of the wages, or if the workman should not complete the work undertaken; in such cases the public authority should intervene, to see that each obtains his due, but not under any other circumstances.

44. To this kind of argument a fair-minded man will not easily or entirely assent; it is not complete, for there are important considerations which it leaves out of account altogether. To labor is to exert oneself for the sake of procuring what is necessary for the various purposes of life, and chief of all for self-preservation. "In the sweat of thy face thou shalt eat bread" (Gen. 3:19). Hence, a man's labor necessarily bears two notes or characters. First of all, it is *personal*, inasmuch as the force which acts is bound up with the personality and

is the exclusive property of him who acts, and, further, was given to him for his advantage. Secondly, man's labor is *necessary*; for without the result of labor a man cannot live, and self-preservation is a law of nature, which it is wrong to disobey. Now, were we to consider labor merely in so far as it is personal, doubtless it would be within the workman's right to accept any rate of wages whatsoever; for in the same way as he is free to work or not, so is he free to accept a small wage or even none at all. But our conclusion must be very different if, together with the personal element in a man's work, we consider the fact that work is also necessary for him to live: these two aspects of his work are separable in thought, but not in reality. The preservation of life is the bounden duty of one and all, and to be wanting therein is a crime. It necessarily follows that each one has a natural right to procure what is required in order to live, and the poor can procure that in no other way than by what they can earn through their work.

45. Let the working man and the employer make free agreements, and in particular let them agree freely as to the wages; nevertheless, there underlies a dictate of natural justice more imperious and ancient than any bargain between man and man, namely, that wages ought not to be insufficient to support a frugal and well-behaved wage-earner. If through necessity or fear of a worse evil the workman accept harder conditions because an employer or contractor will afford him no better, he is made the victim of force and injustice. In these and similar questions, however—such as, for example, the hours of labor in different trades, the sanitary precautions to be observed in factories and workshops, etc.—in order to supersede undue interference on the part of the State, especially as circumstances, times, and localities differ so widely, it is advisable that recourse be had to societies or boards such as We shall mention presently, or to some other mode of safeguarding the interests of the wage-earners; the State being appealed to, should circumstances require, for its sanction and protection.

46. If a workman's wages be sufficient to enable him comfortably to support himself, his wife, and his children, he will find it easy, if he be a sensible man, to practice thrift, and he will not fail, by cutting down expenses, to put by some little savings and thus secure a modest source of income. Nature itself would urge him to this. We have seen that this great labor question cannot be solved save by assuming as a principle that private ownership must be held sacred and inviolable. The law, therefore, should favor ownership, and its policy should be to induce as many as possible of the people to become owners.

47. Many excellent results will follow from this; and, first of all, property will certainly become more equitably divided. For the result of civil change and revolution has been to divide cities into two classes separated by a wide chasm. On the one side, there is the party which holds power because it holds wealth; which has in its grasp the whole of labor and trade; which manipulates for its own benefit and its own purposes all the sources of supply, and which is not without influence even in the administration of the commonwealth. On the other side, there is the needy and powerless multitude, sick and sore in spirit and ever ready for disturbance. If working people can be encouraged to look forward to obtaining a share in the land, the consequence will be that the gulf between vast wealth and sheer poverty will be bridged over, and the respective classes will be brought nearer to one another. A further consequence will result in the great abundance of the fruits of the earth. Men always work harder and more readily when they work on that which belongs to them; nay, they learn to love the very soil that yields in response to the labor of their hands, not only food to eat, but an abundance of good things for themselves and those that are dear to them. That such a spirit of willing labor would add to the produce of the earth and to the wealth of the community is self-evident. And a third advantage would spring from this: Men would cling to the country in which they were born, for no one would exchange his country for a foreign land if his own

afforded him the means of living a decent and happy life. These three important benefits, however, can be reckoned on only provided that a man's means be not drained and exhausted by excessive taxation. The right to possess private property is derived from nature, not from man; and the State has the right to control its use in the interests of the public good alone, but by no means to absorb it altogether. The State would therefore be unjust and cruel if under the name of taxation it were to deprive the private owner of more than is fair.

48. In the last place, employers and workmen may of themselves effect much, in the matter We are treating, by means of such associations and organizations as afford opportune aid to those who are in distress, and which draw the two classes more closely together. Among these may be enumerated societies for mutual help; various benevolent foundations established by private persons to provide for the workman, and for his widow or his orphans, in case of sudden calamity, in sickness, and in the event of death; and institutions for the welfare of boys and girls, young people, and those more advanced in years.

49. The most important of all are workingmen's unions, for these virtually include all the rest. History attests what excellent results were brought about by the artificers' guilds of olden times. They were the means of affording not only many advantages to the workmen, but in no small degree of promoting the advancement of art, as numerous monuments remain to bear witness. Such unions should be suited to the requirements of this our age—an age of wider education, of different habits, and of far more numerous requirements in daily life. It is gratifying to know that there are actually in existence not a few associations of this nature, consisting either of workmen alone, or of workmen and employers together, but it is greatly to be desired that they should become more numerous and more efficient. We have spoken of them more than once, yet it will be well to explain here how notably they are needed, to show that they exist of their

own right, and what should be their organization and their mode of action.

50. The consciousness of his own weakness urges man to call in aid from without. We read in the pages of Holy Writ: "It is better that two should be together than one; for they have the advantage of their society. If one fall he shall be supported by the other. Woe to him that is alone, for when he falleth he hath none to lift him up" (Eccl. 4:9–10). And further: "A brother that is helped by his brother is like a strong city" (Prov. 18:19). It is this natural impulse which binds men together in civil society; and it is likewise this which leads them to join together in associations which are, it is true, lesser and not independent societies, but, nevertheless, real societies.

51. These lesser societies and the larger society differ in many respects, because their immediate purpose and aim are different. Civil society exists for the common good, and hence is concerned with the interests of all in general, albeit with individual interests also in their due place and degree. It is therefore called a public society, because by its agency, as St. Thomas of Aquinas says, "Men establish relations in common with one another in the setting up of a commonwealth."[9] But societies which are formed in the bosom of the commonwealth are styled *private,* and rightly so, since their immediate purpose is the private advantage of the associates. "Now, a private society," says St. Thomas again, "is one which is formed for the purpose of carrying out private objects; as when two or three enter into partnership with the view of trading in common."[10] Private societies, then, although they exist within the body politic, and are severally part of the commonwealth, cannot nevertheless be absolutely, and as such, prohibited by public authority. For to enter into a "society" of this kind is the natural right of man; and the State has for its office to protect natural

9. *Contra impugnantes Dei cultum et religionem,* II, 8.
10. Ibid.

rights, not to destroy them; and, if it forbid its citizens to form associations, it contradicts the very principle of its own existence, for both they and it exist in virtue of the like principle, namely, the natural tendency of man to dwell in society.

52. There are occasions, doubtless, when it is fitting that the law should intervene to prevent certain associations, as when men join together for purposes which are evidently bad, unlawful, or dangerous to the State. In such cases, public authority may justly forbid the formation of such associations and may dissolve them if they already exist. But every precaution should be taken not to violate the rights of individuals and not to impose unreasonable regulations under pretense of public benefit. For laws only bind when they are in accordance with right reason, and, hence, with the eternal law of God.[11]

53. And here we are reminded of the confraternities, societies, and religious orders which have arisen by the Church's authority and the piety of Christian men. The annals of every nation down to our own days bear witness to what they have accomplished for the human race. It is indisputable that on grounds of reason alone such associations, being perfectly blameless in their objects, possess the sanction of the law of nature. In their religious aspect they claim rightly to be responsible to the Church alone. The rulers of the State accordingly have no rights over them, nor can they claim any share in their control; on the contrary, it is the duty of the State to respect and cherish them, and, if need be, to defend them from attack. It is notorious that a very different course has been followed, more especially in our own times. In many places the State authorities have laid violent hands on these communities, and committed manifold injustice against them;

11. "Human law is law only by virtue of its accordance with right reason; and thus it is manifest that it flows from the eternal law. And in so far as it deviates from right reason it is called an unjust law; in such case it is no law at all, but rather a species of violence." *Summa theologiae* I-II, q. 93, a. 3, ad 2.

it has placed them under control of the civil law, taken away their rights as corporate bodies, and despoiled them of their property, in such property the Church had her rights, each member of the body had his or her rights, and there were also the rights of those who had founded or endowed these communities for a definite purpose, and, furthermore, of those for whose benefit and assistance they had their being. Therefore, We cannot refrain from complaining of such spoliation as unjust and fraught with evil results; and with all the more reason do We complain because, at the very time when the law proclaims that association is free to all, We see that Catholic societies, however peaceful and useful, are hampered in every way, whereas the utmost liberty is conceded to individuals whose purposes are at once hurtful to religion and dangerous to the commonwealth.

54. Associations of every kind, and especially those of working men, are now far more common than heretofore. As regards many of these there is no need at present to inquire whence they spring, what are their objects, or what the means they imply. Now, there is a good deal of evidence in favor of the opinion that many of these societies are in the hands of secret leaders and are managed on principles ill-according with Christianity and the public well-being; and that they do their utmost to get within their grasp the whole field of labor, and force working men either to join them or to starve. Under these circumstances, Christian working men must do one of two things: either join associations in which their religion will be exposed to peril or form associations among themselves and unite their forces so as to shake off courageously the yoke of so unrighteous and intolerable an oppression. No one who does not wish to expose man's chief good to extreme risk will for a moment hesitate to say that the second alternative should by all means be adopted.

55. Those Catholics are worthy of all praise—and they are not a few—who, understanding what the times require, have striven, by various undertakings and endeavors, to better the condition of the

working class by rightful means. They have taken up the cause of the working man, and have spared no efforts to better the condition both of families and individuals; to infuse a spirit of equity into the mutual relations of employers and employed; to keep before the eyes of both classes the precepts of duty and the laws of the Gospel—that Gospel which, by inculcating self-restraint, keeps men within the bounds of moderation, and tends to establish harmony among the divergent interests and the various classes which compose the body politic. It is with such ends in view that we see men of eminence, meeting together for discussion, for the promotion of concerted action, and for practical work. Others, again, strive to unite working men of various grades into associations, help them with their advice and means, and enable them to obtain fitting and profitable employment. The bishops, on their part, bestow their ready good will and support; and with their approval and guidance many members of the clergy, both secular and regular, labor assiduously in behalf of the spiritual interest of the members of such associations. And there are not wanting Catholics blessed with affluence, who have, as it were, cast in their lot with the wage-earners, and who have spent large sums in founding and widely spreading benefit and insurance societies, by means of which the working man may without difficulty acquire through his labor not only many present advantages, but also the certainty of honorable support in days to come. How greatly such manifold and earnest activity has benefited the community at large is too well known to require Us to dwell upon it. We find therein grounds for most cheering hope in the future, provided always that the associations We have described continue to grow and spread, and are well and wisely administered. The State should watch over these societies of citizens banded together in accordance with their rights, but it should not thrust itself into their peculiar concerns and their organization, for things move and live by the spirit inspiring them and may be killed by the rough grasp of a hand from without.

56. In order that an association may be carried on with unity of purpose and harmony of action, its administration and government should be firm and wise. All such societies, being free to exist, have the further right to adopt such rules and organization as may best conduce to the attainment of their respective objects. We do not judge it possible to enter into minute particulars touching the subject of organization; this must depend on national character, on practice and experience, on the nature and aim of the work to be done, on the scope of the various trades and employments, and on other circumstances of fact and of time—all of which should be carefully considered.

57. To sum up, then, We may lay it down as a general and lasting law that working men's associations should be so organized and governed as to furnish the best and most suitable means for attaining what is aimed at, that is to say, for helping each individual member to better his condition to the utmost in body, soul, and property. It is clear that they must pay special and chief attention to the duties of religion and morality, and that social betterment should have this chiefly in view; otherwise they would lose wholly their special character, and end by becoming little better than those societies which take no account whatever of religion. What advantage can it be to a working man to obtain by means of a society material well-being, if he endangers his soul for lack of spiritual food? "What doth it profit a man, if he gain the whole world and suffer the loss of his soul?" (Matt. 16:26). This, as our Lord teaches, is the mark or character that distinguishes the Christian from the heathen. "After all these things do the heathen seek.... Seek ye first the Kingdom of God and His justice: and all these things shall be added unto you" (Matt. 6:32–33). Let our associations, then, look first and before all things to God; let religious instruction have therein the foremost place, each one being carefully taught what is his duty to God, what he has to believe, what to hope for, and how he is to work out his salvation; and let all be warned and strengthened with special care against wrong principles and false

teaching. Let the working man be urged and led to the worship of God, to the earnest practice of religion, and, among other things, to the keeping holy of Sundays and holy days. Let him learn to reverence and love holy Church, the common Mother of us all; and hence to obey the precepts of the Church, and to frequent the sacraments, since they are the means ordained by God for obtaining forgiveness of sin and for leading a holy life.

58. The foundations of the organization being thus laid in religion, We next proceed to make clear the relations of the members one to another, in order that they may live together in concord and go forward prosperously and with good results. The offices and charges of the society should be apportioned for the good of the society itself, and in such mode that difference in degree or standing should not interfere with unanimity and good-will. It is most important that office bearers be appointed with due prudence and discretion, and each one's charge carefully mapped out, in order that no members may suffer harm. The common funds must be administered with strict honesty, in such a way that a member may receive assistance in proportion to his necessities. The rights and duties of the employers, as compared with the rights and duties of the employed, ought to be the subject of careful consideration. Should it happen that either a master or a workman believes himself injured, nothing would be more desirable than that a committee should be appointed, composed of reliable and capable members of the association, whose duty would be, conformably with the rules of the association, to settle the dispute. Among the several purposes of a society, one should be to try to arrange for a continuous supply of work at all times and seasons; as well as to create a fund out of which the members may be effectually helped in their needs, not only in the cases of accident, but also in sickness, old age, and distress.

59. Such rules and regulations, if willingly obeyed by all, will sufficiently ensure the well-being of the less well-to-do; whilst such

mutual associations among Catholics are certain to be productive in no small degree of prosperity to the State. It is not rash to conjecture the future from the past. Age gives way to age, but the events of one century are wonderfully like those of another, for they are directed by the providence of God, who overrules the course of history in accordance with His purposes in creating the race of man. We are told that it was cast as a reproach on the Christians in the early ages of the Church that the greater number among them had to live by begging or by labor. Yet, destitute though they were of wealth and influence, they ended by winning over to their side the favor of the rich and the good-will of the powerful. They showed themselves industrious, hard-working, assiduous, and peaceful, ruled by justice, and, above all, bound together in brotherly love. In presence of such mode of life and such example, prejudice gave way, the tongue of malevolence was silenced, and the lying legends of ancient superstition little by little yielded to Christian truth.

60. At the time being, the condition of the working classes is the pressing question of the hour, and nothing can be of higher interest to all classes of the State than that it should be rightly and reasonably settled. But it will be easy for Christian working men to solve it aright if they will form associations, choose wise guides, and follow on the path which with so much advantage to themselves and the common weal was trodden by their fathers before them. Prejudice, it is true, is mighty, and so is the greed of money; but if the sense of what is just and rightful be not deliberately stifled, their fellow citizens are sure to be won over to a kindly feeling towards men whom they see to be in earnest as regards their work and who prefer so unmistakably right dealing to mere lucre, and the sacredness of duty to every other consideration.

61. And further great advantage would result from the state of things We are describing; there would exist so much more ground for hope, and likelihood, even, of recalling to a sense of their duty

those working men who have either given up their faith altogether, or whose lives are at variance with its precepts. Such men feel in most cases that they have been fooled by empty promises and deceived by false pretexts. They cannot but perceive that their grasping employers too often treat them with great inhumanity and hardly care for them outside the profit their labor brings; and if they belong to any union, it is probably one in which there exists, instead of charity and love, that internal strife which ever accompanies poverty when unresigned and unsustained by religion. Broken in spirit and worn down in body, how many of them would gladly free themselves from such galling bondage! But human respect, or the dread of starvation, makes them tremble to take the step. To such as these, Catholic associations are of incalculable service, by helping them out of their difficulties, inviting them to companionship and receiving the returning wanderers to a haven where they may securely find repose.

62. We have now laid before you, Venerable Brethren, both who are the persons and what are the means whereby this most arduous question must be solved. Everyone should put his hand to the work which falls to his share, and that at once and straightway, lest the evil which is already so great become through delay absolutely beyond remedy. Those who rule the commonwealths should avail themselves of the laws and institutions of the country; masters and wealthy owners must be mindful of their duty; the working class, whose interests are at stake, should make every lawful and proper effort; and since religion alone, as We said at the beginning, can avail to destroy the evil at its root, all men should rest persuaded that main thing needful is to re-establish Christian morals, apart from which all the plans and devices of the wisest will prove of little avail.

63. In regard to the Church, her cooperation will never be found lacking, be the time or the occasion what it may; and she will intervene with all the greater effect in proportion as her liberty of action is the more unfettered. Let this be carefully taken to heart by those

whose office it is to safeguard the public welfare. Every minister of holy religion must bring to the struggle the full energy of his mind and all his power of endurance. Moved by your authority, Venerable Brethren, and quickened by your example, they should never cease to urge upon men of every class, upon the high-placed as well as the lowly, the Gospel doctrines of Christian life; by every means in their power, they must strive to secure the good of the people; and above all must earnestly cherish in themselves and try to arouse in others, charity, the mistress and the queen of virtues. For the happy results we all long for must be chiefly brought about by the plenteous outpouring of charity; of that true Christian charity which is the fulfilling of the whole Gospel law, which is always ready to sacrifice itself for others' sake, and is man's surest antidote against worldly pride and immoderate love of self; that charity whose office is described and whose Godlike features are outlined by the Apostle St. Paul in these words: "Charity is patient, is kind...seeketh not her own...suffereth all things...endureth all things" (1 Cor. 13:4–7).

64. On each of you, Venerable Brethren, and on your clergy and people, as an earnest of God's mercy and a mark of Our affection, we lovingly in the Lord bestow the Apostolic Benediction.

Given at St. Peter's, in Rome, the fifteenth day of May, 1891, the fourteenth year of Our Pontificate.

LEO PP. XIII

ENCYCLICAL LETTER

AU MILIEU DES SOLLICITUDES

OF THE SUPREME PONTIFF

LEO XIII

TO OUR VENERABLE BROTHERS
THE ARCHBISHOPS, BISHOPS, CLERGY
AND FAITHFUL OF FRANCE
ON THE CHURCH AND STATE IN FRANCE

1. Amid the cares of the universal Church We have many times, in the course of Our Pontificate, been pleased to testify Our affection for France and her noble people, and in one of Our Encyclicals, still within the memory of all, We endeavored solemnly to express the innermost feelings of Our soul on this subject. It is precisely this affection that has caused Us to watch with deep interest and then to revolve in Our mind the succession of events, sometimes sad, sometimes consoling, which, of late years, has taken place in your midst.

2. Again, at present, when contemplating the depths of the vast conspiracy that certain men have formed for the annihilation of Christianity in France and the animosity with which they pursue the realization of their design, trampling underfoot the most elementary notions of liberty and justice for the sentiment of the greater part of the nation, and of respect for the inalienable rights of the Catholic Church, how can We but be stricken with deepest grief? And when We behold, one after another, the dire consequences of these sinful

attacks which conspire to ruin morals, religion, and even political interests, wisely understood, how express the bitterness that overwhelms Us and the apprehensions that beset Us?

3. On the other hand, We feel greatly consoled when We see this same French people increasing its zeal and affection for the Holy See in proportion as that See is abandoned—We should rather say warred with upon earth. Moved by deeply religious and patriotic sentiments, representatives of all the social classes have repeatedly come to Us from France, happy to aid the Church in her incessant needs and eager to ask us for light and counsel, so as to be sure that amid present tribulations they would in nowise deviate from the teachings of the Head of the Faithful. And We, in Our turn, either in writing or by word of mouth, have openly told Our sons what they had a right to demand of their Father, and, far from discouraging them, we have strongly exhorted them to increase their love and efforts in defense of the Catholic faith and likewise of their native land: two duties of paramount importance and from which, in this life, no man can exempt himself.

4. Now We deem it opportune, nay, even necessary, once again to raise Our voice entreating still more earnestly, We shall not say Catholics only, but all upright and intelligent Frenchmen, utterly to disregard all germs of political strife in order to devote their efforts solely to the pacification of their country. All understand the value of this pacification; all continue to desire it more and more. And We who crave it more than anyone, since We represent on earth the God of peace, urge by these present Letters all righteous souls, all generous hearts, to assist Us in making it stable and fruitful.

5. First of all, let us take as a starting-point a well-known truth admitted by all men of good sense and loudly proclaimed by the history of all peoples; namely, that religion, and religion only, can create the social bond; that it alone maintains the peace of a nation on a solid foundation. When different families, without giving up the

rights and duties of domestic society, unite under the inspiration of nature, in order to constitute themselves members of another larger family circle called civil society, their object is not only to find therein the means of providing for their material welfare, but, above all, to draw thence the boon of moral improvement. Otherwise society would rise but little above the level of an aggregation of beings devoid of reason, and whose whole life would consist in the satisfaction of sensual instincts. Moreover, without this moral improvement it would be difficult to demonstrate that civil society was an advantage rather than a detriment to man, as man.

6. Now, morality, in man, by the mere fact that it should establish harmony among so many dissimilar rights and duties, since it enters as an element into every human act, necessarily supposes God, and with God, religion, that sacred bond whose privilege is to unite, anteriorly to all other bonds, man to God. Indeed, the idea of morality signifies, above all, an order of dependence in regard to truth which is the light of the mind; in regard to good which is the object of the will; and without truth and good there is no morality worthy of the name. And what is the principal and essential truth, that from which all truth is derived? It is God. What, therefore, is the supreme good from which all other good proceeds? God. Finally, who is the creator and guardian of our reason, our will, our whole being, as well as the end of our life? God; always God. Since, therefore, religion is the interior and exterior expression of the dependence which, in justice, we owe to God, there follows a grave obligation. All citizens are bound to unite in maintaining in the nation true religious sentiment, and to defend it in case of need, if ever, despite the protestations of nature and of history, an atheistical school should set about banishing God from society, thereby surely annihilating the moral sense even in the depths of the human conscience. Among men who have not lost all notion of integrity there can exist no difference of opinion on this point.

7. In French Catholics, the religious sentiment should be even deeper and more universal because they have the happiness of belonging to the true religion. If, indeed, religious beliefs were, always and everywhere, given as a basis of the morality of human actions and the existence of all well-ordained society, it is evident that the Catholic religion, by the mere fact that it is the true Church of Jesus Christ, possesses, more than any other, the efficacy required for the regulation of life in society and in the individual. Would you have a brilliant example of this? France herself furnishes the same.... In proportion as France progressed in the Christian faith, she was seen to rise gradually to the moral greatness which she attained as a political and military power. To the natural generosity of her heart Christian charity came and added an abundant source of new energy; her wonderful activity received still greater impetus from contact with the light that guides and is the pledge of constancy, the Christian faith, which, by the hand of France, traced such glorious pages in the history of mankind. And even today does not her faith continue to add new glories to those of the past? We behold France, inexhaustible in her genius and resources, multiplying works of charity at home; we admire her enterprises in foreign lands where, by means of her gold and the labors of her missionaries who work even at the price of their blood, she simultaneously propagates her own renown and the benefits of the Catholic religion. No Frenchman, whatever his convictions in other respects, would dare to renounce glory such as this, for to do so would be to deny his native land.

8. Now the history of a nation reveals in an incontestable way the generating and preserving element of its moral greatness, and should this element ever be missing, neither a superabundance of gold nor even force of arms could save it from moral decadence and perhaps death. Who then but understands that for all Frenchmen professing the Catholic religion the great anxiety should be to insure its preservation, and that with all the more devotedness since in their midst

the sects are making Christianity an object of implacable hostility. Therefore, on this ground, they can afford neither indolence of action nor party divisions; the one would bespeak cowardice unworthy of a Christian, the other would bring about disastrous weakness.

9. And now, before going any further, We must indicate a craftily circulated calumny making most odious imputations against Catholics, and even against the Holy See itself. It is maintained that that vigor of action inculcated in Catholics for the defense of their faith has for a secret motive much less the safeguarding of their religious interests than the ambition of securing to the Church political domination over the State. Truly this is the revival of a very ancient calumny, as its invention belongs to the first enemies of Christianity. Was it not first of all formulated against the adorable person of the Redeemer? Yes, when He illuminated souls by His preaching and alleviated the corporal or spiritual sufferings of the unfortunate with the treasures of His divine bounty, he was accused of having political ends in view. "We have found this man perverting our nation, and forbidding to give tribute to Caesar, and saying that he is Christ, the king" (Luke 23:2). "If thou release this man, thou are not Caesar's friend. For whomsoever maketh himself a king, speaketh against Caesar.... We have no king but Caesar" (John 19:12–15).

10. It was these threatening calumnies which drew from Pilate the sentence of death against Him whom he had repeatedly declared innocent. And the authors of these lies, or of others of equal strength, omitted nothing that would aid their emissaries in propagating them far and wide; and thus did St. Justin, martyr, rebuke the Jews of his time: "Far from repenting when you had learned of His resurrection from the dead, you sent to Jerusalem shrewdly chosen men to announce that a heresy and an impious sect had been started by a certain seducer called Jesus of Galilee."[1]

1. *Dialog. cum Tryphone.*

11. In so audaciously defaming Christianity its enemies know well what they did; their plan was to raise against its propagation a formidable adversary, the Roman Empire. The calumny made headway; and in their credulity the pagans called the first Christians "useless creatures, dangerous citizens, factionists, enemies of the Empire and the Emperors. "[2] But in vain did the apologists of Christianity by their writings, and Christians by their splendid conduct, endeavor to demonstrate the absurdity and criminality of these qualifications. They were not heeded. Their very name was equivalent to a declaration of war; and Christians, by the mere fact of their being such, and for no other reason, were forced to choose between apostasy and martyrdom, being allowed no alternative. During the following centuries, the same grievances and the same severity prevailed to a greater or less extent, whenever governments were unreasonably jealous of their power and maliciously disposed against the Church. They never failed to call public attention to the pretended encroachment of the Church upon the State in order to furnish the State with some apparent right to violently attack the Catholic religion.

12. We have expressly recalled some features of the past that Catholics might not be dismayed by the present. Substantially, the struggle is ever the same: Jesus Christ is always exposed to the contradictions of the world, and the same means are always used by modern enemies of Christianity, means old in principle and scarcely modified in form; but the same means of defense are also clearly indicated to Christians of the present day by our apologists, doctors and martyrs. What they have done it is incumbent upon us to do in our turn. Let us place above all else the glory of God and of His Church; let us work for her with an assiduity at once constant and effective, and leave all care of success to Jesus Christ, who tells us: "In the world you shall have distress: but have confidence, I have overcome the world" (John 16:33).

2. Tertullian, *In Apolog.*; Minutius Felix, *In Octavio.*

13. To attain this, We have already remarked that a great union is necessary, and if it is to be realized, it is indispensable that all preoccupation capable of diminishing its strength and efficacy must be abandoned. Here We intend alluding principally to the political differences among the French in regard to the actual republic—a question We would treat with the clearness which the gravity of the subject demands, beginning with the principles and descending thence to practical results.

14. Various political governments have succeeded one another in France during the last century, each having its own distinctive form: the Empire, the Monarchy, and the Republic. By giving one's self up to abstractions, one could at length conclude which is the best of these forms, considered in themselves; and in all truth it may be affirmed that each of them is good, provided it lead straight to its end—that is to say, to the common good for which social authority is constituted; and finally, it may be added that, from a relative point of view, such and such a form of government may be preferable because of being better adapted to the character and customs of such or such a nation. In this order of speculative ideas, Catholics, like all other citizens, are free to prefer one form of government to another precisely because no one of these social forms is, in itself, opposed to the principles of sound reason nor to the maxims of Christian doctrine. What amply justifies the wisdom of the Church is that in her relations with political powers she makes abstraction of the forms which differentiate them and treats with them concerning the great religious interests of nations, knowing that hers is the duty to undertake their tutelage above all other interests. Our preceding Encyclicals have already exposed these principles, but it was nevertheless necessary to recall them for the development of the subject which occupies us today.

15. In descending from the domain of abstractions to that of facts, we must beware of denying the principles just established: they remain fixed. However, becoming incarnated in facts, they are clothed

with a contingent character, determined by the center in which their application is produced. Otherwise said, if every political form is good by itself and may be applied to the government of nations, the fact still remains that political power is not found in all nations under the same form; each has its own. This form springs from a combination of historical or national, though always human, circumstances which, in a nation, give rise to its traditional and even fundamental laws, and by these is determined the particular form of government, the basis of transmission of supreme power.

16. It is useless to recall that all individuals are bound to accept these governments and not to attempt their overthrow or a change in their form. Hence it is that the Church, the guardian of the truest and highest idea of political sovereignty, since she has derived it from God, has always condemned men who rebelled against legitimate authority and disapproved their doctrines. And that too at the very time when the custodians of power used it against her, thereby depriving themselves of the strongest support given their authority and of efficacious means of obtaining from the people obedience to their laws. And apropos of this subject, We cannot lay too great stress upon the precepts given to the first Christians by the Prince of the Apostles in the midst of persecutions: "Honor all men; love the brotherhood; fear God; honor the king" (1 Pet. 2:17); and those of St. Paul: "I desire, therefore, first of all, that supplications, prayers, intercessions, and thanksgivings be made for all men: For kings and for all who are in high station, that we may lead a quiet and peaceable life, in all piety and chastity. For this is good and acceptable in the sight of God, our Savior" (1 Tim. 2:1–3).

17. However, here it must be carefully observed that whatever be the form of civil power in a nation, it cannot be considered so definitive as to have the right to remain immutable, even though such were the intention of those who, in the beginning, determined it.... Only the Church of Jesus Christ has been able to preserve, and surely will

preserve unto the consummation of time, her form of government. Founded by Him who was, who is, and who will be forever (Heb. 13:8), she has received from Him, since her very origin, all that she requires for the pursuing of her divine mission across the changeable ocean of human affairs. And, far from wishing to transform her essential constitution, she has not the power even to relinquish the conditions of true liberty and sovereign independence with which Providence has endowed her in the general interest of souls.... But, in regard to purely human societies, it is an oft-repeated historical fact that time, that great transformer of all things here below, operates great changes in their political institutions. On some occasions it limits itself to modifying something in the form of the established government; or, again, it will go so far as to substitute other forms for the primitive ones—forms totally different, even as regards the mode of transmitting sovereign power.

18. And how are these political changes of which We speak produced? They sometimes follow in the wake of violent crises, too often of a bloody character, in the midst of which pre-existing governments totally disappear; then anarchy holds sway, and soon public order is shaken to its very foundations and finally overthrown. From that time onward, a social need obtrudes itself upon the nation; it must provide for itself without delay. Is it not its privilege or, better still, its duty to defend itself against a state of affairs troubling it so deeply, and to re-establish public peace in the tranquility of order? Now, this social need justifies the creation and the existence of new governments, whatever form they take; since, in the hypothesis wherein we reason, these new governments are a requisite to public order, all public order being impossible without a government. Thence it follows that, in similar junctures, all the novelty is limited to the political form of civil power, or to its mode of transmission; it in no wise affects the power considered in itself. This continues to be immutable and worthy of respect, as, considered in its nature, it is

constituted to provide for the common good, the supreme end which gives human society its origin. To put it otherwise, in all hypotheses, civil power, considered as such, is from God, always from God: "For there is no power but from God" (Rom. 13.1).

19. Consequently, when new governments representing this immutable power are constituted, their acceptance is not only permissible but even obligatory, being imposed by the need of the social good which has made and which upholds them. This is all the more imperative because an insurrection stirs up hatred among citizens, provokes civil war, and may throw a nation into chaos and anarchy, and this great duty of respect and dependence will endure as long as the exigencies of the common good shall demand it, since this good is, after God, the first and last law in society.

20. Thus, the wisdom of the Church explains itself in the maintenance of her relations with the numerous governments which have succeeded one another in France in less than a century, each change causing violent shocks. Such a line of conduct would be the surest and most salutary for all Frenchmen in their civil relations with the republic, which is the actual government of their nation. Far be it from them to encourage the political dissensions which divide them; all their efforts should be combined to preserve and elevate the moral greatness of their native land.

21. But a difficulty presents itself. "This Republic," it is said, "is animated by such anti-Christian sentiments that honest men, Catholics particularly, could not conscientiously accept it." This, more than anything else, has given rise to dissensions, and in fact aggravated them.... These regrettable differences would have been avoided if the very considerable distinction between constituted power and legislation had been carefully kept in view. In so much does legislation differ from political power and its form, that under a system of government most excellent in form legislation could be detestable; while quite the opposite under a regime most imperfect in form, might be found excellent

legislation. It is an easy task to prove this truth, history in hand, but what would be the use? All are convinced of it. And who, better than the Church, is in position to know it—she who has striven to maintain habitual relations with all political governments? Assuredly she, better than any other power, could tell the consolation or sorrow occasioned her by the laws of the various governments by which nations have been ruled from the Roman Empire down to the present.

22. If the distinction just established has its major importance, it is likewise manifestly reasonable: Legislation is the work of men invested with power, and who, in fact, govern the nation; therefore, it follows that, practically, the quality of the laws depends more upon the quality of these men than upon the power. The laws will be good or bad accordingly as the minds of the legislators are imbued with good or bad principles, and as they allow themselves to be guided by political prudence or by passion.

23. That several years ago different important acts of legislation in France proceeded from a tendency hostile to religion, and therefore to the interests of the nation, is admitted by all, and unfortunately confirmed by the evidence of facts. We Ourselves, in obedience to a sacred duty, made earnest appeals to him who was then at the head of the Republic, but these tendencies continued to exist; the evil grew, and it was not surprising that the members of the French Episcopate chosen by the Holy Spirit to rule over their respective illustrious churches should even quite recently have considered it an obligation publicly to express their grief concerning the condition of affairs in France in regard to the Catholic religion. Poor France! God alone can measure the abyss of evil into which she will sink if this legislation, instead of improving, will stubbornly continue in a course which must end in plucking from the minds and hearts of Frenchmen the religion which has made them so great.

24. And here is precisely the ground on which, political dissensions aside, upright men should unite as one to combat, by all lawful

and honest means, these progressive abuses of legislation. The respect due to constituted power cannot prohibit this: Unlimited respect and obedience cannot be yielded to all legislative measures, of no matter what kind, enacted by this same power. Let it not be forgotten that law is a precept ordained according to reason and promulgated for the good of the community by those who, for this end, have been entrusted with power. Accordingly, such points in legislation as are hostile to religion and to God should never be approved; to the contrary, it is a duty to disapprove them. It was this that St. Augustine, the great Bishop of Hippo, brought out so strongly in his eloquent reasoning: "Sometimes the powerful ones of earth are good and fear God; at other times they fear Him not. Julian was an emperor unfaithful to God, an apostate, a pervert, an idolator. Christian soldiers served this faithless emperor, but as soon as there was question of the cause of Jesus Christ they recognized only Him who was in heaven. Julian commanded them to honor idols and offer them incense, but they put God above the prince. However, when he made them form into ranks and march against a hostile nation, they obeyed instantly. They distinguished the eternal from the temporal master and still in view of the eternal Master they submitted to such a temporal master."[3]

25. We know that, by a lamentable abuse of his reason, and still more so of his will, the atheist denies these principles. But, in a word, atheism is so monstrous an error that it could never, be it said to the honor of humanity, annihilate in it the consciousness of God's claims and substitute them with idolatry of the State.

26. The principles which should regulate our conduct towards God and towards human governments being thus defined, no unprejudiced man can censure French Catholics if, sparing themselves neither fatigue nor sacrifice, they labor to preserve a condition essential to their country's salvation, one which embodies so many

3. *Enarrat. in Psalm* 124, n. 7, fin.

glorious traditions registered by history, and which every Frenchmen is in duty bound not to forget.

27. Before closing Our Letter, We wish to touch upon two points bearing an affinity to each other and which, because so closely connected with religious interests, have stirred up some division among Catholics. One of them is the Concordat, which for so many years has facilitated in France the harmony between the government of the Church and that of the State. On the observance of this solemn, bilateral compact, always faithfully kept by the Holy See, the enemies of the Catholic religion do not themselves agree. The more violent among them desire its abolition, that the State may be entirely free to molest the Church of Jesus Christ. On the contrary, others, being more astute, wish, or rather claim to wish, the preservation of the Concordat: not because they agree that the State should fulfil toward the Church the subscribed engagements, but solely that the State may be benefited by the concessions made by the Church; as if one could, at will, separate engagements entered into from concessions obtained, when both of these things form a substantial part of one whole. For them the Concordat would amount to no more than a chain forged to fetter the liberty of the Church, that holy liberty to which she has a divine and inalienable right. Of these two opinions which will prevail? We know not. We desired to recall them only to recommend Catholics not to provoke a secession by interfering in a matter with which it is the business of the Holy See to deal.

28. We shall not hold to the same language on another point, concerning the principle of the separation of the State and Church, which is equivalent to the separation of human legislation from Christian and divine legislation. We do not care to interrupt Ourselves here in order to demonstrate the absurdity of such a separation; each one will understand for himself. As soon as the State refuses to give to God what belongs to God, by a necessary consequence it refuses to give to citizens that to which, as men, they have

a right; as, whether agreeable or not to accept, it cannot be denied that man's rights spring from his duty toward God. Whence if follows that the State, by missing in this connection the principal object of its institution, finally becomes false to itself by denying that which is the reason of its own existence. These superior truths are so clearly proclaimed by the voice of even natural reason, that they force themselves upon all who are not blinded by the violence of passion; therefore, Catholics cannot be too careful in defending themselves against such a separation. In fact, to wish that the State would separate itself from the Church would be to wish, by a logical sequence, that the Church be reduced to the liberty of living according to the law common to all citizens.... It is true that in certain countries this state of affairs exists. It is a condition which, if it have numerous and serious inconveniences, also offers some advantages—above all when, by a fortunate inconsistency, the legislator is inspired by Christian principles—and, though these advantages cannot justify the false principle of separation nor authorize its defense, they nevertheless render worthy of toleration a situation which, practically, might be worse.

29. But in France, a nation Catholic in her traditions and by the present faith of the great majority of her sons, the Church should not be placed in the precarious position to which she must submit among other peoples; and the better that Catholics understand the aim of the enemies who desire this separation, the less will they favor it. To these enemies, and they say it clearly enough, this separation means that political legislation be entirely independent of religious legislation; nay, more, that Power be absolutely indifferent to the interests of Christian society, that is to say, of the Church; in fact, that it deny her very existence. But they make a reservation formulated thus: As soon as the Church, utilizing the resources which common law accords to the least among Frenchmen, will, by redoubling her native activity, cause her work to prosper, then the State intervening, can and will put French Catholics outside the common law itself. In

a word: the ideal of these men would be a return to paganism: the State would recognize the Church only when it would be pleased to persecute her.

30. We have explained, Venerable Brethren, in an abridged though clear way, some if not all the points upon which French Catholics and all intelligent men should be at peace and unity, so as to remedy, in so far as still remains possible, the evils with which France is afflicted, and to elevate its moral greatness. The points in question are: Religion and country, political power and legislation, the conduct to be observed in regard to this power and legislation, the Concordat, the separation of Church and State.... We cherish the hope and the confidence that the elucidation of these points will dissipate the prejudices of many honest, well-meaning men, facilitate the pacification of minds, and thereby cement the union of all Catholics for the sustaining of the great cause of Christ, who loves the Franks.

31. How consoling to Our heart to encourage you all in this way and to behold you all responding with docility to Our appeal! You, Venerable Brethren, by your authority and with the enlightened zeal for Church and Fatherland which so distinguishes you, will give able support to this peace-making work. We delight in the hope that those who are in power will appreciate Our words, which aim at the happiness and prosperity of France.

32. Meanwhile, as a pledge of Our paternal affection, we bestow upon you, Venerable Brethren, upon your clergy and also upon all the Catholics of France, the apostolic blessing.

Given at Rome, the sixteenth day of February, 1892, in the fourteenth year of Our Pontificate.

LEO PP. XIII

ENCYCLICAL LETTER

LONGINQUA

OF THE SUPREME PONTIFF

LEO XIII

TO THE ARCHBISHOPS AND BISHOPS OF THE UNITED STATES ON CATHOLICISM IN THE UNITED STATES

1. We traverse in spirit and thought the wide expanse of ocean; and although We have at other times addressed you in writing—chiefly when We directed Encyclical Letters to the bishops of the Catholic world—yet have We now resolved to speak to you separately, trusting that We shall be, God willing, of some assistance to the Catholic cause amongst you. To this We apply Ourselves with the utmost zeal and care; because We highly esteem and love exceedingly the young and vigorous American nation, in which We plainly discern latent forces for the advancement alike of civilization and of Christianity.

2. Not long ago, when your whole nation, as was fitting, celebrated, with grateful recollection and every manifestation of joy, the completion of the fourth century since the discovery of America, We, too, commemorated together with you that most auspicious event, sharing in your rejoicings with equal goodwill. Nor were We on that occasion content with offering prayers at a distance for your welfare and greatness. It was Our wish to be in some manner present with you in your festivities. Hence, We cheerfully sent one who should

represent Our person. Not without good reason did We take part in your celebration. For when America was, as yet, but a newborn babe, uttering in its cradle its first feeble cries, the Church took it to her bosom and motherly embrace. Columbus, as We have elsewhere expressly shown, sought, as the primary fruit of his voyages and labors, to open a pathway for the Christian faith into new lands and new seas. Keeping this thought constantly in view, his first solicitude, wherever he disembarked, was to plant upon the shore the sacred emblem of the cross. Wherefore, like as the Ark of Noe, surmounting the overflowing waters, bore the seed of Israel together with the remnants of the human race, even thus did the barks launched by Columbus upon the ocean carry into regions beyond the seas as well the germs of mighty States as the principles of the Catholic religion.

3. This is not the place to give a detailed account of what thereupon ensued. Very rapidly did the light of the Gospel shine upon the savage tribes discovered by the Ligurian. For it is sufficiently well known how many of the children of Francis, as well as of Dominic and of Loyola, were accustomed during the two following centuries to voyage thither for this purpose; how they cared for the colonies brought over from Europe; but primarily and chiefly how they converted the natives from superstition to Christianity, sealing their labors in many instances with the testimony of their blood. The names newly given to so many of your towns and rivers and mountains and lakes teach and clearly witness how deeply your beginnings were marked with the footprints of the Catholic Church.

4. Nor, perchance did the fact which We now recall take place without some design of divine providence. Precisely at the epoch when the American colonies, having, with Catholic aid, achieved liberty and independence, coalesced into a constitutional Republic the ecclesiastical hierarchy was happily established amongst you; and at the very time when the popular suffrage placed the great Washington at the helm of the Republic, the first bishop was set by apostolic

authority over the American Church. The well-known friendship and familiar intercourse which subsisted between these two men seems to be an evidence that the United States ought to be conjoined in concord and amity with the Catholic Church. And not without cause; for without morality the State cannot endure—a truth which that illustrious citizen of yours, whom We have just mentioned, with a keenness of insight worthy of his genius and statesmanship perceived and proclaimed. But the best and strongest support of morality is religion. She, by her very nature, guards and defends all the principles on which duties are founded, and setting before us the motives most powerful to influence us, commands us to live virtuously and forbids us to transgress. Now what is the Church other than a legitimate society, founded by the will and ordinance of Jesus Christ for the preservation of morality and the defense of religion? For this reason have We repeatedly endeavored, from the summit of the pontifical dignity, to inculcate that the Church, whilst directly and immediately aiming at the salvation of souls and the beatitude which is to be attained in heaven, is yet, even in the order of temporal things, the fountain of blessings so numerous and great that they could not have been greater or more numerous had the original purpose of her institution been the pursuit of happiness during the life which is spent on earth.

5. That your Republic is progressing and developing by giant strides is patent to all; and this holds good in religious matters also. For even as your cities, in the course of one century, have made a marvelous increase in wealth and power, so do we behold the Church, from scant and slender beginnings, grown with rapidity to be great and exceedingly flourishing. Now if, on the one hand, the increased riches and resources of your cities are justly attributed to the talents and active industry of the American people, on the other hand, the prosperous condition of Catholicity must be ascribed, first indeed, to the virtue, the ability, and the prudence of the bishops and clergy; but in so slight measure also, to the faith and generosity of the Catholic

laity. Thus, while the different classes exerted their best energies, you were enabled to erect unnumbered religious and useful institutions, sacred edifices, schools for the instruction of youth, colleges for the higher branches, homes for the poor, hospitals for the sick, and convents and monasteries. As for what more closely touches spiritual interests, which are based upon the exercise of Christian virtues, many facts have been brought to Our notice, whereby We are animated with hope and filled with joy, namely, that the numbers of the secular and regular clergy are steadily augmenting, that pious sodalities and confraternities are held in esteem, that the Catholic parochial schools, the Sunday-schools for imparting Christian doctrine, and summer schools are in a flourishing condition; moreover, associations for mutual aid, for the relief of the indigent, for the promotion of temperate living, add to all this the many evidences of popular piety.

6. The main factor, no doubt, in bringing things into this happy state were the ordinances and decrees of your synods, especially of those which in more recent times were convened and confirmed by the authority of the Apostolic See. But, moreover (a fact which it gives pleasure to acknowledge), thanks are due to the equity of the laws which obtain in America and to the customs of the well-ordered Republic. For the Church amongst you, unopposed by the Constitution and government of your nation, fettered by no hostile legislation, protected against violence by the common laws and the impartiality of the tribunals, is free to live and act without hindrance. Yet, though all this is true, it would be very erroneous to draw the conclusion that in America is to be sought the type of the most desirable status of the Church, or that it would be universally lawful or expedient for State and Church to be, as in America, dissevered and divorced. The fact that Catholicity with you is in good condition, nay, is even enjoying a prosperous growth, is by all means to be attributed to the fecundity with which God has endowed His Church, in virtue of which unless men or circumstances interfere, she spontaneously expands and

propagates herself; but she would bring forth more abundant fruits if, in addition to liberty, she enjoyed the favor of the laws and the patronage of the public authority.

7. For Our part We have left nothing undone, as far as circumstances permitted, to preserve and more solidly establish amongst you the Catholic religion. With this intent, We have, as you are well aware, turned Our attention to two special objects: first, the advancement of learning; second, a perfecting of methods in the management of Church affairs. There already, indeed, existed several distinguished universities. We, however, thought it advisable that there should be one founded by authority of the Apostolic See and endowed by Us with all suitable powers, in which Catholic professors might instruct those devoted to the pursuit of learning. The design was to begin with philosophy and theology, adding, as means and circumstances would allow, the remaining branches, those particularly which the present age has introduced or perfected. An education cannot be deemed complete which takes no notice of modern sciences. It is obvious that in the existing keen competition of talents, and the widespread and, in itself, noble and praiseworthy passion for knowledge, Catholics ought to be not followers but leaders. It is necessary, therefore, that they should cultivate every refinement of learning, and zealously train their minds to the discovery of truth and the investigation, so far as it is possible, of the entire domain of nature. This in every age has been the desire of the Church; upon the enlargement of the boundaries of the sciences has she been wont to bestow all possible labor and energy. By a letter, therefore, dated the seventh day of March, in the year of our Lord 1889, directed to you, Venerable Brethren, We established at Washington, your capital city, esteemed by a majority of you a very proper seat for the higher studies, a university for the instruction of young men desirous of pursuing advanced courses. In announcing this matter to Our Venerable Brethren, the Cardinals of the Holy Roman Church, in Consistory,

We expressed the wish that it should be regarded as the fixed law of the university to unite erudition and learning with soundness of faith and to imbue its students not less with religion than with scientific culture. To the Bishops of the United States We entrusted the task of establishing a suitable course of studies and of supervising the discipline of the students; and We conferred the office and authority of Chancellor, as it is called, upon the Archbishop of Baltimore. And, by divine favor, a quite happy beginning was made. For without any delay, whilst you were celebrating the hundredth anniversary of the establishment of your ecclesiastical hierarchy, under the brightest auspices, in the presence of Our delegate, the divinity classes were opened. From that time onward, We know that theological science has been imparted by the diligence of eminent men the renown of whose talents and learning receives a fitting crown in their recognized loyalty and devotion to the Apostolic See. Nor is it long since We were apprised that, thanks to the liberality of a pious priest, a new building had been constructed, in which young men, cleric as well as lay, are to receive instruction in the natural sciences and in literature. From Our knowledge of the American character, We are fully confident that the example set by this noble man will incite others of your citizens to imitate him; they will not fail to realize that liberality exercised towards such an object will be repaid by the very greatest advantages to the public.

8. No one can be ignorant how powerfully similar institutions of learning, whether originally founded by the Roman Church herself from time to time or approved and promoted by her legislation, have contributed to the spread of knowledge and civilization in every part of Europe. Even in Our own day, though other instances might be given, it is enough to mention the University of Louvain, to which the entire Belgian nation ascribes its almost daily increase in prosperity and glory. Equally abundant will be the benefits proceeding from the Washington University, if the professors and students (as

We doubt not they will) be mindful of Our injunctions, and, shunning party spirit and strife, conciliate the good opinion of the people and the clergy.

9. We wish now, Venerable Brethren, to commend to your affection and to the generosity of your people the college which Our predecessor, Pius IX, founded in this city for the ecclesiastical training of young men from North America, and which We took care to place upon a firm basis by a letter dated the twenty-fifth day of October, in the year of our Lord 1884. We can make this appeal the more confidently, because the results obtained from this institution have by no means belied the expectations commonly entertained regarding it. You yourselves can testify that during its brief existence it has sent forth a very large number of exemplary priests, some of whom have been promoted for their virtue and learning to the highest degrees of ecclesiastical dignity. We are, therefore, thoroughly persuaded that you will continue to be solicitous to send hither select young men who are in training to become the hope of the Church. For they will carry back to their homes and utilize for the general good the wealth of intellectual attainments and moral excellence which they shall have acquired in the city of Rome.

10. The love which We cherish towards the Catholics of your nation moved Us, likewise, to turn Our attention at the very beginning of Our Pontificate to the convocation of a third Plenary Council of Baltimore. Subsequently, when the archbishops, at Our invitation, had come to Rome, We diligently inquired from them what they deemed most conducive to the common good. We finally, and after mature deliberation, ratified by apostolic authority the decrees of the prelates assembled at Baltimore. In truth the event has proven, and still proves, that the decrees of Baltimore were salutary and timely in the extreme. Experience has demonstrated their power for the maintenance of discipline; for stimulating the intelligence and zeal of the clergy; for defending and developing the Catholic education of youth.

Wherefore, Venerable Brethren, if We make acknowledgement of your activity in these matters, if We laud your firmness tempered with prudence, We but pay tribute due to your merit; for We are fully sensible that so great a harvest of blessings could by no means have so swiftly ripened to maturity, had you not exerted yourselves, each to the utmost of his ability, sedulously and faithfully to carry into effect the statutes you had wisely framed at Baltimore.

11. But when the Council of Baltimore had concluded its labors, the duty still remained of putting, so to speak, a proper and becoming crown upon the work. This, We perceived, could scarcely be done in a more fitting manner than through the due establishment by the Apostolic See of an American Legation. Accordingly, as you are well aware, We have done this. By this action, as We have elsewhere intimated, We have wished, first of all, to certify that, in Our judgment and affection, America occupies the same place and rights as other States, be they ever so mighty and imperial. In addition to this We had in mind to draw more closely the bonds of duty and friendship which connect you and so many thousands of Catholics with the Apostolic See. In fact, the mass of the Catholics understood how salutary Our action was destined to be; they saw, moreover, that it accorded with the usage and policy of the Apostolic See. For it has been, from earliest antiquity, the custom of the Roman Pontiffs in the exercise of the divinely bestowed gift of the primacy in the administration of the Church of Christ to send forth legates to Christian nations and peoples. And they did this, not by an adventitious but an inherent right. For "the Roman Pontiff, upon whom Christ has conferred ordinary and immediate jurisdiction, as well over all and singular churches, as overall and singular pastors and faithful,[1] since he cannot personally visit the different regions and thus exercise the pastoral office over the flock entrusted to him, finds it necessary from time to time, in the discharge of

1. Vatican Council, Session 4, c. 3.

the ministry imposed on him, to dispatch legates into different parts of the world, according as the need arises; who, supplying his place, may correct errors, make the rough ways plain, and administer to the people confided to their care increased means of salvation."[2]

12. But how unjust and baseless would be the suspicion, should it anywhere exist, that the powers conferred on the legate are an obstacle to the authority of the bishops! Sacred to Us (more than to any other) are the rights of those "whom the Holy Spirit has placed as bishops to rule the Church of God." That these rights should remain intact in every nation in every part of the globe, We both desire and ought to desire, the more so since the dignity of the individual bishop is by nature so interwoven with the dignity of the Roman Pontiff that any measure which benefits the one necessarily protects the other. "My honor is the honor of the Universal Church. My honor is the unimpaired vigor of my brethren. Then am I truly honored when to each one due honor is not denied."[3] Therefore, since it is the office and function of an apostolic legate, with whatsoever powers he may be vested, to execute the mandates and interpret the will of the Pontiff who sends him, thus, so far from his being of any detriment to the ordinary power of the bishops, he will rather bring an accession of stability and strength. His authority will possess no slight weight for preserving in the multitude a submissive spirit; in the clergy discipline and due reverence for the bishops, and in the bishops mutual charity and an intimate union of souls. And since this union, so salutary and desirable, consists mainly in harmony of thought and action, he will, no doubt, bring it to pass that each one of you shall persevere in the diligent administration of his diocesan affairs; that one shall not impede another in matters of government; that one shall not pry into the counsels and conduct of another; finally, that with

2. Cap. *Un. Extrav. Comm. De Consuet*, 1, 1.
3. St. Gregory the Great, *Epist. ad Eulog. Alex.*, VIII, 30.

disagreements eradicated and mutual esteem maintained, you may all work together with combined energies to promote the glory of the American Church and the general welfare. It is difficult to estimate the good results which will flow from this concord of the bishops. Our own people will receive edification; and the force of example will have its effect on those without who will be persuaded by this argument alone that the divine apostolate has passed by inheritance to the ranks of the Catholic episcopate.

13. Another consideration claims our earnest attention. All intelligent men are agreed, and We Ourselves have with pleasure intimated it above, that America seems destined for greater things. Now, it is Our wish that the Catholic Church should not only share in, but help to bring about, this prospective greatness. We deem it right and proper that she should, by availing herself of the opportunities daily presented to her, keep equal step with the Republic in the march of improvement, at the same time striving to the utmost, by her virtue and her institutions, to aid in the rapid growth of the States. Now, she will attain both these objects the more easily and abundantly, in proportion to the degree in which the future shall find her constitution perfected. But what is the meaning of the legation of which we are speaking, or what is its ultimate aim except to bring it about that the constitution of the Church shall be strengthened, her discipline better fortified? Wherefore, We ardently desire that this truth should sink day by day more deeply into the minds of Catholics—namely, that they can in no better way safeguard their own individual interests and the common good than by yielding a hearty submission and obedience to the Church. Your faithful people, however, are scarcely in need of exhortation on this point; for they are accustomed to adhere to the institutions of Catholicity with willing souls and a constancy worthy of all praise.

14. To one matter of the first importance and fraught with the greatest blessings, it is a pleasure at this place to refer, on account of

the holy firmness in principle and practice respecting it which, as a rule, rightly prevails amongst you; We mean the Christian dogma of the unity and indissolubility of marriage; which supplies the firmest bond of safety not merely to the family but to society at large. Not a few of your citizens, even of those who dissent from us in other doctrines, terrified by the licentiousness of divorce, admire and approve in this regard the Catholic teaching and the Catholic customs. They are led to this judgment not less by love of country than by the wisdom of the doctrine. For difficult it is to imagine a more deadly pest to the community than the wish to declare dissoluble a bond which the law of God has made perpetual and inseverable. Divorce "is the fruitful cause of mutable marriage contracts; it diminishes mutual affection; it supplies a pernicious stimulus to unfaithfulness; it is injurious to the care and education of children; it gives occasion to the breaking up of domestic society; it scatters the seeds of discord among families; it lessens and degrades the dignity of women, who incur the danger of being abandoned when they shall have subserved the lust of their husbands. And since nothing tends so effectually as the corruption of morals to ruin families and undermine the strength of kingdoms, it may easily be perceived that divorce is especially hostile to the prosperity of families and States."[4]

15. As regards civil affairs, experience has shown how important it is that the citizens should be upright and virtuous. In a free State, unless justice be generally cultivated, unless the people be repeatedly and diligently urged to observe the precepts and laws of the Gospel, liberty itself may be pernicious. Let those of the clergy, therefore, who are occupied with the instruction of the multitude, treat plainly this topic of the duties of citizens, so that all may understand and feel the necessity, in political life, of conscientiousness, self-restraint, and integrity; for that cannot be lawful in public which is unlawful

4. Encyclical Letter *Arcanum*.

in private affairs. On this whole subject there are to be found, as you know, in the Encyclical Letters written by Us from time to time in the course of Our pontificate, many things which Catholics should attend to and observe. In these writings and expositions, We have treated of human liberty, of the chief Christian duties, of civil government, and of the Christian constitution of States, drawing Our principles from the teaching of the Gospels as well as from reason. They, then, who wish to be good citizens and discharge their duties faithfully may readily learn from Our Letters the ideal of an upright life. In like manner, let the priests be persistent in keeping before the minds of the people the enactments of the Third Council of Baltimore, particularly those which inculcate the virtue of temperance, the frequent use of the sacraments and the observance of the just laws and institutions of the Republic.

16. Now, with regard to entering societies, extreme care should be taken not to be ensnared by error. And We wish to be understood as referring in a special manner to the working classes, who assuredly have the right to unite in associations for the promotion of their interests; a right acknowledged by the Church and unopposed by nature. But it is very important to take heed with whom they are to associate, lest whilst seeking aid for the improvement of their condition they may be imperiling far weightier interests. The most effectual precaution against this peril is to determine with themselves at no time or in any matter to be parties to the violation of justice. Any society, therefore, which is ruled by and servilely obeys persons who are not steadfast for the right and friendly to religion is capable of being extremely prejudicial to the interests as well of individuals as of the community; beneficial it cannot be. Let this conclusion, therefore, remain firm: to shun not only those associations which have been openly condemned by the judgment of the Church, but those also which, in the opinion of intelligent men, and especially of the bishops, are regarded as suspicious and dangerous.

17. Nay, rather, unless forced by necessity to do otherwise, Catholics ought to prefer to associate with Catholics, a course which will be very conducive to the safeguarding of their faith. As presidents of societies thus formed among themselves, it will be well to appoint either priests or upright laymen of weight and character, guided by whose counsels they should endeavor peacefully to adopt and carry into effect such measures as may seem most advantageous to their interests, keeping in view the rules laid down by Us in Our Encyclical, *Rerum Novarum*. Let them, however, never allow this to escape their memory: that whilst it is proper and desirable to assert and secure the rights of the many, yet this is not to be done by a violation of duty; and that these are very important duties; not to touch what belongs to another; to allow everyone to be free in the management of his own affairs; not to hinder anyone to dispose of his services when he please and where he please. The scenes of violence and riot which you witnessed last year in your own country sufficiently admonish you that America too is threatened with the audacity and ferocity of the enemies of public order. The state of the times, therefore, bids Catholics to labor for the tranquility of the commonwealth, and for this purpose to obey the laws, abhor violence, and seek no more than equity or justice permits.

18. Towards these objects much may be contributed by those who have devoted themselves to writing, and in particular by those who are engaged on the daily press. We are aware that already there labor in this field many men of skill and experience, whose diligence demands words of praise rather than of encouragement. Nevertheless, since the thirst for reading and knowledge is so vehement and widespread amongst you, and since, according to circumstances, it can be productive either of good or evil, every effort should be made to increase the number of intelligent and well-disposed writers who take religion for their guide and virtue for their constant companion. And this seems all the more necessary in America, on account of the familiar

intercourse and intimacy between Catholics and those who are estranged from the Catholic name, a condition of things which certainly exacts from our people great circumspection and more than ordinary firmness. It is necessary to instruct, admonish, strengthen and urge them on to the pursuit of virtue and to the faithful observance, amid so many occasions of stumbling, of their duties towards the Church. It is, of course, the proper function of the clergy to devote their care and energies to this great work; but the age and the country require that journalists should be equally zealous in this same cause and labor in it to the full extent of their powers. Let them, however, seriously reflect that their writings, if not positively prejudicial to religion, will surely be of slight service to it unless in concord of minds they all seek the same end. They who desire to be of real service to the Church, and with their pens heartily to defend the Catholic cause, should carry on the conflict with perfect unanimity, and, as it were, with serried ranks, for they rather inflict than repel war if they waste their strength by discord. In like manner their work, instead of being profitable and fruitful, becomes injurious and disastrous whenever they presume to call before their tribunal the decisions and acts of bishops, and, casting off due reverence, cavil and find fault; not perceiving how great a disturbance of order, how many evils are thereby produced. Let them, then, be mindful of their duty, and not overstep the proper limits of moderation. The bishops, placed in the lofty position of authority, are to be obeyed, and suitable honor befitting the magnitude and sanctity of their office should be paid them. Now, this reverence, "which it is lawful to no one to neglect," should of necessity be eminently conspicuous and exemplary in Catholic journalists. For journals, naturally circulating far and wide, come daily into the hands of everybody, and exert no small influence upon the opinions and morals of the multitude.[5]

---

5. *Ep. Cognita Nobis ad Archiepp. et Epp., Taurinen, Mediolanen, et Vercellen* (January 25, 1882).

19. We have Ourselves, on frequent occasions, laid down many rules respecting the duties of a good writer; many of which were unanimously inculcated as well by the Third Council of Baltimore as by the archbishops in their meeting at Chicago in the year 1893. Let Catholic writers, therefore, bear impressed on their minds Our teachings on this point as well as yours; and let them resolve that their entire method of writing shall be thereby guided, if they indeed desire, as they ought to desire, to discharge their duty well.

20. Our thoughts now turn to those who dissent from us in matters of Christian faith; and who shall deny that, with not a few of them, dissent is a matter rather of inheritance than of will? How solicitous We are of their salvation, with what ardor of soul We wish that they should be at length restored to the embrace of the Church, the common mother of all, Our Apostolic Epistle *Praeclara* has in very recent times declared. Nor are we destitute of all hope; for He is present and has a care whom all things obey and who laid down His life that He might "gather in one the children of God who were dispersed" (John 11:52).

21. Surely, we ought not to desert them nor leave them to their fancies; but with mildness and charity draw them to us, using every means of persuasion to induce them to examine closely every part of the Catholic doctrine and to free themselves from preconceived notions. In this matter, if the first place belongs to the bishops and clergy, the second belongs to the laity, who have it in their power to aid the apostolic efforts of the clergy by the probity of their morals and the integrity of their lives. Great is the force of example; particularly with those who are earnestly seeking the truth, and who, from a certain inborn virtuous disposition, are striving to live an honorable and upright life, to which class very many of your fellow-citizens belong. If the spectacle of Christian virtues exerted the powerful influence over the heathens blinded, as they were, by inveterate superstition, which the records of history attest, shall we think it powerless

to eradicate error in the case of those who have been initiated into the Christian religion?

22. Finally, We cannot pass over in silence those whose long-continued unhappy lot implores and demands succor from men of apostolic zeal; We refer to the Indians and the Negroes who are to be found within the confines of America, the greatest portion of whom have not yet dispelled the darkness of superstition. How wide a field for cultivation! How great a multitude of human beings to be made partakers of the blessing derived through Jesus Christ!

23. Meanwhile, as a presage of heavenly graces and a testimony of Our benevolence, We most lovingly in the Lord impart to you, Venerable Brethren, and to your clergy and people, Our Apostolic Benediction.

Given at Rome, at St. Peter's, on the feast of the Epiphany, the sixth day of January, 1895, in the seventeenth year of Our Pontificate.

LEO PP. XIII

APOSTOLIC LETTER

TESTEM BENEVOLENTIAE NOSTRAE

OF THE SUPREME PONTIFF

LEO XIII

TO OUR BELOVED SON, JAMES CARDINAL GIBBONS, CARDINAL PRIEST OF THE TITLE SANCTA MARIA, BEYOND THE TIBER, ARCHBISHOP OF BALTIMORE ON NEW OPINIONS, VIRTUE, NATURE AND GRACE, WITH REGARD TO AMERICANISM

WE send to you by this letter a renewed expression of that good will which we have not failed during the course of our pontificate to manifest frequently to you and to your colleagues in the episcopate and to the whole American people, availing ourselves of every opportunity offered us by the progress of your church or whatever you have done for safeguarding and promoting Catholic interests. Moreover, we have often considered and admired the noble gifts of your nation which enable the American people to be alive to every good work which promotes the good of humanity and the splendor of civilization. Although this letter is not intended, as preceding ones, to repeat the words of praise so often spoken, but rather to call attention to some things to be avoided and corrected; still because it is conceived in that same spirit of apostolic charity which has inspired all our letters, we shall expect that you will take it as another proof of our love; the more so because it is intended to suppress certain contentions which have arisen lately among you to the detriment of the peace of many souls.

It is known to you, beloved son, that the biography of Isaac Thomas Hecker, especially through the action of those who under took to translate or interpret it in a foreign language, has excited not a little controversy, on account of certain opinions brought forward concerning the way of leading Christian life.

We, therefore, on account of our apostolic office, having to guard the integrity of the faith and the security of the faithful, are desirous of writing to you more at length concerning this whole matter.

The underlying principle of these new opinions is that, in order to more easily attract those who differ from her, the Church should shape her teachings more in accord with the spirit of the age and relax some of her ancient severity and make some concessions to new opinions. Many think that these concessions should be made not only in regard to ways of living, but even in regard to doctrines which belong to the deposit of the faith. They contend that it would be opportune, in order to gain those who differ from us, to omit certain points of her teaching which are of lesser importance, and to tone down the meaning which the Church has always attached to them. It does not need many words, beloved son, to prove the falsity of these ideas if the nature and origin of the doctrine which the Church proposes are recalled to mind. The Vatican Council says concerning this point: "For the doctrine of faith which God has revealed has not been proposed, like a philosophical invention to be perfected by human ingenuity, but has been delivered as a divine deposit to the Spouse of Christ to be faithfully kept and infallibly declared. Hence that meaning of the sacred dogmas is perpetually to be retained which our Holy Mother, the Church, has once declared, nor is that meaning ever to be departed from under the pretense or pretext of a deeper comprehension of them."[1]

1. Vatican Council, Constitution *De fide catholica*, c. 4.

We cannot consider as altogether blameless the silence which purposely leads to the omission or neglect of some of the principles of Christian doctrine, for all the principles come from the same Author and Master, "the only-begotten Son, who is in the bosom of the Father" (John 1:18). They are adapted to all times and all nations, as is clearly seen from the words of our Lord to His Apostles: "Going, therefore, teach all nations; teaching them to observe all things whatsoever I have commanded you, and behold, I am with you all days, even to the end of the world" (Matt. 28:19). Concerning this point the Vatican Council says: "All those things are to be believed with divine and catholic faith which are contained in the Word of God, written or handed down, and which the Church, either by a solemn judgment or by her ordinary and universal magisterium, proposes for belief as having been divinely revealed."[2]

Let it be far from anyone's mind to suppress for any reason any doctrine that has been handed down. Such a policy would tend rather to separate Catholics from the Church than to bring in those who differ. There is nothing closer to our heart than to have those who are separated from the fold of Christ return to it, but in no other way than the way pointed out by Christ. The rule of life laid down for Catholics is not of such a nature that it cannot accommodate itself to the exigencies of various times and places. The Church has, guided by her divine Master, a kind and merciful spirit, for which reason from the very beginning she has been what St. Paul said of himself: "I became all things to all men that I might save all" (1 Cor. 9:22).

History proves clearly that the Apostolic See, to which has been entrusted the mission not only of teaching but of governing the whole Church, has continued "in one and the same doctrine, one and the same sense, and one and the same judgment."[3]

---

2. Ibid., c. 3.
3. Ibid., c. 4.

But in regard to ways of living she has been accustomed to so yield that, the divine principle of morals being kept intact, she has never neglected to accommodate herself to the character and genius of the nations which she embraces.

Who can doubt that she will act in this same spirit again if the salvation of souls requires it? In this matter, the Church must be the judge, not private men who are often deceived by the appearance of right. In this, all must concur with our predecessor, Pius VI, who condemned, as injurious to the Church and the spirit of God who guides her, the doctrine contained in the seventy-eighth proposition of the Synod of Pistoia because that proposition subjected to scrutiny the discipline made and approved by the Church, "as if the Church could frame a code of laws useless or heavier than human liberty can bear."

But, beloved son, in this present matter of which we are speaking, there is even a greater danger and a more manifest opposition to Catholic doctrine and discipline in that opinion of the lovers of novelty, according to which they hold such liberty should be allowed in the Church, that her supervision and watchfulness being in some sense lessened, allowance be granted the faithful, each one to follow out more freely the leading of his own mind and the trend of his own proper activity. They are of opinion that such liberty has its counterpart in the newly given civil freedom which is now the right and the foundation of almost every secular state.

In the Apostolic Letters concerning the constitution of states, addressed by us to the bishops of the whole Church, we discussed this point at length; and there set forth the difference existing between the Church, which is a divine society, and all other social human organizations which depend simply on free will and choice of men.

It is well, then, to particularly direct attention to the opinion which serves as the argument in behalf of this greater liberty sought for and recommended to Catholics.

It is alleged that now the Vatican decree concerning the infallible teaching authority of the Roman Pontiff having been proclaimed that nothing further on that score can give any solicitude, and accordingly, since that has been safeguarded and put beyond question a wider and freer field both for thought and action lies open to each one. But such reasoning is evidently faulty, since, if we are to come to any conclusion from the infallible teaching authority of the Church, it should rather be that no one should wish to depart from it, and moreover that the minds of all being leavened and directed thereby, greater security from private error would be enjoyed by all. And further, those who avail themselves of such a way of reasoning seem to depart seriously from the over-ruling wisdom of the Most High—which wisdom, since it was pleased to set forth by most solemn decision the authority and supreme teaching rights of this Apostolic See—willed that decision precisely in order to safeguard the minds of the Church's children from the dangers of these present times.

These dangers, namely, the confounding of license with liberty, the passion for discussing and pouring contempt upon any possible subject, the assumed right to hold whatever opinions one pleases upon any subject and to set them forth in print to the world, have so wrapped minds in darkness that there is now a greater need of the Church's teaching office than ever before, lest people become unmindful both of conscience and of duty.

We, indeed, have no thought of rejecting everything that modern industry and study has produced; so far from it that we welcome to the patrimony of truth and to an ever-widening scope of public well-being whatsoever helps toward the progress of learning and virtue. Yet all this, to be of any solid benefit, nay, to have a real existence and growth, can only be on the condition of recognizing the wisdom and authority of the Church.

Coming now to speak of the conclusions which have been deduced from the above opinions, and for them, we readily believe there was no thought of wrong or guile, yet the things themselves certainly merit some degree of suspicion. First, all external guidance is set aside for those souls who are striving after Christian perfection as being superfluous or indeed, not useful in any sense—the contention being that the Holy Spirit pours richer and more abundant graces than formerly upon the souls of the faithful, so that without human intervention He teaches and guides them by some hidden instinct of His own. Yet it is the sign of no small over-confidence to desire to measure and determine the mode of the divine communication to mankind, since it wholly depends upon His own good pleasure, and He is a most generous dispenser of his own gifts. "The Spirit breatheth whereso He listeth" (John 3:8). "And to each one of us grace is given according to the measure of the giving of Christ" (Eph. 4:7).

And shall anyone who recalls the history of the Apostles, the faith of the nascent Church, the trials and deaths of the martyrs—and, above all, those olden times, so fruitful in saints—dare to measure our age with these, or affirm that they received less of the divine outpouring from the Spirit of Holiness? Not to dwell upon this point, there is no one who calls in question the truth that the Holy Spirit does work by a secret descent into the souls of the just and that He stirs them alike by warnings and impulses, since unless this were the case all outward defense and authority would be unavailing. "For if any persuades himself that he can give assent to saving, that is, to Gospel truth when proclaimed, without any illumination of the Holy Spirit, who gives unto all sweetness both to assent and to hold, such a one is deceived by a heretical spirit."[4]

Moreover, as experience shows, these promptings and impulses of the Holy Spirit are for the most part felt through the medium of the aid and light of an external teaching authority. To quote St. Augustine. "He [the Holy Spirit] cooperates to the fruit gathered from the good trees, since He externally waters and cultivates them by the

4. Second Council of Orange, Canon 7.

outward ministry of men, and yet of Himself bestows the inward increase."[5] This, indeed, belongs to the ordinary law of God's loving Providence that as He has decreed that men for the most part shall be saved by the ministry also of men, so has He wished that those whom He calls to the higher planes of holiness should be led thereto by men; hence St. Chrysostom declares we are taught of God through the instrumentality of men.[6]

Of this a striking example is given us in the very first days of the Church. For though Saul, intent upon blood and slaughter, had heard the voice of our Lord Himself and had asked, "What dost Thou wish me to do?" yet he was bidden to enter Damascus and search for Ananias (Acts 9: "Enter the city and it shall be there told to thee what thou must do").

Nor can we leave out of consideration the truth that those who are striving after perfection, since by that fact they walk in no beaten or well-known path, are the most liable to stray, and hence have greater need than others of a teacher and guide. Such guidance has ever obtained in the Church; it has been the universal teaching of those who throughout the ages have been eminent for wisdom and sanctity—and hence to reject it would be to commit one's self to a belief at once rash and dangerous.

A thorough consideration of this point, in the supposition that no exterior guide is granted such souls, will make us see the difficulty of locating or determining the direction and application of that more abundant influx of the Holy Spirit so greatly extolled by innovators. To practice virtue there is absolute need of the assistance of the Holy Spirit, yet we find those who are fond of novelty giving an unwarranted importance to the natural virtues, as though they better responded to the customs and necessities of the times and that having

5. *De Gratia Christi*, c. 19.
6. *Homily* 1, *in Inscrib. Altar.*

these as his outfit man becomes more ready to act and more strenuous in action. It is not easy to understand how persons possessed of Christian wisdom can either prefer natural to supernatural virtues or attribute to them a greater efficacy and fruitfulness. Can it be that nature conjoined with grace is weaker than when left to herself?

Can it be that those men illustrious for sanctity, whom the Church distinguishes and openly pays homage to, were deficient, came short in the order of nature and its endowments, because they excelled in Christian strength? And although it be allowed at times to wonder at acts worthy of admiration which are the outcome of natural virtue—is there anyone at all endowed simply with an outfit of natural virtue? Is there anyone not tried by mental anxiety, and this in no light degree? Yet ever to master such, as also to preserve in its entirety the law of the natural order, requires an assistance from on high. These single notable acts to which we have alluded will frequently upon a closer investigation be found to exhibit the appearance rather than the reality of virtue. Grant that it is virtue, unless we would "run in vain" and be unmindful of that eternal bliss which a good God in his mercy has destined for us, of what avail are natural virtues unless seconded by the gift of divine grace? Hence St. Augustine well says: "Wonderful is the strength, and swift the course, but outside the true path."[7] For as the nature of man, owing to the primal fault, is inclined to evil and dishonor, yet by the help of grace is raised up, is borne along with a new greatness and strength, so, too, virtue, which is not the product of nature alone, but of grace also, is made fruitful unto everlasting life and takes on a more strong and abiding character.

This over-esteem of natural virtue finds a method of expression in assuming to divide all virtues in active and passive, and it is alleged that whereas passive virtues found better place in past times, our age is to be characterized by the active. That such a division and

7. *In Psalm* 31.

distinction cannot be maintained is patent—for there is not, nor can there be, merely passive virtue. "Virtue," says St. Thomas Aquinas, "designates the perfection of some faculty, but the end of such faculty is an act, and an act of virtue is naught else than the good use of free will," acting, that is to say, under the grace of God if the act be one of supernatural virtue.

He alone could wish that some Christian virtues be adapted to certain times and different ones for other times who is unmindful of the apostle's words: "That those whom He foreknew, He predestined to be made conformable to the image of His Son" (Rom. 8:29). Christ is the teacher and the exemplar of all sanctity, and to His standard must all those conform who wish for eternal life. Nor does Christ know any change as the ages pass, "for He is yesterday and today and the same forever" (Heb. 8:8). To the men of all ages was the precept given: "Learn of me, because I am meek and humble of heart" (Matt. 9:29.)

To every age has He been made manifest to us as obedient even unto death (Phil. 2:8); in every age the apostle's dictum has its force: "Those who are Christ's have crucified their flesh with its vices and concupiscences" (Gal. 5:24). Would to God that more nowadays practiced these virtues in the degree of the saints of past times, who in humility, obedience and self-restraint were powerful "in word and in deed" to the great advantage not only of religion, but of the state and the public welfare.

From this disregard of the evangelical virtues, erroneously styled passive, the step was a short one to a contempt of the religious life which has in some degree taken hold of minds. That such a value is generally held by the upholders of new views, we infer from certain statements concerning the vows which religious orders take. They say vows are alien to the spirit of our times, in that they limit the bounds of human liberty; that they are more suitable to weak than to strong minds; that so far from making for human perfection and the good of human organization, they are hurtful to both. But that this is as false as possible from the practice and the doctrine of the Church is clear, since she has always given the very highest approval to the religious method of life; nor without good cause, for those who under the divine call have freely embraced that state of life did not content themselves with the observance of precepts, but, going forward to the evangelical counsels, showed themselves ready and valiant soldiers of Christ. Shall we judge this to be a characteristic of weak minds, or shall we say that it is useless or hurtful to a more perfect state of life?

Those who so bind themselves by the vows of religion, far from having suffered a loss of liberty, enjoy that fuller and freer kind, that liberty, namely, by which Christ has made us free. And this further view of theirs, namely, that the religious life is either entirely useless or of little service to the Church, besides being injurious to the religious orders cannot be the opinion of anyone who has read the annals of the Church. Did not your country, the United States, derive the beginnings both of faith and of culture from the children of these religious families? For one of whom but very lately, a thing greatly to your praise, you have decreed that a statue be publicly erected. And even at the present time, wherever the religious families are found, how speedy and yet how fruitful a harvest of good works do they not bring forth! How very many leave home and seek strange lands to impart the truth of the Gospel and to widen the bounds of civilization; and this they do with the greatest cheerfulness amid manifold dangers! Out of their number not less, indeed, than from the rest of the clergy, the Christian world finds the preachers of God's word, the directors of conscience, the teachers of youth, and the Church itself the examples of all sanctity.

Nor should any difference of praise be made between those who follow the active state of life and those others who, charmed with solitude, give themselves to prayer and bodily mortification. And how much, indeed, of good report these have merited, and do merit, is known surely to all who do not forget that the "continual prayer of the just man" (James 5:16) avails to placate and to bring down the blessings of heaven when to such prayers bodily mortification is added.

But if there be those who prefer to form one body without the obligation of the vows let them pursue such a course. It is not new in the Church, nor in any wise censurable. Let them be careful, however, not to set forth such a state above that of religious orders. But rather, since mankind are more disposed at the present time to indulge themselves in pleasures, let those be held in greater esteem "who having left all things have followed Christ."

Finally, not to delay too long, it is stated that the way and method hitherto in use among Catholics for bringing back those who have fallen away from the Church should be left aside and another one chosen, in which matter it will suffice to note that it is not the part of prudence to neglect that which antiquity in its long experience has approved and which is also taught by apostolic authority. The scriptures teach us that it is the duty of all to be solicitous for the salvation of one's neighbor, according to the power and position of each. The faithful do this by religiously discharging the duties of their state of life, by the uprightness of their conduct, by their works of Christian charity and by earnest and continuous prayer to God. On the other hand, those who belong to the clergy should do this by an enlightened fulfillment of their preaching ministry, by the pomp and splendor of ceremonies, but especially by setting forth that sound form of doctrine which St. Paul inculcated upon Titus and Timothy. But if, among the different ways of preaching the word of God that one sometimes seems to be preferable, which directed to non-Catholics, not in churches, but in some suitable place, in such wise that controversy is not sought, but friendly conference, such a method is certainly without fault. But let those who undertake such ministry be set apart by the authority of the bishops and let them be men whose science and virtue has been previously ascertained. For we think that there are many in your country who are separated from Catholic truth more by ignorance than by ill-will, who might perchance more easily be drawn to the one fold of Christ if this truth be set forth to them in a friendly and familiar way.

From the foregoing it is manifest, beloved son, that we are not able to give approval to those views which, in their collective sense, are called by some "Americanism." But if by this name are to be understood certain endowments of mind which belong to the American people, just as other characteristics belong to various other nations, and if, moreover, by it is designated your political condition and the laws and customs by which you are governed, there is no reason to take exception to the name. But if this is to be so understood that the doctrines which have been adverted to above are not only indicated, but exalted, there can be no manner of doubt that our Venerable Brethren, the bishops of America, would be the first to repudiate and condemn it as being most injurious to themselves and to their country. For it would give rise to the suspicion that there are among you some who conceive and would have the Church in America to be different from what it is in the rest of the world.

But the true Church is one, as by unity of doctrine, so by unity of government, and she is catholic also. Since God has placed the center and foundation of unity in the chair of Blessed Peter, she is rightly called the Roman Church, for "where Peter is, there is the Church." Wherefore, if anybody wishes to be considered a real Catholic, he ought to be able to say from his heart the selfsame words which Jerome addressed to Pope Damasus: "I, acknowledging no other leader than Christ, am bound in fellowship with Your Holiness; that is, with the chair of Peter. I know that the Church was built upon him as its rock, and that whosoever gathereth not with you, scattereth."[8]

8. *Epist.* 15, *ad Damasum*, n. 2.

We having thought it fitting, beloved son, in view of your high office, that this letter should be addressed specially to you. It will also be our care to see that copies are sent to the bishops of the United States, testifying again that love by which we embrace your whole country, a country which in past times has done so much for the cause of religion, and which will by the divine assistance continue to do still greater things. To you, and to all the faithful of America, we grant most lovingly, as a pledge of divine assistance, our Apostolic Benediction.

Given at Rome, from St. Peter's, the twenty-second day of January, 1899, the twenty-first year of our pontificate.

LEO PP. XIII

ENCYCLICAL LETTER
GRAVES DE COMMUNI RE
OF THE SUPREME PONTIFF
LEO XIII

TO OUR VENERABLE BRETHREN THE PATRIARCHS, PRIMATES, ARCHBISHOPS, BISHOPS, AND OTHER ORDINARIES IN PEACE AND COMMUNION WITH THE APOSTOLIC SEE ON CHRISTIAN DEMOCRACY

1. The grave discussions on economical questions which for same time past have disturbed the peace of several countries of the world are growing in frequency and intensity to such a degree that the minds of thoughtful men are filled, and rightly so, with worry and alarm. These discussions take their rise in the bad philosophical and ethical teaching which is now widespread among the people. The changes, also, which the mechanical inventions of the age have introduced, the rapidity of communication between places, and the devices of every kind for diminishing labor and increasing gain, all add bitterness to the strife; and, lastly, matters have been brought to such a pass by the struggle between capital and labor, fomented as it is by professional agitators, that the countries where these disturbances most frequently occur find themselves confronted with ruin and disaster.

2. At the very beginning of Our pontificate, We clearly pointed out what the peril was which confronted society on this head, and

We deemed it Our duty to warn Catholics, in unmistakable language, how great the error was which was lurking in the utterances of socialism, and how great the danger was that threatened not only their temporal possessions, but also their morality and religion. That was the purpose of Our Encyclical Letter *Quod apostolici muneris* which We published on the twenty-eighth of December in the year 1878; but, as these dangers day by day threatened still greater disaster, both to individuals and the commonwealth, We strove with all the more energy to avert them. This was the object of Our Encyclical *Rerum novarum* of the fifteenth of May, 1891, in which we dwelt at length on the rights and duties which both classes of society—those, namely, who control capital, and those who contribute labor—are bound in relation to each other; and at the same time, We made it evident that the remedies which are most useful to protect the cause of religion, and to terminate the contest between the different classes of society, were to be found in the precepts of the Gospel.

3. Nor, with God's grace, were Our hopes entirely frustrated. Even those who are not Catholics, moved by the power of truth, avowed that the Church must be credited with a watchful care over all classes of society, and especially those whom fortune had least favored. Catholics, of course, profited abundantly by these Letters, for they not only received encouragement and strength for the excellent undertakings in which they were engaged, but also obtained the light which they needed in order to study this order of problems with great sureness and success. Hence it happened that the differences of opinion which prevailed among them were either removed or lessened. In the order of action, much has been done in favor of the proletariat, especially in those places where poverty was at its worst. Many new institutions were set on foot, those which were already established were increased, and all reaped the benefit of a greater stability. Such are, for instance, the popular bureaus which supply information to the uneducated; the rural banks which make loans to small farmers;

the societies for mutual help or relief; the unions of working men and other associations or institutions of the same kind. Thus, under the auspices of the Church, a measure of united action among Catholics was secured, as well as some planning in the setting up of agencies for the protection of the masses which, in fact, are as often oppressed by guile and exploitation of their necessities as by their own indigence and toil.

4. This work of popular aid had, at first, no name of its own. The name of Christian Socialism, with its derivatives, which was adopted by some was very properly allowed to fall into disuse. Afterwards, some asked to have it called the popular Christian Movement. In the countries most concerned with this matter, there are some who are known as Social Christians. Elsewhere, the movement is described as Christian Democracy and its partisans as Christian Democrats, in opposition to what the socialists call Social Democracy. Not much exception is taken to the first of these two names, i.e., Social Christians, but many excellent men find the term Christian Democracy objectionable. They hold it to be very ambiguous and for this reason open to two objections. It seems by implication covertly to favor popular government and to disparage other methods of political administration. Secondly, it appears to belittle religion by restricting its scope to the care of the poor, as if the other sections of society were not of its concern. More than that, under the shadow of its name, there might easily lurk a design to attack all legitimate power, either civil or sacred. Wherefore, since this discussion is now so widespread, and so bitter, the consciousness of duty warns Us to put a check on this controversy and to define what Catholics are to think on this matter. We also propose to describe how the movement may extend its scope and be made more useful to the commonwealth.

5. What Social Democracy is and what Christian Democracy ought to be, assuredly no one can doubt. The first, with due consideration to the greater or less intemperance of its utterance, is carried

to such an excess by many as to maintain that there is really nothing existing above the natural order of things, and that the acquirement and enjoyment of corporal and external goods constitute man's happiness. It aims at putting all government in the hands of the masses, reducing all ranks to the same level, abolishing all distinction of class, and finally introducing community of goods. Hence, the right to own private property is to be abrogated, and whatever property a man possesses, or whatever means of livelihood he has, is to be common to all.

6. As against this, Christian Democracy, by the fact that it is Christian, is built, and necessarily so, on the basic principles of divine faith, and it must provide better conditions for the masses, with the ulterior object of promoting the perfection of souls made for things eternal. Hence, for Christian Democracy, justice is sacred; it must maintain that the right of acquiring and possessing property cannot be impugned, and it must safeguard the various distinctions and degrees which are indispensable in every well-ordered commonwealth. Finally, it must endeavor to preserve in every human society the form and the character which God ever impresses on it. It is clear, therefore, that there in nothing in common between Social and Christian Democracy. They differ from each other as much as the sect of socialism differs from the profession of Christianity.

7. Moreover, it would be a crime to distort this name of Christian Democracy to politics, for, although democracy, both in its philological and philosophical significations, implies popular government, yet in its present application it must be employed without any political significance, so as to mean nothing else than this beneficent Christian action in behalf of the people. For the laws of nature and of the Gospel, which by right are superior to all human contingencies, are necessarily independent of all particular forms of civil government, while at the same time they are in harmony with everything that is not repugnant to morality and justice. They are, therefore, and they

must remain absolutely free from the passions and the vicissitudes of parties, so that, under whatever political constitution, the citizens may and ought to abide by those laws which command them to love God above all things, and their neighbors as themselves. This has always been the policy of the Church. The Roman Pontiffs acted upon this principle, whenever they dealt with different countries, no matter what might be the character of their governments. Hence, the mind and the action of Catholics devoted to promoting the welfare of the working classes can never be actuated with the purpose of favoring and introducing one government in place of another.

8. In the same manner, we must remove from Christian Democracy another possible subject of reproach, namely, that while looking after the advantage of the working people it should seem to overlook the upper classes of society, for they also are of the greatest use in preserving and perfecting the commonwealth. The Christian law of charity, which has just been mentioned, will prevent us from so doing. For it embraces all men, irrespective of ranks, as members of one and the same family, children of the same most beneficent Father, redeemed by the same Savior, and called to the same eternal heritage. Hence the doctrine of the Apostle, who warns us: "We are one body and one spirit called to the one hope in our vocation; one Lord, one faith and one baptism; one God and the Father of all who is above all, and through all, and in us all" (Eph. 4:4–6). Wherefore, on account of the union established by nature between the common people and the other classes of society, and which Christian brotherhood makes still closer, whatever diligence we devote to assisting the people will certainly profit also the other classes, the more so since, as will be thereafter shown, their cooperation is proper and necessary for the success of this undertaking.

9. Let there be no question of fostering under this name of Christian Democracy any intention of diminishing the spirit of obedience, or of withdrawing people from their lawful rulers. Both the natural

and the Christian law command us to revere those who in their various grades are shown above us in the State, and to submit ourselves to their just commands. It is quite in keeping with our dignity as men and Christians to obey, not only exteriorly, but from the heart, as the Apostle expresses it, "for conscience's sake," when he commands us to keep our soul subject to the higher powers (cf. Rom. 13:1, 5). It is abhorrent to the profession of Christianity that anyone should feel unwilling to be subject and obedient to those who rule in the Church, and first of all to the bishops whom (without prejudice to the universal power of the Roman Pontiff) "the Holy Spirit has placed to rule the Church of God which Christ has purchased by His blood" (Acts 20:28). He who thinks or acts otherwise is guilty of ignoring the grave precept of the Apostle who bids us to obey our rulers and to be subject to them, for they watch as having to give an account of our souls (Heb. 13:17). Let the faithful everywhere implant these principles deep in their souls, and put them in practice in their daily life, and let the ministers of the Gospel meditate on them profoundly, and incessantly labor, not merely by exhortation but especially by example, to teach them to others.

10. We have recalled these principles, which on other occasions We had already elucidated, in the hope that all dispute about the name of Christian Democracy will cease and that all suspicion of any danger coming from what the name signifies will be put at rest. And with reason do We hope so; for, neglecting the opinions of certain men whose views on the nature and efficacy of this kind of Christian Democracy are not free from exaggeration and from error, let no one condemn that zeal which, in accordance with the natural and divine laws, aims to make the condition of those who toil more tolerable; to enable them to obtain, little by little, those means by which they may provide for the future; to help them to practice in public and in private the duties which morality and religion inculcate; to aid them to feel that they are not animals but men, not heathens but

Christians, and so to enable them to strive more zealously and more eagerly for the one thing which is necessary; namely, that ultimate good for which we are born into this world. This is the intention, this is the work of those who wish that the people should be animated by Christian sentiments and should be protected from the contamination of socialism which threatens them.

11. We have designedly made mention here of virtue and religion. For it is the opinion of some, and the error is already very common, that the social question is merely an economic one, whereas in point of fact it is, above all, a moral and religious matter, and for that reason must be settled by the principles of morality and according to the dictates of religion. For even though wages are doubled and the hours of labor are shortened and food is cheapened, yet, if the working man hearkens to the doctrines that are taught on this subject, as he is prone to do, and is prompted by the examples set before him to throw off respect for God and to enter upon a life of immorality, his labors and his gain will avail him naught.

12. Trial and experience have made it abundantly clear that many a workman lives in cramped and miserable quarters, in spite of his shorter hours and larger wages, simply because he has cast aside the restraints of morality and religion. Take away the instinct which Christian wisdom has planted and nurtured in men's hearts, take away foresight, temperance, frugality, patience, and other rightful, natural habits, no matter how much he may strive, he will never achieve prosperity. That is the reason why We have incessantly exhorted Catholics to enter these associations for bettering the condition of the laboring classes, and to organize other undertakings with the same object in view; but We have likewise warned them that all this should be done under the auspices of religion, with its help and under its guidance.

13. The zeal of Catholics on behalf of the masses is especially praiseworthy because it is engaged in the very same field in which,

under the benign inspiration of the Church, the active industry of charity has always labored, adapting itself in all cases to the varying exigencies of the times. For the law of mutual charity perfects, as it were, the law of justice, not merely by giving each man his due and in not impeding him in the exercise of his rights, but also by befriending him, "not with the word alone, or the lips, but in deed and in truth" (1 John 3:18), being mindful of what Christ so lovingly said to His own: "A new commandment I give unto you, that you love one another, as I have loved you, that you love also one another. By this shall all men know that you are my disciples, if you have love one for the other" (John 13:34–35). This zeal in coming to the rescue of our fellow men should, of course, be solicitous first for the eternal good of souls, but it must not neglect what is good and helpful for this life.

14. We should remember what Christ said to the disciple of the Baptist who asked him: "Art thou he that art to come or look we for another?" (Matt. 11:3). He invoked, as proof of the mission given to Him among men, His exercise of charity, quoting for them the text of Isaiah: "The blind see, the lame walk, the lepers are cleansed, the deaf hear, the dead rise again, the poor have the Gospel preached to them" (Matt. 11:4–5). And speaking also of the last judgment and of the rewards and punishments He will assign, He declared that He would take special account of the charity men exercised toward each other. And in that discourse there is one thing that especially excites our surprise, namely, that Christ omits those works of mercy which comfort the soul and referring only to those which comfort the body, He regards them as being done to Himself: "For I was hungry and you gave me to eat; I was thirsty and you gave me to drink; I was a stranger and you took me in; naked and you covered me; sick and you visited me; I was in prison and you came to me" (Matt. 25:35–36).

15. To the teachings which enjoin the twofold charity of spiritual and corporal works, Christ adds His own example, so that no one may fail to recognize the importance which He attaches to it. In the

present instance we recall the sweet words that came from His paternal heart: "I have pity on the multitude" (Mark 8:2), as well as the desire He had to assist them even if it were necessary to invoke His miraculous power. Of His tender compassion we have the proclamation made in Holy Writ, namely, that "He went about doing good and healing all that were oppressed by the devil" (Acts 10:38). This law of charity which He imposed upon His Apostles, they in the most holy and zealous way put into practice; and after them those who embraced Christianity originated that wonderful variety of institutions for alleviating all the miseries by which mankind is afflicted. And these institutions carried on and continually increased their powers of relief and were the especial glories of Christianity and of the civilization of which it was the source, so that right-minded men never fail to admire those foundations, aware as they are of the proneness of men to concern themselves about their own and neglect the needs of others.

16. Nor are we to eliminate from the list of good works the giving of money for charity, in pursuance of what Christ has said: "But yet that which remaineth, give alms" (Luke 11:41). Against this, the socialist cries out and demands its abolition as injurious to the native dignity of man. But, if it is done in the manner which the Scripture enjoins (Matt. 6:2–4) and in conformity with the true Christian spirit, it neither connotes pride in the giver nor inflicts shame upon the one who receives. Far from being dishonorable for man, it draws closer the bonds of human society of augmenting the force of the obligation of the duties which men are under with regard to each other. No one is so rich that he does not need another's help; no one so poor as not to be useful in some way to his fellow man; and the disposition to ask assistance from others with confidence and to grant it with kindness is part of our very nature. Thus, justice and charity are so linked with each other, under the equable and sweet law of Christ, as to form an admirable cohesive power in human society and to lead all

of its members to exercise a sort of providence in looking after their own and in seeking the common good as well.

17. As regards not merely the temporary aid given to the laboring classes, but the establishment of permanent institutions in their behalf, it is most commendable for charity to undertake them. It will thus see that more certain and more reliable means of assistance will be afforded to the necessitous. That kind of help is especially worthy of recognition which forms the minds of mechanics and laborers to thrift and foresight, so that in course of time they may be able, in part at least, to look out for themselves. To aim at that is not only to dignify the duty of the rich toward the poor, but to elevate the poor themselves, for, while it urges them to work in order to improve their condition, it preserves them meantime from danger, it refrains immoderation in their desires, and acts as a spur in the practice of virtue. Since, therefore, this is of such great avail and so much in keeping with the spirit of the times, it is a worthy object for the charity of righteous men to undertake with prudence and zeal.

18. Let it be understood, therefore, that this devotion of Catholics to comfort and elevate the mass of the people is in keeping with the spirit of the Church and is most conformable to the examples which the Church has always held up for imitation. It matters very little whether it goes under the name of the Popular Christian Movement or Christian Democracy, if the instructions that have been given by Us be fully carried out with fitting obedience. But it is of the greatest importance that Catholics should be one in mind, will, and action in a matter of such great moment. And it is also of importance that the influence of these undertakings should be extended by the multiplication of men and means devoted to the same object.

19. Especially must there be appeals to the kindly assistance of those whose rank, wealth, and intellectual as well as spiritual culture give them a certain standing in the community. If their help is not extended, scarcely anything can be done which will help in promoting

the well-being of the people. Assuredly, the more earnestly many of those who are prominent citizens conspire effectively to attain that object, the quicker and surer will the end be reached. We would, however, have them understand that they are not at all free to look after or neglect those who happen to be beneath them, but that it is a strict duty which binds them. For no one lives only for his personal advantage in a community; he lives for the common good as well, so that, when others cannot contribute their share for the general good, those who can do so are obliged to make up the deficiency. The very extent of the benefits they have received increases the burden of their responsibility, and a stricter account will have to be rendered to God who bestowed those blessings upon them. What should also urge all to the fulfilment of their duty in this regard is the widespread disaster which will eventually fall upon all classes of society if this assistance does not arrive in time; and therefore is it that he who neglects the cause of the distressed masses is disregarding his own interest as well as that of the community.

20. If this action, which is social in the Christian sense of the term, develops and grows in accordance with its own nature, there will be no danger, as is feared, that those other institutions, which the piety of our ancestors have established and which are now flourishing, will decline or be absorbed by new foundations. Both of them spring from the same root of charity and religion, and not only do not conflict with each other, but can easily be made to coalesce and combine so perfectly as to provide, all the better by the pooling of their beneficent efforts, for the needs of the masses and for the daily increasing perils to which they are exposed.

21. The condition of things at present proclaims, and proclaims vehemently, that there is need for a union of brave minds with all the resources they can command. The harvest of misery is before our eyes, and the dreadful projects of the most disastrous national upheavals are threatening us from the growing power of the socialistic

movement. They have insidiously worked their way into the very heart of the community, and in the darkness of their secret gatherings, and in the open light of day, in their writings and their harangues, they are urging the masses onward to sedition; they fling aside religious discipline; they scorn duties; they clamor only for rights; they are working incessantly on the multitudes of the needy which daily grow greater, and which, because of their poverty are easily deluded and led into error. It is equally the concern of the State and of religion, and all good men should deem it a sacred duty to preserve and guard both in the honor which is their due.

22. That this most desirable agreement of wills should be maintained, it is essential that all refrain from giving any cause of dissension which hurt and divide minds. Hence, in newspapers and in speeches to the people, let them avoid subtle and practically useless questions which are neither easy to solve nor easy to understand except by minds of unusual ability and after the most serious study. It is quite natural for people to hesitate on doubtful subjects, and that different men should hold different opinions, but those who sincerely seek after truth will preserve equanimity, modesty, and courtesy in matters of dispute. They will not let differences of opinion deteriorate into conflicts of wills. Besides, to whatever opinion a man's judgment may incline, if the matter is yet open to discussion, let him keep it, provided he be always disposed to listen with religious obedience to what the Holy See may decide on the question.

23. The action of Catholics, of whatever description it may be, will work with greater effect if all of the various associations, while preserving their individual rights, move together under one primary and directive force. In Italy, We desire that this directive force should emanate from the Institute of Catholic Congresses and Reunions so often praised by Us, to which Our predecessor and We Ourselves have committed the charge of controlling the common action of Catholics under the authority and direction of the bishops of the country. So

let it be for other nations, in case there be any leading organization of this description to which this matter has been legitimately entrusted.

24. Now, in all questions of this sort where the interests of the Church and the Christian people are so closely allied, it is evident what they who are in the sacred ministry should do, and it is clear how industrious they should be in inculcating right doctrine and in teaching the duties of prudence and charity. To go out and move among the people, to exert a healthy influence on them by adapting themselves to the present condition of things, is what more than once in addressing the clergy We have advised. More frequently, also, in writing to the bishops and other dignitaries of the Church, and especially of late,[1] We have lauded this affectionate solicitude for the people and declared it to be the special duty of both the secular and regular clergy. But in the fulfilment of this obligation let there be the greatest caution and prudence exerted, and let it be done after the fashion of the saints. Francis, who was poor and humble, Vincent of Paul, the father of the afflicted classes, and very many others whom the Church keeps ever in her memory were wont to lavish their care upon the people, but in such wise as not to be engrossed overmuch or to be unmindful of themselves or to let it prevent them from laboring with the same assiduity in the perfection of their own soul and the cultivation of virtue.

25. There remains one thing upon which We desire to insist very strongly, in which not only the ministers of the Gospel, but also all those who are devoting themselves to the cause of the people, can

1. Letter to the Minister General of the Minorites, November 25, 1898. In this letter, the Pope recalled the instructions given in *Aeterni patris* concerning the way to be followed in higher studies; the doctrine of Thomas Aquinas should be followed by all the religious who wish truly to philosophize (*qui vere philosophari volunt*); paramount importance of the study of holy Scripture; how to preach the word of God; forceful exhortation addressed to the Franciscans to go out of their monasteries and, following the example of St. Francis, devote themselves to the salvation of the masses; importance of the Third Order of St. Francis with regard to this work.

with very little difficulty bring about a most commendable result. That is to inculcate in the minds of the people, in a brotherly way and whenever the opportunity presents itself, the following principles; namely: to keep aloof on all occasions from seditious acts and seditious men; to hold inviolate the rights of others; to show a proper respect to superiors; to willingly perform the work in which they are employed; not to grow weary of the restraint of family life which in many ways is so advantageous; to keep to their religious practices above all, and in their hardships and trials to have recourse to the Church for consolation. In the furtherance of all this, it is of great help to propose the splendid example of the Holy Family of Nazareth, and to advise the invocation of its protection, and it also helps to remind the people of the examples of sanctity which have shone in the midst of poverty, and to hold up before them the reward that awaits them in the better life to come.

26. Finally, We recur again to what We have already declared and We insist upon it most solemnly; namely, that whatever projects individuals or associations form in this matter should be formed under episcopal authority. Let them not be led astray by an excessive zeal in the cause of charity. If it leads them to be wanting in proper submission, it is not a sincere zeal; it will not have any useful result and cannot be acceptable to God. God delights in the souls of those who put aside their own designs and obey the rulers of His Church as if they were obeying Him; He assists them even when they attempt difficult things and benignly leads them to their desired end. Let them show, also, examples of virtue, so as to prove that a Christian is a hater of idleness and self indulgence, that he stands firm and unconquered in the midst of adversity. Examples of that kind have a power of moving people to dispositions of soul that make for salvation, and have all the greater force as the condition of those who give them is higher in the social scale.

27. We exhort you, Venerable Brethren, to provide for all this,

as the necessities of men and of places may require, according to your prudence and your zeal, meeting as usual in council to combine with each other in your plans for the furtherance of these projects. Let your solicitude watch and let your authority be effective in controlling, compelling, and also in preventing, lest anyone under the pretext of good should cause the vigor of sacred discipline to be relaxed or the order which Christ has established in His Church to be disturbed. Thus, by the rightful, harmonious and ever-increasing labor of all Catholics, let it become more and more evident that the tranquility of order and the true prosperity flourish especially among those peoples whom the Church controls and influences; and that she holds it as her sacred duty to admonish everyone of what the law of God enjoins, to unite the rich and the poor in the bonds of fraternal charity, and to lift up and strengthen men's souls in the times when adversity presses heavily upon them.

28. Let Our commands and Our wishes be confirmed by the words so full of apostolic charity which the blessed Paul addressed to the Romans: "I beseech you therefore brethren, be reformed in the newness of your mind; he that giveth, with simplicity; he that ruleth, with carefulness; he that showeth mercy, with cheerfulness. Let love be without dissimulation. Hating that which is evil; cleaving to that which is good; loving one another with the charity of brotherhood; with honor preventing one another; in carefulness, not slothful; rejoicing in hope; patient in tribulation; instant in prayer. Communicating to the necessities of the saints. Pursuing hospitality. Rejoice with them that rejoice; weep with them that weep; being of one mind to one another; to no man rendering evil for evil; providing good things not only in the sight of God but also in the sight of men" (Rom. 12:1, 2, 8–13, 15–17).

29. As a pledge of these benefits receive the Apostolic Benediction which, Venerable Brethren, We grant most lovingly in the Lord to you and your clergy and people.

Given at St. Peter's, in Rome, the eighteenth day of January, 1901, the twenty-third year of Our Pontificate.

LEO PP. XIII

Designed by Fiona Cecile Clarke, the CLUNY MEDIA *logo*
depicts a monk at work in the scriptorium,
with a cat sitting at his feet.

The monk represents our mission to emulate
the invaluable contributions of the monks
of Cluny in preserving the libraries of the West,
our strivings to know and love the truth.

The cat at the monk's feet is Pangur Bán, from the
eponymous Irish poem of the 9th century.
The anonymous poet compares his scholarly
pursuit of truth with the cat's happy hunting of mice.
The depiction of Pangur Bán is an homage to the work
of the monks of Irish monasteries and a sign
of the joy we at Cluny take in our trade.

"Messe ocus Pangur Bán,
cechtar nathar fria saindan:
bíth a menmasam fri seilgg,
mu memna céin im saincheirdd."